CW00926440

RESEARCHING ENGLISH LANGUA(

Routle   nd are
one-stc
    As   erview
of the   es and
key rea   sional'
structu   on and
extensi   e read
across t   ained.
    Re

❏ prc   ndent
    res
❏ off   f Eng-
    lisk   ic lin-
    gui
❏ gui   to the
    sut
❏ inc
❏ illu   lished
    stu
❏ inc   uding
    Ro   n and
John McH. Sinclair.

LIBREX-

This title will be essential reading for students undertaking research within the areas
of English Language, Linguistics and Applied Linguistics.

Alison Sealey is Senior Lecturer in the Department of English at the University of
Birmingham. She has published extensively on a range of topics in sociolinguistics
and applied linguistics, and is the author, with Bob Carter, of *Applied Linguistics as
Social Science* (2004).

ROUTLEDGE ENGLISH LANGUAGE INTRODUCTIONS

SERIES EDITOR: PETER STOCKWELL

Peter Stockwell is Professor of Literary Linguistics in the School of English Studies at the University of Nottingham, UK, where his interests include sociolinguistics, stylistics and cognitive poetics. His recent publications include *Language in Theory*, Routledge 2005 (with Mark Robson), *Cognitive Poetics: An Introduction*, Routledge, 2002, *The Poetics of Science Fiction*, *Investigating English Language* (with Howard Jackson), and *Contextualized Stylistics* (edited with Tony Bex and Michael Burke).

SERIES CONSULTANT: RONALD CARTER

Ronald Carter is Professor of Modern English Language in the School of English Studies at the University of Nottingham, UK. He is the co-series editor of the forthcoming *Routledge Applied Linguistics* series, series editor of *Interface*, and was co-founder of the Routledge *Intertext* series.

OTHER TITLES IN THE SERIES:

Introducing English Language
Louise Mullany and Peter Stockwell

Language and Power
Paul Simpson and Andrea Mayr

Language and Media
Alan Durant and Marina Lambrou

World Englishes 2nd edition
Jennifer Jenkins

Practical Phonetics and Phonology 2nd edition
Beverley Collins and Inger Mees

Sociolinguistics 2nd edition
Peter Stockwell

Pragmatics and Discourse 2nd edition
Joan Cutting

Psycholinguistics
John Field

Grammar and Vocabulary
Howard Jackson

Stylistics
Paul Simpson

Language in Theory
Mark Robson and Peter Stockwell

Child Language
Jean Stilwell Peccei

RESEARCHING ENGLISH LANGUAGE

A resource book for students

A
B
C
D

ALISON SEALEY

Routledge
Taylor & Francis Group

LONDON AND NEW YORK

First published 2010
by Routledge
2 Park Square, Milton Park, Abingdon, Oxon OX14 4RN

Routledge is an imprint of the Taylor & Francis Group, an informa business

Typeset in 10 on 12.5 pt Minion by
The Running Head Limited, Cambridge, www.therunnninghead.com
Printed and bound in Great Britain by TJ International Ltd, Padstow, Cornwall

British Library Cataloguing in Publication Data
A catalogue record for this book is available from the British Library

Library of Congress Cataloging in Publication Data
Sealey, Alison.
Researching English language: a resource book for students / Alison Sealey.
    p.   cm.—(Routledge English language introductions)
  1. English language—Research—Data processing. 2. English language—History—
Data processing. 3. English language–Rhetoric. I. Title.
PE1074.5.S43 2010
420.72—dc22

                                                                    2009053124

ISBN10: 0–415–46897–3 (hbk)
ISBN10: 0–415–46898–1 (pbk)

ISBN13: 978–0–415–46897–8 (hbk)
ISBN13: 978–0–415–46898–5 (pbk)

HOW TO USE THIS BOOK

The Routledge English Language Introductions are 'flexi-texts' that you can use to suit your own style of study. The books are divided into four sections:

A Introduction – sets out the key concepts for the area of study. The units of this section take you step-by-step through the foundational terms and ideas, carefully providing you with an initial toolkit for your own study. By the end of the section, you will have a good overview of the whole field.

B Development – adds to your knowledge and builds on the key ideas already introduced. Units in this section might also draw together several areas of interest. By the end of this section, you will already have a good and fairly detailed grasp of the field, and will be ready to undertake your own exploration and thinking.

C Exploration – provides examples of language data and guides you through your own investigation of the field. The units in this section will be more open-ended and exploratory, and you will be encouraged to try out your ideas and think for yourself, using your newly acquired knowledge.

D Extension – offers you the chance to compare your expertise with key readings in the area. These are taken from the work of important writers, and are provided with guidance and questions for your further thought.

You can read this book like a traditional textbook, 'vertically' straight through each unit from beginning to end. This will take you comprehensively through the broad field of study. However, the Routledge English Language Introductions have been carefully designed so that you can read them in another dimension, 'horizontally' as a *strand* across the numbered units. For example, Unit A1 corresponds with B1, C1 and D1 as a coherent strand; A2 with B2, C2 and D2, and so on. Reading across a strand will take you rapidly from the key concepts of a specific area, to a level of expertise in that precise area, all with a very close focus. You can match your way of reading with the way that you work best.

The glossary and index at the end, together with the suggestions for further reading, will help to keep you orientated. Each textbook has a supporting website with extra commentary, suggestions, additional material and support for teachers and students.

RESEARCHING ENGLISH LANGUAGE

The aim of this book is to support students throughout the process of doing a research project in some aspect of their study of English Language. It has been written to help people who are relatively new to the demands of devising and managing an independent piece of research. Each strand deals with a stage of the process, from identifying ideas for a possible project (strand 1), through the planning and design stages, leading to doing the research (strands 2–7), and finally writing it up, perhaps as a dissertation, as well as reflecting on how to build on the experience (strands 8 and 9). You can use the book as a guide throughout your research project, in which case it will probably be most useful to read 'horizontally' across each strand. For example, at the stage when you are consulting existing literature, it would make sense to read each of the units in strand 2, as the units in each section in that strand deal in increasing depth with that topic. However, if you progress in the conventional 'vertical' direction, reading all of Section A before looking at Section B, you will gain an overview of the main aspects of the whole research process first, and you can extend this by reading the other sections when you are ready. There are activities throughout, designed to encourage you to apply the ideas presented to your own situation, and these can be tackled in various ways. Readers can do them independently, working alone, or with peers – either informally in self-study groups or as part of a course on research design or dissertation preparation.

CONTENTS

C EXPLORATION

FIGURES AND TABLES

Figures

Tables

ACKNOWLEDGEMENTS

I am greatly indebted to the many people who have made contributions to this book in various ways. A number of students at the University of Birmingham, both undergraduates and postgraduates, have generously allowed me to draw some of my examples from their work, as well as to be interviewed about their experiences of doing dissertations and research projects. Where I have quoted individuals' work I have used pseudonyms, but I would like to thank them all, including Gena Bennett, Joe Bennett, Helena Blazkova, Chandani Borhara, David Bunker, Rachel Clarke, Louise Davenport, Jennifer Davies, Steve Dentith, Elizabeth Doole, Joanna Hall, Robert Jones, Rochelle Jones, William Kennedy, Oliver McCall, Kathryn Minchin, Jacquie Mullender, Garry Plappert, James Price, Caroline Tagg, Holly Waite, Hayley Wells, Louise Whitaker and Ruth Wright.

Parts of the book were made available in draft form via a wiki to which more than 50 people had access, and I thank them for their comments and encouragement.

Colleagues at the University of Birmingham facilitated access to people, ideas and technology, and I am grateful to them, in particular Esther Asprey, Suganthi John, Bill Miller, Rosamund Moon and Paul Thompson.

Via the email list of the British Association for Applied Linguistics (BAAL), I sought suggestions and contributions at different stages of writing, and really appreciate the generous responses I received. I take this opportunity to thank David Barton, Mike Baynham, Malcolm Benson, Meriel Bloor, Martin Edwardes, Sheena Gardner, Anthea Fraser Gupta, Clare Furneaux, Valerie Hobbs, Amanda Howard, Susan Hunston, Veronica Koller, Helen Moore, Sian Preece, Brian Richards, Philip Riley, Frances Rock, Julia Snell, Jane Sunderland, Geoff Thompson, Graham Turner and Karin Tusting.

Four undergraduate students (at the universities of Birmingham and Reading) and one anonymous reviewer read an earlier draft, and their comments and suggestions were very helpful. Thanks to Rachael Arbon, Jennifer Davies, Darren Gothard and Kathryn Minchin, all of whom also piloted the activities, which led to some useful modifications. Thanks also to Bob Carter, Vanessa Cheung, Deborah James and Leon Sealey-Huggins, who commented on various parts of the draft text.

Finally, thanks to the staff at Routledge who suggested this project and provided support throughout.

Permissions

C7.1.5 Image taken from 'Creating a conversational context through video blogging: a case study of Geriatric 1927', p. 684. This article was published in *Computers in Human Behavior* 25, pp. 679–89, Dave Harley and Geraldine Fitzpatrick. Copyright Elsevier (2009). Reproduced with permission of the authors and publisher.

D1.1 Preface in John McH. Sinclair, *International Journal of Corpus Linguistics* 12 (2) (2006) pp. 155–7. Reprinted with the kind permission of John Benjamins Publishing Company, Amsterdam/Philadelphia [www.benjamins.com].

D1.2 S. D. Fischer (2000) 'More than just handwaving: the mutual contributions of sign language and linguistics', in K. Emmorey and H. Lane (eds) *The Signs of Language Revisited: an anthology to honor Ursula Bellugi and Edward Klima*, Mahwah, New Jersey: Lawrence Erlbaum Associates. Reproduced with permission of Taylor & Francis.

D1.3 R. Carter (2004) *Language and Creativity: the art of common talk*, London: Routledge, pp. 1–6. Reproduced with the kind permission of the publishers.

D2.1 E. A. Schegloff, Irene Koshik, S. Jacoby and D. Olsher (2002) 'Conversation analysis and applied linguistics', *Annual Review of Applied Linguistics* 22, pp. 3–31. © Cambridge Journals, published by Cambridge University Press, reproduced with permission.

D2.2 This article was published in *Journal of Pragmatics* 37, N. R. Norrick, 'Interactional remembering in conversational narrative', pp. 1819–44. Copyright Elsevier (2005).

D2.3 Extract from pp. 414–16 of R. Hasan (1996) 'Literacy, everyday talk and society', in R. Hasan and G. Williams (eds) *Literacy in Society*, London: Addison Wesley Longman. © Addison Wesley Longman Limited 1996. Reproduced with permission of Pearson Education Ltd.

D3.1 This article was published in *Journal of Pragmatics* 37, S. W. Smith, H. P. Noda, S. Andrews and A. H. Jucker, 'Setting the stage: how speakers prepare listeners for the introduction of referents in dialogues and monologues', pp. 1865–95. Copyright Elsevier (2005).

D3.2 Reproduced with permission of Oxford University Press from *Oxford Applied Linguistics: individual freedom in language teaching* by Christopher Brumfit. © Oxford University Press 2001.

D4.1 Reprinted with permission of the publisher from 'Experimental paradigms for studying language acquisition', in *Pathways to Language: from fetus to adolescent* by Kyra Karmiloff and Annette Karmiloff-Smith, pp. 21–5, Cambridge, MA: Harvard University Press. Copyright © 2001 by the President and Fellows of Harvard College.

D4.2 *Local Literacies: reading and writing in one community*, D. Barton and M. Hamilton. Copyright © 1998 Routledge. Reproduced with permission of Taylor & Francis Books UK.

D4.3 A. Cumming (1994) 'Alternatives in TESOL research: descriptive, interpretive, and ideological orientations', *TESOL Quarterly* 28 (4), pp. 673–5. Reproduced with permission.

D5.1 J. Coates, *Women Talk: conversation between women friends*, Oxford: Blackwell, pp. 3–6. Copyright © 1996, Jennifer Coates. Reproduced with permission of Blackwell Publishing Ltd.

D5.2 'Data collection: real stories from the field (5.5)', by Vasiliki Papaioannou, Nora

Basurto Santos, and Amanda Howard, in B. Beaven (ed.), *IATEFL 2007 Aberdeen Conference Selections*, IATEFL (2008), Darwin College, University of Kent, Canterbury, Kent CT2 7NY (www.iatefl.org). Reproduced with permission of the authors and IATEFL.

D6.1   Reprinted from *System* 31, B. Petrić and B. Czárl, 'Validating a writing strategy questionnaire', pp. 187–215. Copyright (2003), with permission of Elsevier.

D6.2   Extracts from 'Methodology: the construction and annotation of the corpus', in E. Semino and M. Short (2004) *Corpus Stylistics*, pp. 19–41, London: Routledge. Reproduced with the kind permission of the publishers.

D6.3   Janet Maybin, *Children's Voices*, published 2005. © Janet Maybin 2006. Reproduced with permission of Palgrave Macmillan.

D7.1   J. Coates and J. Thornborrow, 'Myths, lies and audiotapes: some thoughts on data transcripts', *Discourse and Society* 10 (4), pp. 594–7. © 1999 by SAGE Publications. Reprinted with permission.

D7.2   C. E. Gildersleeve-Neumann, E. S. Kester, B. L. Davis and E. D. Peňa (2008) 'English speech sound development in preschool-aged children from bilingual English–Spanish environments', *Language, Speech, and Hearing Services in Schools* 39, pp. 314–28. Reprinted with permission.

D7.3   R. Macksoud (2009) 'Using interview data in case studies', in S. Hunston and D. Oakey (eds) *Introducing Applied Linguistics: key concepts and skills*, London: Routledge.

D8.1   M. R. Lea and B. V. Street (1998) 'Student writing in higher education: an academic literacies approach', *Studies in Higher Education* 23 (2), pp. 157–72. Reprinted with permission of the publisher (Taylor & Francis Ltd, www.tandf.co.uk/journals).

D8.2   *The Politics of Writing*, R. Clark and R. Ivanič. Copyright © 1997 Routledge. Reproduced with permission of Taylor & Francis Books UK.
        Image 4.3 from R. Clark and R. Ivanič (1991) 'Consciousness raising about the writing process', in P. Garret and C. James (eds) *Language Awareness in the Classroom*, pp. 168–85. Reproduced with permission of Pearson Education.

D9.1   Extracts from P. Smagorinsky, L. Wright, S. M. Augustine, C. O'Donnell-Allen and B. Konopak, 'Student engagement in the teaching and learning of grammar: a case study of an early-career secondary school English teacher', *Journal of Teacher Education* 58 (1), pp. 76–90. © 2007 by SAGE Publications. Reprinted with permission.

D9.2   Extracts from B. Rampton (2007) 'Neo-Hymesian linguistic ethnography in the United Kingdom', *Journal of Sociolinguistics* 11 (5), pp. 584–607. Copyright © 2007, Blackwell Publishing Ltd. Reproduced with permission of Blackwell Publishing Ltd.

D9.3   Extracts from A. Curzan and R. Queen (2006) 'In the profession: academic publication', *Journal of English Linguistics* 34, pp. 367–72. Copyright © 2006 by SAGE Publications. Reprinted.

Section A

INTRODUCTION
THE BASICS OF RESEARCHING ENGLISH LANGUAGE

A1 THE FIRST STAGES: GETTING STARTED AND SETTLING ON A TOPIC

A1.1 Why research English Language?

I assume that if you're reading this, it's at least partly because you need to conduct a piece of independent research into some aspect of English Language. It's also likely that you need to do this for accreditation – for a diploma or degree qualification where the development of research skills and experience is a requirement. So there are, no doubt, pragmatic reasons for reading this to find out more about how to do a research project and/or write a dissertation.

However, you may also have somewhat less instrumental reasons: many undergraduates look forward to their dissertation as the first opportunity in their university studies to exercise real choice about their academic work. Students often find the word limits of their routine assignments constraining, and welcome the chance to explore something that interests them in real depth. And for those studying at a more advanced level – either currently or planning to do so – the extended piece of research is an important milestone.

A1.2 Choosing a topic to research

At some point you will need to make a decision about the area of English Language studies that you want to research further. There are likely to be three main ways in which you can identify something to work on.

First, there are always aspects of our own biographies and interests that are connected with language. For example, it is often when students first go to university that they become aware that their own ways of using English are not shared by all English speakers. Suddenly their local accent or dialect words get them noticed, and this may be the motivation for researching the language features of their home region – or of the student community they now belong to. If you are bilingual, you may well have become even more aware, as you have studied language(s) in a formal way, of things that interest you about bilingualism. A student in my department, whose mother taught in an international school in the Netherlands, and who was herself fluent in English and Dutch, identified 'bilingualism' as her area of interest at the start of the dissertation writing process. (The study she eventually submitted was entitled 'An investigation into second language acquisition amongst 4- to 5-year-old children in a multilingual community'.) Other students capitalise on their familiarity with particular areas of culture, such as music, film, graphic novels, and so on, using the research process as an opportunity to explore the linguistic aspects of texts that interest them more generally. It may simply be that you have begun to notice features of language in your daily experience, especially changes and variations, and to wonder how and why they are developing as they are. One student stated in her initial proposal that she wanted to research the change in the use of the capital letter, 'which seems to be disappearing, not only from electronic language but newspapers/magazines/film and TV credits too'. There have been successful dissertations on environmental language such as graffiti, shop names and the discourse of shared spaces (how, for example, does your students' union building communicate its function and ethos from the printed material, both official and more ephemeral, to be seen as you wander round it?). So, in short, if you are looking for a topic, keep your eyes and ears open, and make a note each time some aspect of language comes to your attention.

Note that injunction to 'make a note' in the last paragraph. If you have not already done so, identify a notebook or folder to keep together all kinds of ideas that may strike you as you work on this project. Something highly portable and instantly accessible is crucial so that you can record ideas wherever you are. If it suits your approach to working, consider using a blog or wiki to record and add to your thoughts about the project – and a dedicated space on your computer is a must too, of course. No one else needs to have access to this, and you can type up and reorganise its contents at convenient times, but this kind of notebook tool is a great facilitator of research and writing, and can be a source of comfort and inspiration when the project seems to be drifting – which it almost certainly will at some point along the way!

A second source of inspiration may come from the studies you have already done. Perhaps there was a module you found particularly interesting, but you had to choose just one topic to write about for assessment and now you can follow up one of the others. Or maybe you have already enjoyed working on a group project, and would like to develop a particular aspect of it on your own. An example of this is the student who worked in a group which researched differences in the ways men and women reacted to regional accents. While the group project highlighted female perceptions, he decided to concentrate on men's attitudes to regional accents. Another way in which you can exploit your wider studying is to make use of the links between different subjects. Many students in my own department take courses in English literature alongside their language courses, while others follow a joint degree programme with subjects such as psychology or history. The overlaps are particularly obvious in some of these cases – where stylistic studies of literary texts bridge these two aspects of English research, for example, and psycholinguistic investigations concerned with language processing may occur in the disciplines of both psychology and linguistics. It may be helpful to look back over all the courses you have studied – or are currently studying – and remind yourself of language-related issues you have found interesting that may warrant further research.

Thirdly, you may feel ready to leave your comfort zone and make good some of the gaps in your knowledge. This is obviously more challenging than building on previous work, but it may be more rewarding too. Sometimes students have not been able to take a course they had hoped to, but can find out more about the issues it covers by doing a dissertation in one of these areas. You may have managed to avoid doing any quantitative research throughout your studies, and realise now that knowing how to handle statistical **data** would be useful in the career you've decided on – so you could choose a research project that allows you to learn new skills. Of course you do not need to move into a completely new area – and this is probably not advisable – but you may simply want to develop your interests in slightly new ways. Several students

I know who had identified teaching as their chosen career decided to do their English Language research in schools. One, for example, settled on the general area of child language acquisition as her focus, eventually submitting a dissertation with the title 'Is the use of language in the classroom an important factor in the underachievement of boys in English lessons?'

So, if you don't already know what area you want to research, try to think about what you are interested in generally that has some linguistic dimension (and this covers a very wide range of possibilities), the aspects of your studies that you have enjoyed most and would like to know more about, and new directions you might choose that would 'round out' your knowledge of English Language and/or be useful to you in the future.

Activity

> You could, if you wish, draw up a list of topics that present themselves as possible areas to use in your research study, and then respond to them using a ranking scale to identify which ones appeal to you most, and also which seem most feasible, in terms of access to data, the timescale required, and so on. This is not just a pointless exercise. Setting out options and working through them systematically can be a useful way of coming to a decision (about all sorts of choices you have to make in life, not just academic ones such as this). Also, research studies in the social sciences often make use of this technique – and you may even devise a research instrument along these lines yourself (see C6). For example, Alford and Struther (1990) were interested in finding out about the perceptions of regional accents on the part of L1 speakers of English (that is, some people for whom English was their first language) and L2 speakers (English Language learners). They played recordings of speakers from different areas of the United States to the listeners, and asked them to rate the speakers on a 7-point scale (known as a **Likert scale**) for various traits, such as 'well educated/poorly educated' and 'trustworthy/untrustworthy'. 'In the ranking', they explain, 'a score of 1 was the most negative and 7 the most positive' (p. 485). What do you think they found? Can you see any problems with this research method?

It is always advisable, where possible, to have experience of being on the receiving end of research procedures that you expect others to use, and although this example – of devising and responding to your own Likert scale – is rather contrived, it does give you that opportunity.

Having thought about what you would most *like* to study further, you will need to think in a bit more detail about what makes a research project successful. Later sections of this book will help you to consider this from various points of view, but one thing you will inevitably need to do is to find out more about your potential research topic, and the way to do that is by beginning to read what others have had to say about it.

READING AROUND YOUR TOPIC   A2

> The research student has the responsibility to find out what already exists in the area in which they propose to do research before doing the research itself. The review forms the foundation for the research proper.
>
> (Hart 1998: 26)

A2.1 Housekeeping

You have no doubt written a great many assignments in the past few years, so you should be familiar with the process of building up a bibliography that reflects the reading you have done as a central component of your learning. Preparing to do a research project is a good time to look again at two sources of information about this – even though the presentation of your list of references may be one of the final things you do in relation to your dissertation.

First, check the requirements of your department or institution in relation to the format expected for including references in assessed written work, especially any guidance that is specific to the dissertation or research project. You will of course need to consult this again as you prepare your work for submission, but for now make sure that you are fully familiar with the details you need to record of the sources you consult, so that you can start as you mean to go on, and keep appropriately detailed records of everything you read *at the time of reading*. Make sure that you know which bibliographic details your tutors expect you to include in your list of references, so that you collect them as you read. These details may vary slightly, but they will almost certainly be something like the following.

For books: name(s) of author(s)/editor(s); year of publication; title of book; edition, if not the first; number of volumes, if more than one; place of publication; name of publisher.

For chapters in books: name(s) of author(s); year of publication; title of chapter; editor(s) of book; title of book; edition, if not the first; number of volumes, if multi-volumed work/series; place of publication; name of publisher; page numbers.

For journal articles: names(s) of author(s); date; title of article; title of journal; volume number; part number (if used by the journal); page numbers.

For online sources: name of author/editor, year of publication, title, edition details, place of publication, publisher (if ascertainable); the web address (for the specific webpage) and the date or range of dates when the page was accessed.

There is much more detail in style guides and other relevant sources, including the format expected for *presenting* these different components, such as which parts should appear in italics or brackets, punctuation conventions, and so on. The important thing at this stage is to be sure to collect the information as you go along. Many people use bibliographic software, and there are many advantages to doing so, but this is not essential. Identify what kind of record-keeping system works best for you and be rigorous about using it.

The second source I suggest you consult now is any feedback you may have received on previous written work about your reading (and referencing). If your tutors have had criticisms of this in the past, make use of these now, if necessary clarifying with them where they have not been satisfied with your work so that you can attend to this in your research project.

A2.2 Identifying what to read

No matter what topic you have chosen to research, someone will already have written about it, so you may be certain that there is a literature to consult. You will probably start with reading you have done already when becoming acquainted with the topic by one of the means considered in A1. Specialist tutors will have provided you with bibliographies for the courses they teach, so this reading has been pre-selected by people who know the subject well. As an undergraduate, it is quite possible to produce successful assessed work without departing very far from the titles suggested on these reading lists, but this will not be adequate for an independent research project. You can of course return to these reading lists and generate a more detailed list for yourself of items relating to your particular interest, but you should also make use of the many and increasingly sophisticated databases and search facilities available from your institution's library. Some students find this rather daunting, but it is very important that you do learn (if you don't know already) how to conduct appropriate searches for reading material and how to convert the results into a manageable work plan for the time you have available.

One possible problem for students researching English Language topics is that, because these are so diverse, there is no single academic discipline and group of journals where all the useful material will necessarily be published. Searches in the 'English' databases may be frustrating because of the concentration on literature topics; some linguistic research is located in the biological and psychological sciences; some is associated with the humanities; many applied linguists are closely associated with educational research, and there is also a close link between this tradition and work in the social sciences (see Sealey and Carter 2004). Be prepared, therefore, to spend a little time identifying which resources are most likely to generate useful results for your own study – and to recognise that there are likely to be areas of research that touch on your interest but are too far outside your knowledge and expertise to be incorporated into a short project at this level. Do make use of your library's training materials, online guidance and manuals – and the staff. There is a lot of support available – although in the end, of course, it is up to you to do the actual research.

An example

Suppose you have decided that your research project is going to be about gender differences in the use of online discourse. You may feel most familiar, and therefore comfortable, with using the basic search facilities available to any computer user with a subscription to the internet. So you could try typing the strings 'gender differences' and 'online discourse' into Google. I did this and returned ten hits. These came from a very mixed set of sources, and few of them seemed to be research findings. Such a limited list suggests that the search terms I chose were not the best ones. This illustrates the need to think about the discourse of academic writing, and the vocabulary that researchers are likely to use to identify their concerns. A more productive term is probably 'computer-mediated communication', and 'gender' alone (rather than 'gender differences') is likely to be a keyword if this is a dimension the researcher is interested in. When I tried again typing these terms into Google, my problem veered to the other extreme: this time I got over a million hits. If you try something like this yourself, you should begin to realise why libraries spend money on subscribing to the resources I am recommending: much of the filtering and evaluating has been done for you, and the results you receive, provided you construct a sensible search, should be of direct use in an academic study.

One of the bibliographic databases where you are likely to find relevant material is CSA Linguistics and Language Behavior Abstracts. Academic journals have a convention of including an 'abstract', which is a brief summary of the whole article, and 'keywords'. To return results that are centrally relevant, rather than those which deal with your area of interest only in passing, it is useful to ask for terms that appear either as keywords or in the abstract. I typed 'computer mediated communication' into the keyword field, and, using what are known as the 'Boolean operators', I chose 'and' – rather than 'or' – with another keyword, 'gender'. This was to ensure that studies about language and gender but not computers, and studies about CMC but not gender, would be excluded from the list of results. This search produced 37 hits, but the results screen also indicated that these included different types of resource. Five were dissertations; four were chapters/essays; 28 were published in journals, of which 21 were identified as peer-reviewed journals. The process of peer reviewing is discussed in B2, but the main point to note here is that readers should be able to have more confidence in findings that have been subjected to this process than in those that have not. As a starting point, a list of 21 journal articles and four book chapters seems a reasonable number to tackle for a student starting out on a modest research project. You will not need to read every word of every article (see below), and you will work outwards from this list to identify further sources, so, if you have a few months to do your project, this is a practically manageable start. This is not to suggest that 25 is an ideal length for a bibliography – or even that there is such a 'magic number'. The optimum length of the list of references for a research project will vary according to a wide range of factors. However, we can safely say that ten is too few and a million too many references to work with successfully.

Another advantage of using dedicated academic databases is that you can see at a glance what each article is about, and so whether it is likely to be of interest. At the same time, you will begin to get a feel for current research priorities and the discourse in which they are expressed. Beginning your literature review will achieve more than simply giving you a list of titles to track down; it should also suggest more specific ideas for your own research. It may help you to narrow down the questions you will try to answer, and it should suggest the means by which you can collect and analyse data.

In my example, a quick scan of the abstracts visible on the results screen revealed that these studies were about a whole range of aspects of the main topic, including eroticism and desire, literacy practices, blogs as a discourse genre, metaphor, cross-cultural issues, pedagogical issues, language play online, and so on. At this point, my next step would be to use my notebook (see A1) to brainstorm some ideas about narrowing down my topic and extending my reading in this more prescribed area.

The initial set of resources identified by these two methods (sources already recommended in taught courses, and sources identified by library searches) will of course be supplemented by the bibliographies included in each of these sources. Cameron (2001: 185) advises, 'do not begin your reading with the earliest references in your list; begin with the most recent references'. Hart (1998: 99), however, warns against leaving older sources unread, or 'only understood through derivative sources'. So which advice is right? Cameron's reasoning is important: taking note of writers whose work is still cited should help you to identify which older work continues to be influential – and to read it for yourself. You can actually construct a 'citation index' of your own based on your early reading: keep a 'score sheet' of authors or sources which keep cropping up in relation to an aspect of your topic; those with several ticks against them should be consulted at first hand.

 Activity

> Identify up to three key words or phrases that are central to your topic. For each term, consider possible variations (e.g. 'language acquisition'/'language development'). Using your institution's library resources, identify an appropriate database and carry out a search. Aim to generate a list of about 30 items, of which 25 are refereed journal articles or chapters in edited collections. Experiment with using different databases, search terms, combinations of Boolean operators, and so on. Make a note of which approaches work better, and of ideas that occur to you as possible ways of developing your research project, even as you skim-read the abstracts produced by your searches. These may be in each of the following areas:
>
> ❏   questions that come to mind as you see what others have studied and discovered,
> ❏   the kinds of data previous researchers have used to answer their questions, and
> ❏   the methods previous researchers have used in their studies.

A2.3 What are you reading for?

This may seem a rather silly question, but give it some thought: how would you answer it? You may be influenced by the pragmatic considerations raised in A1. Obviously you won't receive a high mark for your work if it fails to include evidence of adequate reading. In addition, earlier sections in this unit have indicated some of the more intellectual reasons for becoming familiar with the existing literature before (and while) doing your own research. These reasons include:

❏   identifying what is already known about your topic and the questions to which
     you want to find answers
❏   raising new questions, or more refined versions of your original questions
❏   becoming more familiar with:
          the core concepts in your areas of interest
          the theories and approaches that have influenced researchers who work in them
          the discourse used in this corner of the wider academic community
❏   identifying appropriate data and methods to research your topic.

This list implies that there can be a range of different approaches you may take when reading any given text. Many study guides list generic skills relevant to all disciplines, and these are useful if you find it difficult to feel that you are reading effectively – especially when undertaking an extended independent research project. Typically, the advice given is to start by gaining a general impression of the text, for example by looking first at the abstract, introduction and conclusion of an article, or the contents list and section headings of books or book chapters. This makes use of the kinds of reading known as *scanning*, where you check for specific items of relevance, and *skimming*, where you gain a general impression of a text. It is also advisable to have some pre-identified purpose for reading the text, which may be one or more questions you hope it will answer; this should help you to concentrate and not try to absorb everything at once. After reading the text (see below), it is helpful to allow yourself time to recall what you have read, and you will of course need to make useful notes. Try to become aware of your strengths and weaknesses as a note-taker: you probably know by now if you have a tendency to highlight everything indiscriminately, or to copy out lengthy extracts, or to use a cryptic shorthand that mystifies you when you return to your notes after a gap. Such habits may be hard to break – but you can improve these skills if you are aware of which things you need to do better. Remember too, of course, that it is from reading other people's work that the possibility of plagiarism arises. Make sure you know your institution's policy on this, and seek clarification if you are in any doubt about the conventions of acknowledging your sources when you incorporate what you have read into your own writing. Do make sure to indicate very clearly in your notes where you have taken verbatim quotes from your source.

A2.4 Reading critically

Research at undergraduate level presents some particular challenges, being a transition from the directed learning experienced at school and in the taught components of university courses to the more independent scholarship expected at the postgraduate level. Universities in the UK provide explicit statements of the criteria by which students' written work will be assessed. The use of reading at undergraduate dissertation level is, typically, required to demonstrate knowledge of the field, but higher marks are awarded to work where this knowledge is shown to be more extensive, and also to work that includes a 'critical' review of the literature. The emphasis on criticality increases at postgraduate level, and this is partly because extensive knowledge and experience are a firmer basis for critique than ignorance and partial understanding.

The more you read, the more you will be able to question assumptions, identify the poor arguments of others, and put forward your own original contribution.

Ideally, a period of sustained reading equips you to move on to the next stage – clarifying what exactly you aim to find out, and how to go about doing so.

A3 **WHAT DO YOU WANT TO KNOW?**

> The process of developing a set of research questions can be the most challenging part of the research project.
>
> (Blaikie 2000: 65)

A3.1 Questions of data and theory

An assumption underlying this book is that readers are currently or imminently engaged in carrying out a small research project themselves. Such projects are likely to have many things in common for many kinds of reader, but there will be differences in the detail, depending on the discipline or department where students are located, the local institution and the national educational system that provide the context for this work.

I am also assuming that most readers will either be required or will choose to do some original data collection, and that their projects will involve **empirical** research. In other words, you plan to find out something about some aspect of the English language by investigating it directly, using techniques of observation and collecting evidence that you and others can 'see with your own eyes'. For some kinds of topic, however, you will not be able to collect your own data, but will make use of what has already been collected by others. One student, Rosie, did this in an investigation of taboo words (see B1), using the Lund **corpus** as her data. In either case, there is bound to be some theoretical work involved, and it may well be at the stage of drafting questions that this will begin to become more apparent.

For some students, the issue that interests them most is not susceptible to empirical investigation at all, and their research project focuses not on new linguistic data but on issues that are predominantly theoretical. As examples of this, Wray and Bloomer (2006: 10) cite 'the evolution or origin of language, philosophy of language, or syntactic theory'. Most students, though, do choose to gain experience of data collection and analysis, and you may be required to do this for assessment – so check before you decide to take a different approach. An example of a successful non-empirical project (at Masters level) consisted of an analysis of the arguments in two texts by eminent linguists: Steven Pinker's *The Language Instinct* (1994) and Geoffrey Sampson's (1997) 'reply', *Educating Eve: the 'language instinct' debate*. In this kind of project, the formulation of precise research questions in advance may be less crucial, and the questions are likely to be of a different kind, but clarity about what you are doing as an investigator of any topic is still important.

A3.2 Making your questions explicit

At the heart of a successful research project, then, is usually (though not invariably – see above) a limited number of tightly specified questions, to which the research carried out provides some clear answers. This seems simple enough, but it is deceptively so. It would also seem obvious that the identification of the questions must come at about this point – after the stage of identifying a topic and finding out more about what is already known about it, and before embarking on the collection of data – and yet this, too, is not always quite such a straightforwardly linear process. Doing a research project, especially when you have limited experience, is almost certain to involve revisions and reworkings of your ideas, including your research questions, as you realise what is feasible with the time and resources available. Students often frame their research questions initially as variants of the statement, 'I'd like to find out more about . . .'. Such formulations are appealing, because they express an interest in an area, but they are unsatisfactory as research questions, because they do not specify what exactly you want to know, nor do they make explicit the kind of knowledge that would constitute an answer to the question.

As a student of English Language, you know about the grammatical structure of questions, and can no doubt identify the lexis and syntax associated with them. Kipling lists in a well-known poem his 'six honest serving men': *what, why, when, how, where* and *who*. As you draft possible questions for your research, try to incorporate the appropriate features of these interrogatives – and to anticipate what the answers to your questions would look like. In other words, how would you know when you had answered the question you have drafted? What would adequate evidence be? If this seems daunting, don't worry – it isn't easy! But thought given to this aspect of your study now will be rewarded if it means that you don't waste time trying to find answers to unanswerable questions. The issue here is not only that referred to in B1, which cites Sebba (2000) on the distinction between 'eternal' and 'research' questions. It's about identifying in your question(s) what kind of knowledge you are intending to pursue. As I have said, this may only become clear after you have done a fair amount of work, so don't let the search for the perfect research question paralyse you at the outset!

Activity

From whatever stage of planning you have currently reached, consider whether your project is of the type that:

❏   necessarily involves the collection of new data,
❏   involves data analysis but can make use of existing data sets, or
❏   aims to explore a theoretical issue, using data primarily in an illustrative way.

Make a note of your research questions as they stand now, and consider the implications of these for the design of your project.

Example

One student, Nina, began with a fairly clear idea about comparing quantitative and qualitative approaches to analysis of the language of a single text, Mary Shelley's *Frankenstein*. In her extended proposal for the dissertation, she expressed her aims as statements:

> I aim to discuss the advantages and disadvantages of each [analytical approach] when I draw conclusions and make interpretations from the findings of the quantitative data (statistics from the target and reference corpus) and the qualitative data, which will seek to explain the patterns found in the language of the text under investigation (comparing it to real life usage in the reference corpus). I will also make a critique of both methods to see which is better in certain aspects of the stylistic analysis.

A useful exercise she could have tried at this point would be to convert these aims into questions. As you will see, the first sentence in the extract quoted is so long that this would not be easy to do – which is a clue as to the feasibility of the intended procedure. In particular, the reference to 'statistics' is very vague and cannot be clarified from this extract as it stands. Nevertheless, we can, with some adjustments, generate some of the questions that could be said to underlie this statement of aims. Here is an indication of how the aims might be rephrased as questions:

1   What are the advantages and disadvantages of (a) qualitative and (b) quantitative approaches to the analysis of the target text (*Frankenstein*)?
2   How can the patterns found in the language of the target text be explained?
3   Which method is better in certain aspects of the stylistic analysis?

Now, let us look at the *kind* of questions these are. Two of them, Q1 and Q3, are questions of judgement or evaluation. There is a place for this kind of enquiry in language research, but it is a different kind of enquiry from that which establishes what something is like, or how much of something there is in a particular set of data. Crucially, a researcher who seeks to establish whether something is 'better' than something else is obliged to make explicit the criteria used to establish this. Q2 is concerned with explanation, another area which is notoriously difficult to research. Again, it is not impossible to find out *why* things are the way they are, but it is usually easier to establish *that* they are this way than to account for the causes. The final observation I would make about this set of questions is that they are very general. Nina refers to 'certain aspects of the stylistic analysis', but it is important to be clear *which* aspects are to be investigated. Looking for 'patterns in the language' of the text is an entirely appropriate enterprise, but in a short, word-limited project, it is nearly always best to narrow such a focus to a particular kind of pattern.

This is in fact what Nina did, and, with the guidance of her supervisor, the questions she eventually investigated included: 'What emotional conceptual metaphors are most frequent in *Frankenstein*?' Nina's research led her to explore various theories about and approaches to analysing metaphor, and to apply what she found to the particular emotions of remorse, anger and sadness – in *Frankenstein* and in the Bank of

English, which she used as a **reference corpus**. So another of her eventual questions was 'Does the Bank of English support the claim that emotional conceptual metaphors are used in everyday language?' From this example, you should be able to see why I claimed above that it is not unusual for the precise questions you will eventually use to guide your research not to be fully specified at the start of the process. Nevertheless, some clarity in your thinking as you draft potential questions will serve you well as you design your study.

The process of drafting your research questions, then, can be helpful in several aspects of planning your project. As you will know from your study of **adjacency pairs**, questions invite answers, so thinking about your questions should lead you to anticipate what kinds of answers you will generate. It should also mean that you begin to identify what kinds of evidence will be needed to answer your question(s), which in turn has implications for data collection and analysis. In relation to any question you devise, you can ask yourself a series of 'meta-questions'. What resources would you need to answer this question? What kind of data and evidence would you generate? What kind of measurement is involved? How long would it take, realistically, to collect and analyse the data that would be used in answering the question? You may not be able to answer all of these definitively, but it is useful to try.

Example
A recent study by Lindquist (2007) focuses on the 'spread and development of a new type of adverb in American and British English'. The formations he is interested in add *-wise* to another word, which, as he notes, is not in itself a new way of forming adverbs in English. He thinks that there has been a subtle innovation in the past few decades, however, resulting in what he calls 'viewpoint adverbs'. Examples include *budget-wise*, *career-wise* and *percentage-wise*. The article begins with an extensive literature review (headed 'previous scholarship' – see strand 2), which precedes a list of research questions, identified as remaining 'wholly or partly unanswered after the studies reviewed above'. Before you read the questions Lindquist thought of, can you anticipate what they are likely to be? This is his list:

1 Is the use of these adverbs more frequent in spoken English than in written English?
2 Has the use increased or decreased during the ten-year period 1990–2000?
3 Is there a difference in frequency between American English and British English, and if so, does it change throughout time?
4 What morphological constraints are there for the formation of the adverbs?
5 In what registers are the adverbs used most frequently?

(Lindquist 2007: 136–7)

For a short, assessed research project, any one of these questions would probably be quite enough on its own, and it is instructive to think through how any one of them could be answered. For this worked example, I have not included the question about how long it would take to collect and analyse the data, but this kind of practicality is important for you to consider – especially as you will have a definite and probably non-negotiable deadline for submitting your work for assessment.

It is obvious that to answer these questions Lindquist needed an extensive set of data, comprising texts where the words he was interested in would be found, and, as he notes, 'For the study of relatively rare lexical phenomena, a large corpus of material is necessary' (p. 137). It is also obvious that the whole study was much more feasible because existing data sets of already digitised texts could be used: to embark on new recordings of speech, transcription and then conversion to corpus format would add considerably to the labour involved. Within the large corpus Lindquist needed, Q1 requires a range of (transcribed) discourse, including both spoken and written sources, Q2 requires sources from the different periods in question, Q3 requires both American and British sources and Q5 requires data representative of different genres. Furthermore, for comparisons such as these, each sub-corpus needs to be similar enough to the one(s) with which it is being compared that any findings are not distorted by some other **variable**. It would clearly not be appropriate, for example, to answer Q3 by comparing an American English corpus of crime fiction with a British English corpus of political speeches! (In fact, he used CDROMs of newspaper texts, partly because 'journalistic prose has been shown to be a . . . genre that picks up new trends quickly' (p. 137).) Q4 is slightly different in kind, and requires knowledge of word formation and etymology to apply in an analysis of the items identified in the other parts of the investigation.

Assuming the study has overcome any problems of access to suitable data, what other practical implications do these questions raise for the research design? Well, search tools were needed to identify all the words of interest, and only those words. Since the sub-corpora were of slightly different sizes, the researcher had to do some mathematical calculations to 'normalise' them for accurate comparison.

Of course this example is only one kind of project, and yours may be of a very different kind in terms of aims, data and area of interest. Nevertheless, you should try to anticipate the issues highlighted in this example in your own planning and drafting of research questions.

A4 WAYS OF FINDING OUT WHAT YOU WANT TO KNOW

If your project involves the collection of empirical data (see A3), then by definition you will need access to the phenomenon or phenomena in which you are interested. These phenomena are as diverse as 'adverbs ending in –*wise*' or 'metaphors in talk about cancer' or 'measures of linguistic accuracy' – or indeed whatever it is that you are trying to investigate. Throughout the book, I use the idea of 'X's and 'Y's, as 'placeholders' for the things which are being studied in any research project. The careful (re) drafting of your research questions should help you to identify what the Xs and Ys are in your particular project, and the next stage is to think about how you can find out more about them.

A4.1 Ways of observing

The most obvious way of doing this is by some kind of observation. Do you have a mental picture of researchers at work? If so, perhaps it includes someone in a white coat looking down a microscope, or watching a chemical reaction taking place in a laboratory: these are certainly the stereotypes we are exposed to in mainstream culture. There are various reasons, some of them obvious and others not so obvious, why observing the Xs and Ys of English language usually needs to be done in rather different ways, but some research methods do make use of direct observation.

> Make a list of the kinds of things likely to be of interest to English Language researchers that can be observed directly. If you can, you should draw on studies you know of that make use of direct observation. What are the Xs and Ys in these studies, and do they have anything in common?

It is worth noting at this point that there are differences between spoken and written Xs and Ys when it comes to research methods. When your target phenomena are originally in a textual form (including writing, printing or images), they will not be aware, as people talking are likely to be, that they are the subject of a research study. The same is true, though to a lesser extent, of 'second-hand' data, such as existing recordings or transcriptions of talk – but of course in these cases you will have reduced control over what is included in your data set. If you observe an interaction, and if you are able to make a visual record of it (whether a video recording or just notes and diagrams) the record of the talk you eventually analyse will include more information than if you have only someone else's basic transcript. In either case, however, the challenges connected with observational research methods in English Language are most acute in respect of spoken data.

One obvious difficulty with observing people using language is that they may either object to you doing so, or, if they do give informed consent, they may use language differently when you are there observing. This leads to the famous 'observer's paradox' noted by Labov (1972: 209): 'The aim of linguistic research in the community must be to find out how people talk when they are not systematically observed; yet we can only obtain these data by systematic observation'. One technique developed by researchers working in the 'ethnographic' tradition (see Reading D4.2), to try to mitigate this problem, is 'participant observation', where the researcher becomes, at least for a while, a member of the (speech) community that she or he is interested in, rather than an observer looking in from outside.

A second problem is that the kind of observation you can do directly as people produce speech in context is of something very fleeting, which leaves no data to be revisited and investigated unless you introduce some apparatus other than your own eyes and ears. This is quite possible, of course, but it is important to be aware that the use of audio and visual recording equipment is an intervention between you and what you are observing. Even the act of taking notes can be very disruptive of spontaneous conversation.

A third challenge is that the Xs or Ys you hope to observe may simply not occur in the contexts where you hoped to observe them. This could be for various reasons, not restricted to the self-monitoring to which Labov drew attention. For example, researchers of politeness phenomena (such as apologies or exchanges of compliments) must either (a) happen to be around and alert when someone apologises or gives someone else a compliment, or (b) find some way of making sure that compliments and apologies are uttered when they are there to observe them. This challenge may be met by the method of elicitation: where the researcher prompts a willing participant to produce the X or Y instead of waiting for it to occur 'naturally'. The disadvantage of this is that elicited data may be rather different from the spontaneously occurring language for which it is intended as a substitute.

Some kinds of research targets cannot be accessed at all via direct observation, because of the kinds of things they are. Examples include nearly everything that we refer to as going on 'inside people's heads'; despite developments in technology that make brain activity potentially more visible, we cannot access directly other people's memories or ideas. In other cases, it would be completely impractical to try to 'harvest' many individual instances of the phenomenon in question, so researchers do not seek to observe these things but instead they ask people about them. Their research instruments then are interviews, questionnaires (including acceptability judgements) or perhaps research diaries kept by the participants.

Note, however, that, because some of these instruments generate linguistic data, they can have more than one function within this typology. The sociolinguistic interview designed for researching the production of particular phonemes, for example, is closer to other kinds of elicitation than the qualitative interview whose goal is to find out about people's experiences or beliefs. A social researcher may analyse participants' research diaries or 'free' responses in questionnaires entirely for their content, regardless of how it is expressed. A linguistic researcher, by contrast, may look at such texts in a 'discourse analytic' way.

These issues provide us with a range of approaches to 'ways of observing' the production of spoken language, each with their own advantages and disadvantages, which are further explored in B4. We can think of them as lying on a continuum, from direct, unmediated observation at one end, through recordings, on to observations of elicited language behaviour, including in experimental conditions, through to, at the opposite end, records of people's accounts of their experiences, attitudes or beliefs, where no direct observation by the researcher is involved. This typology is represented by Figure A4.1.1. The sloping line suggesting how far each approach provides direct access to authentic, or 'naturally occurring', language behaviour is merely indicative and not intended as a firm quantitative measure, of course.

Potter and Hepburn (2007) express well an important difference between the types of data generated using different kinds of observation:

> If the researcher was taken ill that morning, interviews and focus groups (and experiments, surveys, and questionnaires) would fail to be done, and so are not naturalistic; phone calls between friends, family mealtimes, relationship counselling sessions, police interviews, records of Parliamentary debates (amongst many other things) would carry on more or less as before.
>
> (Potter and Hepburn 2007: 277)

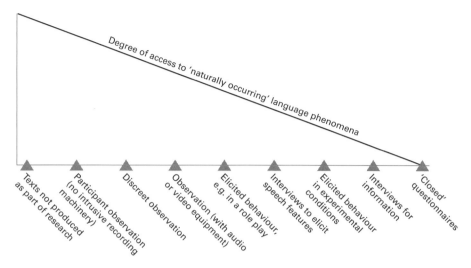

Figure A4.1.1 Continuum showing kinds of observation and degree of access each provides to 'authentic' language behaviour

A4.2 Ways of classifying

Another way to identify methods appropriate for your research study is to clarify a little further the nature of your own Xs and Ys. The process of classifying or categorising phenomena lies somewhere between the two very broad research traditions referred to as 'qualitative' and 'quantitative'. This division relates to the kinds of questions researchers ask, which is explored in strand 3. Usually, questions that are framed in terms such as 'What is X like?' are answered using 'qualitative' methods, because they are concerned with the 'qualities' that X possesses. By contrast, questions that ask 'How much of X is there in Y?' or 'How many Xs are there compared to the number of Ys?' or 'How much effect does X have on Y?' entail some measurement and counting, and are thus answered with reference to 'quantitative' methods.

For examples from the English Language field, we might cite, as a 'What is X like?' kind of question, investigations into the discourse produced by children in their friendship groups, such as those documented in Maybin (2005) or Sealey (2000). Maybin's concerns are very much with the way children collaborate in their talk to construct versions of themselves and their world, and she champions ethnographic methods as the most appropriate way to access these dynamic processes. A very different approach to researching (younger) children's language is used by Parker and Brorson (2005), who investigated whether there was a correlation between an 'X' – in this case, mean length of utterance in morphemes (MLUm) – and a 'Y', in this case, mean length of utterance in words (MLUw). To do this, they counted and compared these Xs and Ys in '40 language transcripts from typically-developing, English-speaking children between the ages of 3;0 and 3;10' (p. 365).

The main point to note here is that both approaches make use of labels and concepts, and that we cannot take these for granted, even when we plan to count and do calculations on instances of, or relationships between, Xs and Ys. It may seem attractive to produce statistics and calculations in a research report, rather than qualitative descriptions, because the former can confer an air of scientific respectability. However, even if the counting is very careful and the statistical procedures impeccable, the findings are meaningless if the classification of things counted is confused, inconsistent or even just naïve. How are we to be sure, for example, which speech acts are to count as 'apologies' or 'compliments'?

These issues need not put you off using either kind of method, but, as discussed in other units in this strand, you should try to be aware of how you are classifying things and whether your categories are defensible. Often, you will use systems devised by previous researchers and this should give you confidence, particularly if you find out about and make sure you understand how they devised their systems of categorising and labelling their Xs and Ys. However, there are still controversies among researchers about how this should be done, so try to be appropriately critical of the categories you use.

A4.3 Ways of measuring and counting

Qualitative and quantitative approaches to research are often contrasted with each other, but, as noted above, even the most quantitative of studies makes use of categories of phenomena that are derived from theories about what things are like and thus contain a qualitative dimension. Conversely, studies that start off as descriptive and interpretive may at some point need to measure and perhaps compare quantities. Furthermore, your reading around a topic will almost certainly lead you to encounters with the findings of studies that have different degrees of emphasis along the qualitative–quantitative continuum, so it is sensible to be aware of some of the theories and methods underlying both.

We are so used to measuring and counting in everyday life that it is easy to forget that, like the observations discussed above, both processes are products of theories and are mediated by language. Obtaining a measurement with a ruler, tape measure or milometer in the car seems like making a direct observation, but it only works because of the social conventions that have established norms of 'centimetres' and 'kilometres', or 'inches' and 'miles' (and the conflict between the two systems is evidence of this). When it is human beings themselves, and their linguistic behaviour or attitudes, that are being measured, it is important to recognise that you are drawing on theories and conventions. It is likely to be impossible to access directly some observable 'variable' about which there is total agreement.

For these reasons, quantitative approaches are better suited to some kinds of enquiry than others. For example, studies of large corpora of language data will usually involve counting the frequency of some lexical or grammatical feature, even if they also include the detailed analysis of some of the specific instances in particular **concordance lines**. Remember, though, that many theoretical decisions have gone into the selection and compilation of material to include in any corpus, as well as into the **tagging systems** used to identify items in the corpus as belonging to particular linguistic categories, and, of course, into the development of the software used in the analysis. So qualitative, interpretive work underpins the counting and measuring that is more readily associated with corpus linguistics.

In another (English) language studies domain, researchers interested in accents often want to establish how frequent a particular sound is in the speech of different speakers, which involves both measuring the quality of sounds produced and counting their frequency. Clark and Hillenbrand (2003) made recordings of 21 speakers from the Michigan area saying 70 sentences that ended with a series of monosyllabic words containing the vowel sounds they were interested in. (The words included, for example, *bead*, *bid*, *heat*, *hit*, *bear*, *hair* and *Bayer*.) They used a spectrogram to measure the formant contours and also devised a listening test. Their conclusions are about the quality of the vowel sounds preceding /r/ in words such as *hear* and *beer* in this particular accent, and are thus derived from multiple examples of the target phenomena produced in tightly controlled conditions. It should be quite apparent that numbers and measurements were indispensable for a study such as this and, even if you are much less well resourced and restricted to an investigation on a much smaller scale, you would probably investigate a similar kind of question using measurement and counting of a similar kind.

Another area of research which is under pressure to generate quantitative evidence is in language teaching – and particularly language testing. This often involves measuring learners' progress, in the hope of identifying which teaching methods work best. Given the time and money invested by individuals, families and governments in the teaching of literacy and of additional languages, it is not surprising that there is a sizeable industry producing and administering tests linked with these enterprises, or that researchers are called upon to investigate 'what works'. The counting and measurement here are even more saturated with underlying theories, and sometimes vested interests, and small-scale projects that can actually generate useful findings are likely to be difficult to carry out. Note, moreover, that the 'what works?' question is a causal one, so any research in this area is inherently more challenging than studies that do not try to find out *why* something is the case.

Nevertheless, such projects are not impossible. A student, Enam, was interested in how children can be taught to spell more accurately. She set up a project in a primary school, where she divided the children to whom she was given access into three groups. One was treated as a 'control' group and given no teaching about a list of target words she identified; a second group was taught a relevant spelling rule; and a third was encouraged to practise the words to be learned using a particular method known as 'look, cover, write, check'. Enam analysed the pre- and post-spelling test results for each group, and concluded that, since overall the control group seemed to make the least progress, 'any intervention seems better than none at all'. However, following conventions in the academic community of practice, she acknowledges: the very small number of children in her study; a number of anomalies in the results which it is hard to account for; the extreme variability in the children's starting point for tackling these spellings, and in their attitudes towards learning and the study itself, and so on. In addition, there were practical challenges in conducting the research, including Enam's own timetable constraints and the absences of some children during part of the project. Overall, such examples suggest that engaging in research that involves the measurement and counting of people's behaviour, particularly when your control over the research context is limited, is best approached with some caution, and may not yield definitive results. What it may help you to do, however, is to learn at first hand some of the techniques and procedures involved in this kind of research.

This unit has invited you to think about the research you plan to do in a slightly different way from that found in some other methods textbooks. Some key points in this unit include:

❏   Be clear about the kinds of things you hope to investigate: work out what the Xs and Ys are in your study.
❏   Identify the questions to which you want to find answers, making sure that they are actually answerable.
❏   Recognise the link between these questions and the methods appropriate for answering them.
❏   The traditional division of research into 'quantitative' and 'qualitative' approaches is not always helpful, and can disguise the fact that both make use of theories, even if these are often left implicit.

Although it is not necessary for you, as a beginning researcher, to become too bogged down by such issues, it can be helpful for you to recognise where in your project you are engaged in observing things, classifying things and measuring things, and that none of these aspects of the research enterprise is without its challenges.

A5   POSSIBILITIES AND PITFALLS

Once you have completed the initial stages of designing your research project, you will no doubt be keen to begin collecting data. This is sensible, and if you are going to meet problems, often the best way of learning to deal with them is by experience. However, while you cannot possibly foresee every eventuality and cover every angle in the abstract, it is useful to be aware of some of the potential problems that may be overcome with planning and forethought. This unit outlines some issues that may arise with reference to people, objects and contexts.

A5.1 Establishing where you stand: researching people

Social attitudes to the practice of research into human behaviour have changed considerably in recent years, and the regulations governing the collection of information about people, including recordings of what they say, are now quite extensive. These may differ from one country to another, but there is a general tendency for legislators to enact laws aimed at protecting people from invasions of their privacy and the misuse of information held about them. The practice of social research has, consistently with this kind of legislation, become increasingly constrained by similar concerns about the privacy and rights of anyone who participates in a research study. As institutions, universities in the UK are required to comply with the Data Protection Act, the Freedom of Information Act and the Human Rights Act: different laws may apply in other countries, but the general tendencies illustrated by UK law are found elsewhere too. The details of these laws are unlikely to affect your research study directly, but if you do want to know more about them, there is a government website which you may consult (www.opsi.gov.uk/ACTS).

Of more obvious, direct relevance to students doing their own research are the institutional regulations (which are likely to be designed in part to ensure compliance with these laws) developed by committees with responsibility for ethical procedures. One of the implications of all this is that you must usually ask people for permission to observe them, especially if you want to make recordings of them, whether audio or video. If you plan to do this, or if you interview them or ask to them to complete questionnaires, you need to think carefully about the ethical implications of this kind of contact, and to obtain their informed consent for precisely the procedures you intend to use. Obviously, if the people involved are not of an age or state of mind to give their consent, then the issues are more complicated, and consent may be needed from someone qualified to act on their behalf. In addition, people doing research in schools in the UK may be required to submit to a Criminal Records Bureau (CRB) check – and this can take several weeks.

The paragraphs above provide a basic indication of the regulatory aspects of these issues, but you should also consult your supervisor and any guidelines issued by your institution to ensure that you follow the appropriate procedures. While research is sub-ject to laws and institutional regulations based on respect for people's rights, including the right to privacy, some of these considerations are much less acute for an individual researcher whose work will be read only by two or three other people and will never reach 'the public domain' (i.e. be available as a publication that anyone can access). However, the principles of confidentiality are the same, and it is not impossible that your dissertation could form the basis of a publication in due course (see strand 9), while there is always the possibility that you may want to develop your early work into a larger project which might be published. Therefore, it is advisable to familiarise your-self with the expectations of good practice from the earliest stages of doing research. Cameron (2001), for example, discusses these issues in some detail, and the British Association for Applied Linguistics (BAAL) has guidelines on its website for employed researchers, with a condensed version for students. You may need to produce a form for your research participants to sign, and you will need to know how this is handled in your particular circumstances. Some institutions and departments provide stu-dents with a pro-forma which they can use with minimal adaptation, while others expect students to develop something specific to their own projects. See Johnstone (2000: 43–7) for some examples based on her own students' projects.

Associated with the official considerations of privacy, consent and legal obliga-tions are some perhaps less obvious ethical issues that can arise when you become a researcher. It is probably anthropologists and ethnographers, in particular, who have published most about the challenges of participating in the life of a community while simultaneously conducting research, but even fleeting contacts with the people who provide you with data constitute relationships, and you may be taken aback to find yourself negotiating what is sometimes an ambiguous role.

For example, suppose you have decided to collect some language data from children. You may have negotiated access to a suitable school, successfully completed a CRB check, obtained appropriate informed consent and begun to collect data as planned. To one of the children you meet, however – perhaps a child who is not involved in your study, but someone who comes across you in a public area of the school building – you represent an unfamiliar adult to talk to. A younger child may 'latch on' to you and unexpectedly disclose some sensitive information; an adolescent may give out signals that s/he finds you attractive. What do you do? Or how would you handle questions from an informant who regards you as a language expert about 'correct' pronunciation, as you attempt to collect data about regional variations in accent? Of course it may be that nothing like this happens in your own project, and you cannot anticipate everything that will happen. Nevertheless, while working towards your own objectives of collecting data, it is important too to be aware of the way in which you may be perceived by those you interact with as a researcher, and to be prepared for that role.

A5.2 Making things work for you

It seems fairly obvious that if you plan to record people talking you need some electronic equipment that works. However, each time I have taught courses involving students recording spoken data someone has discovered the frustration of the dying battery, or the poor sound quality produced by an inappropriate machine, or has lost the precious recording through inadvertent wiping of the tape or unsuccessful transferring of the file. So, if your research involves the use of any equipment at all, take some time to make sure that it is the best available tool for the job, that you know how to use it, that you are fully equipped with the right discs, batteries, mains electricity leads, and so on. Always do a dry run before you plunge in to the first session of actually collecting data, preferably in the same location you will be using when you start in earnest. Do you need an extension lead in case the plug sockets are nowhere near where you need to sit with your interviewee, for example?

Even if you have decided that you need no electronic equipment for the study you have planned, it is embarrassing and unhelpful to your project to have your note-taking pencil break or pen run out of ink in the middle of an interview. So always be fully equipped for the data collection process you plan to use, and have back-up materials to hand.

Think, too, about how you will carry what you need and make sure you have something appropriate that makes access to everything straightforward. Always remember that if people are giving their time to participate in your research they have a right to expect you to be efficient and well organised.

Some other inanimate objects that may seem to conspire against you are books, connections to the internet, hard drives and data storage devices, printers, mobile phones, and so on. If you need resources from the library (and you will), make sure that you can access them when you need them, and if there is to be a delay, take account of this in your planning. If you are building a corpus of texts, make sure you know what is involved in the preparation of hard copies for scanning, and electronic versions for analysis. Again, do a dry run on a small quantity of your data in case you discover that any stage is not working as you expected or takes a lot longer. If your texts are available only online, check that you can practically – and legally – download them in the form you need.

Most universities no longer accept problems with computing equipment as valid grounds for not submitting assessed work on time. Everyone who routinely works with computers knows the importance of keeping back-up copies of data and files, and yet everyone can probably cite instances when they, or someone they know well, failed to observe this basic procedure. Try not to let the obviously disastrous consequences of this afflict you: do regular housekeeping and make copies of your data, notes, plans and draft reports of the project. Be systematic in labelling files and folders so that you know where to put your hands on the material you need.

A5.3 Fitting into the bigger picture

It will often be the case that the less experienced you are as a researcher, the less time you have to devote to your research, as you progress from a short independent study prior to your dissertation, perhaps, as an undergraduate, towards the three or more years of doctoral work and possibly funded studies lasting several years if your job eventually entails a research component. So management of limited time is very important from the outset of research projects, and I suggest constructing a timeline that works backwards from the deadline for submission, with at least a few days built in at that point for printer problems, final proof-reading and the like, and identifies milestones between then and the point you are at now. Having planned such an overview, you can then 'zoom in' to each stage as you approach it and include more specific detail to help you use each week, day and even hour that you have available in the most productive way.

Figure A5.3.1 is an example of the tasks that Rosie (whose project is cited in units A3 and B1) set herself for a short period between meetings with her supervisor. She was at the stage when she had decided on her study and was about to collect her data, using an existing corpus.

Note that Rosie is working simultaneously on several fronts. As well as clarifying for herself which corpus or corpora might contain the data she needs, she is continuing to read about her topic, focusing at this stage on the methods previous researchers have used, and also thinking ahead to the help she needs from staff in her department other than her supervisor.

Many students find that their research projects become a very absorbing dimension of their lives, and it is easy to forget that your particular project is less central to everyone else's concerns. Your tutors, even though they have a responsibility to see you at agreed times, may not be available immediately when you have questions, and even short delays can add up and result in your work being slowed down. One way to counteract this problem is to have several aspects of your work in hand at any one time, making it possible to switch between tasks and still make progress if one aspect has to be temporarily put on hold.

Timing can also present problems when other people's arrangements don't coincide

For Next Supervision: WEEK 5 end /6 if staff name is around?

- Draft critical review - 2'000 words (approx)
- ask library about COLT CD-ROM.   }
- do internet search for COLT (full corpus).   }   staff name has staff name co-ordinating - waiting for email /appthment.
- ask   staff name   for COLT cd-ROM.   }
- See if I can find BNC - full corpus - what data is on it (speaker/hearer) participant! none - but is it!
- Chat room search - top 3 no. of hits   - hard info to find - only current users online.
- look into methodologies of : T labov ✓
                                D James ✓
                                T McEnery
                                A Deigan (lang+desire) ✓
                                AB Stenström (teenage talk) ✓ - corpus compilation? but
                                EL Battistella (Bad lang) ✓
- choose word selection for study.

Figure A5.3.1 One dissertation student's plan of tasks to tackle during a two-week period

with the requirements of your department. Longitudinal studies (where the X to be investigated is some kind of change over time, such as 'Does a specific feature of the language use of boys and girls respectively diverge between the ages of two and five years?') are impossible if you have only five weeks for data collection. Even a very feasible project with a short timescale, though, may need something to be happening during exactly the five weeks that are available to you that simply does not occur then. School terms and holidays, for example, may fall at just the wrong times for you to collect data from children's first few days in a new class; the family with whom you have negotiated access to information may have a holiday booked for the one weekend when you hoped to tape-record them, and so on.

Texts are generally less of a problem in this respect than people, but access to a published corpus or a collection of your friends' text messages may be secured more slowly than you hoped. As with spoken data, you must make sure you are not breaking any rules of copyright or confidentiality; this could apply with personal documents or those which are commercially sensitive, for example, or material such as internal communications in an institution such as a school. A growing research field is that associated with computer-mediated communication, where, again, personal 'interaction' can be analysed without the labour of transcribing speech – but, if this is email correspondence, chat-rooms or similar forums, you may well need the authors' permission.

If your project involves statistical calculations, additional forward planning may be required, especially if you need help from a facility such as a statistics advisory service. Such support services are typically very busy, and are often unable to sort out problems with data once it has been collected or processed in a particular way. Online guidance from the Statistical Advisory Service at the University of Reading, for example, informs students that 'statistical inputs to a project at its planning stage can help to lead to better designed studies, as well as saving time and resources. This is as important as, if not more important than collaborating in data analysis' (Statistical Advisory Service, University of Reading 2007).

Other obstacles that may interfere with your plans are on an even larger scale, such as, for one researcher, the outbreak of war which coincided with a limited window for data collection (Piquemal and Kouritzin 2006). Illness, transportation failures, changes in the institutional or political context: all these things can interfere with your research plans. However, you would need to be very unlucky indeed to be beset by more than one or two of these contingencies in the course of any single study!

DOING THE RESEARCH: COLLECTING DATA   A6

Most student research projects involve the collection of some new data – and doing this is an experience that is likely to prove valuable in all sorts of ways. Some departments, institutions or specific programmes of study will specify that this is an essential component of the dissertation or research project. (See B1 on checking any regulations like this that may apply to your own study.) However, it is possible to produce an extended piece of scholarship that does not rely on collecting new data. So, if your research is of the more theoretical, library-based type, this strand may not seem directly relevant to you. On the other hand, as a reader of other people's research articles and books, it is useful to be aware of the practicalities of data collection, not least because these may account for aspects of published research that you find less than wholly satisfactory. There is also a third possibility, which is that you bring your own analysis to an existing data set. You might, for example, use the extensive database of recordings and transcriptions of children's language, CHILDES, to investigate a question of your own devising, without making new recordings yourself.

While B6 explores general issues in data collection, such as what kind of data you need, where you can obtain it, how much you need, and so on, this unit takes a very practical approach to a range of methods of collecting the kind of data likely to be useful in answering questions about English Language topics. Do remember that the reading you do will provide you with potential models for appropriate methods of collecting data: you should not need to reinvent the wheel!

A6.1 Collecting and processing written data

Putting together a set of written texts which are already published, especially if they are in electronic form, is probably one of the most straightforward ways of collecting data. You will need to take into account issues of privacy, copyright, and so on (see A5), but you have more control over the data collection process than if your project involves negotiating with other people. If your texts are not already digitised, you should consider whether to scan them using software with optical character recognition (OCR), so that you can process and mark them electronically. If you prefer to work on hard copies, consider making several, so that you can identify different kinds of features, correct mistakes or revise your annotations.

If your texts include components other than language, such as images, consider whether these will become part of your data or be excluded from it. You should recognise that this is a theoretical decision: indeed any data that is derived from acts of communication has already been transformed to some extent by being used in research rather than for its original purpose. The typographical features of texts are integral to them in their original communicative form, and you need to think about how thoroughly you include information about these dimensions in your processing and analysis of the language. Try to make principled decisions, and to be explicit about these, rather than taking the easy option – which may often be to ignore everything but the strictly linguistic aspects of your texts.

Keep notes in your project notebook of what you do as you go along: it's surprising how easily you can be baffled by your own work if you leave it for a while and return to it partly processed.

A6.2 Collecting and processing spoken data

For many students, the idea of collecting and analysing spontaneous spoken language is a motivating aspect of doing some independent research. Much of their study up to this point has described the features of this ubiquitous component of human interaction. They have learned to identify patterns and variations in its sounds and grammatical structure, the lexical choices speakers make and the subtle and impressive cues they use to negotiate turn-taking as well as self-presentation, the management of mutual 'face' needs, and so on. The prospect of arranging to investigate some brand new material, which no linguist has seen before, and to seek out equivalent patterns in this material, is very exciting. It is also quite daunting – and quite a challenge to work through all the steps entailed in such research projects. Succeeding in such an enterprise, however, is immensely satisfying.

Textbooks about social research tend to list 'observation' as a method separate from recording speech, but I have not done so here as I am assuming that your interest is in some dimension of language behaviour, rather than in the other kinds of behaviour which may be the subject of observational methods in social research. One particular dimension of this method is significant to note, however. Ethnographic research often includes an element of 'participant observation', where the researcher explores a social setting and its associated behaviour 'from the inside', participating in the life of those being researched. It may be appropriate for you to take such a role in your own study, but do be aware of the very difficult balance you will need to strike between your two roles. In particular, if you are collecting spoken language data, your own participation in any interaction is likely to influence it, making your study susceptible to the criticism that your data is less 'authentic' than it would be if none of the speakers was simultaneously a researcher, with a particular aspect of language behaviour in mind.

If you do need spontaneous spoken language, and if you plan to analyse it in detail, then you will probably need to make and transcribe high quality recordings. You will also need to identify the circumstances in which the kind of language you are interested in is likely to be produced. Transactional language, for example, is by definition likely to be found in public settings, while studies of how in-groups and friendships are maintained require access to 'closed' settings (such as people's own homes) or informal contexts. If your interest is in regional dialect or accent, you will inevitably need to be in a particular geographical location, but remember, too, the potential sources of television, radio and the internet; Wray and Bloomer (2006: 143) advise that, if you intend to gather recorded data for this purpose from the media, you could 'target "passer-by" interviews on news broadcasts, schools programmes that use interviews with children, and "fly-on-the-wall" documentaries'. Do be sure to give careful thought to the process of collecting spoken language data. It may seem relatively easy to get a group of your friends round for a drink and leave a recorder running, but the resulting data is likely to be appropriate for only a limited kind of investigation – so think more imaginatively about the possibilities.

Table A6.2.1 shows some examples of potential projects involving unscripted, unelicited spoken language. They are drawn from various sources, including projects undertaken by students in departments where I have worked. They should give you some idea of the range of ways in which you can collect spoken data for an English Language research project.

Table A6.2.1 Types of spoken data associated with a range of research topics

Broad research topic	Data collected
Child language development	Several recordings of a young child over a period of weeks as s/he learns to read (Wray and Bloomer 2006)
Pragmatics	A lesson in a school, with a specific focus on teacher's instructions to pupils
Power and accountability in spoken interaction	One or more broadcast interviews with political figures
Power relationships within the family	A series of recordings of a family at the dinner table
Transactional language	Recordings of interactions at the desk in a university library
Discourse markers	15 minutes of relaxed conversation, to include instances of *oh, well, you know, I mean* (Cameron 2001)

Data on some topics researched within spoken language is harder to collect because it is unpredictable. Part of my own MA dissertation on children's metalinguistic awareness included utterances produced by my son (then aged 4) where language itself was the topic of what he said. They included lots of questions, such as 'Why do people say, "Say the magic word," when it isn't "abracadabra" or anything like that, it's just "please"?' (Sealey 1990: 45), and, from the back seat of the car I was driving, when I muttered 'thank you' in the direction of a fellow motorist who had not acknowledged that I'd let him into the traffic, 'Are you being sarcastic?' (I was!). Although the approach is open to a range of criticisms, the only method I could use was to record such examples in writing as soon as possible after they occurred. Similar methods have been used by researchers collecting examples of exchanges between speakers in public places, such as apologies or compliments.

Another option is to collect data from broadcast sources, such as dramas or films, recognising that scripted talk, while different in well-documented ways from spontaneous talk, nevertheless draws on the norms and conventions of the culture in which it is produced, and so may be a source of data about these, if only indirectly. The same is true of much comedy material, which may work by disrupting expectations about social interaction, and can thus be another source of spoken language data – provided the scripted provenance of any such data is acknowledged and taken into account in the analysis.

As with the written material you collect, you have a lot of work to do before your raw recordings are ready for detailed analysis. The most obvious first stage is to transcribe some or all of your material, and how you do this will, as you would expect, depend largely on what you intend to use the data for. This is where the 'data collection' phase of your study begins to merge into the 'data analysis' phase – as is discussed at length in Reading D7.1, and these issues are dealt with in more detail in strand 7.

A6.3 Collecting and processing elicited data

The diagram in Figure A4.1.1 illustrates the different degrees to which the researcher is involved in the production of data. To access certain kinds of knowledge, it may be impractical or inappropriate to rely on collecting examples of language produced for purposes other than your study, and you may need to engineer contexts in which people provide you with data by responding to your questions or other kinds of stimulus. Approaches to the collection of elicited data include interviews, questionnaires, diaries, discourse completion instruments and experiments. Some **methodological** issues associated with these methods are discussed in B4 and C6, and you should think carefully about whether these methods really can elicit the kind of evidence you need to answer your research questions. More practically, each of these methods has its operational advantages and challenges, and these will be our concern here.

Both questionnaires and interviews are, obviously, ways of accessing information by asking 'informants' to tell you something. Both can take a variety of forms, from very open-ended questions which can generate a wide range of responses, to much more tightly circumscribed questions to which responses must be selected from a predetermined list. From a practical point of view, the tightly controlled 'tick-box'

DOING THE RESEARCH: COLLECTING DATA   29

questionnaire is less time-consuming, and so can be used with a much larger number of informants than the unstructured, free-form interview. Moreover, the resulting data can be coded much more quickly, and potentially automatically, if the forms have been designed to be machine-readable. On the other hand, the material you may obtain from an interview in which the informant has free rein to respond very much in their own terms to the issues you want to know about may give you much greater insight into those issues than you can obtain from a set of 'yes/no' responses to your questions. The careful design of both questionnaires and interview schedules is a crucial aspect of using these methods to collect data, and it is dealt with in many textbooks for social researchers. What follows is a digest of the main points you will read about if you consult such sources – I have drawn particularly on Blaxter et al. (2001).

A6.3.1 Types of interview

❏   *medium of communication*: face-to-face; by email; by telephone
❏   *medium of recording*: video and audio; audio only; notes
❏   *place*: home of interviewee or interviewer; public place; place of work
❏   *degree of structure*: tightly prescribed; semi-structured; open-ended
❏   *approach*: direct questions; stimuli for informants to respond to, such as statements, photographs or audio recordings; artefacts (such as, if your informants are children for example, toys or puzzles), invitations to talk, such as 'Can you tell me about . . .?'
❏   *information given to interviewee about interview in advance*: very little; general summary of themes to be covered; detailed questions, to encourage prior reflection
❏   *participants*: one interviewer and one interviewee; one interviewer and pairs of interviewees; 'focus group' of interviewees and one or more interviewers
❏   *aim*: to elicit particular linguistic behaviour (e.g. for a dialect study); to elicit factual information (e.g. about experiences of using different language varieties in different social contexts); to elicit information about attitudes and values (e.g. for a survey on attitudes to accents).

A6.3.2 Questionnaires

Questionnaires may seem to be straightforward ways to gather quite a lot of information efficiently, but, especially as you have studied language and the challenges of negotiating meaning, you probably know by now that this is not always the case. Also, questionnaires, like interviews, range in style from highly structured to more open-ended formats, and you should think carefully about what is most likely to generate the data you need.

Some designs are very close to tightly structured interviews, such as those used by market researchers, who may have stopped you in the street and read questions out to you. An advantage of this method is that you get immediate responses from any informant willing to speak to you, whereas questionnaires emailed or posted to potential respondents are likely to be completed by only a limited proportion of those you target.

Blaxter et al. (2001: 179) list seven basic types of question, based on the kinds of surveys typically carried out in the social sciences. You may need to use some or all of these types, because even if your main interest is in some aspect of language, you are likely to want 'demographic' information, too, about categories such as your respondents' age, sex, place of birth, and so on (plan this carefully: don't collect information you don't need, but don't neglect to record something that is relevant to your analysis). The question types listed by Blaxter et al. are 'quantity or information, category, list or multiple choice, scale, ranking, complex grid or table, and open-ended'. Types of question are illustrated in greater detail in C6, but you will be familiar with most of them if you have filled out evaluations of courses you have studied in your educational institution, when you may have been asked to indicate, for example:

1   what percentage of the lectures you attended (quantity or information),
2   whether you opted to be assessed by exam, assignment or a mixture (category),
3   which of a possible set of topics you found particularly rewarding (list or multiple choice),
4   how well you thought the course fulfilled its aims (on a scale of, say, 1–5),
5   which three of six possible reforms to the course you would rate in order of greatest importance (ranking),
6   your views on several aspects of the course, in a nine-cell grid containing, along one dimension, the contribution of each of 'lectures', 'seminars', 'assignment topics' to, on another dimension, 'enjoyment', 'relevance' and 'interest' (complex grid or table), and
7   your own comments about the course in free text boxes (open-ended).

The kinds of problem which novice (and even experienced) researchers find with their questionnaires have been identified by many commentators. Foddy (1994: 181) lists several types of question that have been shown to cause respondents some difficulty, and these include questions that: 'required more than one answer; contained too many meaningful words; included qualifying clauses or phrases; included reference to two or more subjects; included difficult vocabulary; or included instructions'. Other question types which textbooks counsel against include loaded or leading questions, and questions which ask for particularly sensitive or personal information. This links with the design of the questionnaire, which should include clear and accessible font size and presentation, information about you and your project, and about the confidentiality of responses, clear instructions (do you want people to circle, tick or delete parts of the response?) and a note of thanks at the end for their time and co-operation. If you need the form returned by post, make sure you make this easy and free to the respondent: include a stamped envelope, but have your address on the form, too, in case the envelope goes astray. The other advice which you will find in anything you read about how to use questionnaires as a form of research data is to do a pilot study. Ask some people who are not going to complete the 'real thing', but whose abilities to do so are equivalent to those of your actual informants, to complete a draft of your questionnaire, and take their feedback very seriously. For some kinds of questionnaire, you may need to include a 'training' session, to make sure your respondents understand precisely what you want from them (see C6).

A6.3.3 Diaries or journals

Like questionnaires and interviews, diaries share the limitations of methods which rely on 'self-reporting'. As well as having knowledge and/or experience of the topic, informants must be willing and able to share this with you honestly, and have the time, motivation and level of literacy necessary to take the trouble to do so. On the other hand, diaries can be a means to access information about your area of interest which avoids the intrusive and potentially distorting aspects of recording interactions; they can also produce evidence of the phenomenon in which you are interested without the need to trawl through masses of irrelevant material. Before electronic sound recordings were possible, the only way people could record developments in young children's language was to make notes in some kind of longitudinal journal of the sounds and then utterances they were heard to make – and this can still be a useful source of evidence if recording equipment is not available at a critical moment. Teachers may ask their students to keep journals, to give them additional insights into aspects of their learning, including language learning (see C6), while other diary studies have focused on literacy practices, asking informants to keep a record of everything they read or write over a specified period of time. If your area of interest is bilingualism, you might ask people to record which variety they use in which contexts, and so on. It is very likely that the method will be more useful if supplemented by others: the diary may well, for example, form the basis of a follow-up interview, structuring the topics to be pursued in greater depth as both interviewer and interviewee have shared knowledge of a very relevant text.

A6.3.4 Elicitation instruments

Linguistic research makes use of various kinds of stimuli to produce data from informants. **Introspection** has a long history as a method used to probe the grammaticality of particular structures, and you will no doubt have read textbooks and articles which have presented you with potential sentences and asked you to reflect on whether these are acceptable in your variety of English. This method has been criticised on a number of grounds (see Milroy and Gordon 2003), but it has the advantage that it is relatively straightforward to use with large numbers of informants and may be appropriate for specific kinds of question.

Sociolinguistic studies use well established methods to elicit speech which includes particular features of interest to the researcher. People may be asked to read a passage aloud, and their pronunciation of particular sounds is noted, perhaps contrasted with the same speakers' pronunciation when asked to concentrate on these sounds, as when reading a list of paired words, and with the more relaxed production elicited by getting them to talk while doing something else at the same time (Harnsberger et al. 2008).

A slightly different kind of elicitation involves asking people to imagine a familiar situation and what they would say – or even what they think others would say, given information about the participants and the context. Researchers have used both role play and written 'discourse completion tasks' to generate data in this way. An obvious criticism is of the artificiality of the evidence produced, but these approaches have the advantage of focusing informants' attention on particular kinds of interaction, typically apologies, requests, refusals and compliments, which do not occur often enough to be recorded in any quantity by chance.

A6.3.5 Experiments

The final type of data collection method to be discussed in this unit is the experiment. I discuss in other units some of the criticisms of experimental methods for language-related research. A core objection is that experiments have their origins in the sciences which can rely on the 'indifference' of their objects of study: the experimenter can control the setting, manipulate variables and observe replicable outcomes as causes produce effects, unaffected by the reflexivity of human beings with their self-awareness, interests and values – and propensity to communicate with each other. Experimental methods are thus most appropriate for collecting data in studies whose interest is less in language at the level of discourse and social interaction, and more linked with its physical and biological dimensions. Typical domains are experiments in auditory and visual perception, including with very young infants. If you decide that the Xs and Ys of your own study do lend themselves to the collection of experimental data, then I would advise you to read extensively about similar experiments, including practical aspects, to plan the procedure in great detail and to do a pilot run before running the actual experiment. As with some kinds of questionnaire, experiments may well require in addition that the participants receive some 'training' before the experiment proper is run.

A6.4 Combined methods

Because language and human beings are both very complex phenomena, it is likely that no single method will give you all the data you would ideally collect about the topic of your research. Although time and resources may be against you conducting, for example, an extended ethnography with lengthy observations, fieldnotes, recordings, interviews and additional elicited data, you should consider the possibility of **triangulating** one kind of data with another. As we have seen, each of the methods used in researching language has its critics and disadvantages, so drawing on more than one approach may help to mitigate some of the problems.

You could follow up some of your questionnaires with interviews, for example, to explore certain issues in more depth; or you could take issues raised in your small number of interviews and ask a larger group of people about them by means of a questionnaire. Some researchers take transcripts of recordings back to the people who made them, and probe aspects of what was said (although don't be surprised if the speakers have forgotten all about what to you is a fascinating utterance in your carefully transcribed record of the interaction!). Your bilingual informant may be willing both to keep a diary and to allow you to record some conversation in which code-switching occurs, so that you can compare their perceptions of how they use each variety with some empirical evidence. Always bear in mind, however, the importance of being as clear as you are able about your methodological decisions: a rag-bag of data of many different kinds is unlikely to help you answer your research questions!

A6.5 Housekeeping

It is important to catalogue your data in a consistent way, giving each component a fairly transparent name. Record your decisions and when you come to write up the whole project, remember that for the reader, who will be much less familiar with the data than you are, a brief summary of what your data consists of can be enormously helpful. This may be in a tabulated form (remembering too that the categories you decide to use are also underpinned by theories – see C5); this will not take up too much of your word limit, but it provides both you and your reader with a snapshot of the evidence on which you are drawing.

CLARIFYING WHAT YOU HAVE FOUND OUT   A7

> A clear and tidy data set is a first step towards a thorough analysis: once we have a rough idea what is going on, it is much easier to investigate individual issues further.
>
> (Rasinger 2008: 109)

In B3 and C3, I explain why I think that it is better to have some idea about how you will analyse your data before you begin collecting it than to start thinking about this only after the collection stage. Otherwise, you can easily be faced with a large amount of material and the sense that you are little further forward with your research project than when you began compiling a list of potentially relevant reading. However, even if you have planned ahead, you will probably find that the stage of analysing your data does not go exactly as you anticipated. It is at this point that you may need to make some amendments to the framework of your study, making the most of what you have even if it is not exactly what you hoped for.

In B5, there are several examples of studies which presented the researchers with unexpected problems. Another applied linguist who responded to my request for examples of such challenges focused on the stage of analysing the data collected. He 'confessed' that his data had not always enabled him to answer the question he set out to research. For example, he identified a node word whose **collocates** he thought would be revealing – but his corpus search revealed no obvious pattern. In spite of this, he realised that there were some significant features of its semanticity. His advice was, 'Never abandon sinking data; and if the data gives you lemons, make lemonade!'

So, assuming you are now at the stage of having identified clear research questions, determined the data you will use to answer them and collected this data, it is sensible to keep up with your 'housekeeping' – taking stock of what you have in the way of data and reminding yourself once again about what you hoped to find out and how you planned to do it.

> Draw up a table to use as a checklist, based on your original plans. Use one
> column for your research questions, another for the Xs and Ys that are the
> object of your investigation, a third for the data you planned to collect that
> represents these Xs and Ys, and a fourth for the data you have actually man-
> aged to collect. Include a fifth column for notes about what needs to be done
> with the data as you analyse it.

Comments

If columns 3 and 4 match exactly, so much the better. However, if for whatever reason
you have less – or different, or perhaps even more – material to analyse than you
expected, then think carefully about the effects of this discrepancy on your questions and approach to analysis. For example, if the response rate on a questionnaire
you have distributed has been disappointingly low, consider whether you can gather
an equivalent amount of data some other way. Would it be possible to find suitable
respondents using a different method to obtain contact details, such as the knowledge
of someone in your initial group who has been supportive of your research? Perhaps
you have been successful in collecting data from young and older adults, but not the
adolescents you intended to include, owing to problems of access to a school site. In
such a case, if it becomes clear that you can realistically compare the responses of only
two groups of informants rather than three, what are the implications for your study?
Can you adjust your questions to reflect the new situation? Obviously this is not ideal,
and you should be honest about what happened when writing up your findings, but it
is also important to recognise how to work with the data you do have and not despair
if you have met problems in collecting your data.

A7.1 Types of data and approaches to analysis

On the assumption that you do arrive at the point where you have questions and data
that match sufficiently for you to start your analysis, how do you proceed? I refer you
again to Figure A4.1.1 (p. 17), which represents a sliding scale of intervention by the
researcher in pursuit of language data. The same continuum may be used to illustrate
the degree to which the resulting data is likely to lend itself to an obvious method of
analysis. That is, the more the researcher has planned and intervened in the production of the data, the fewer the options are likely to be about how to analyse it. This
should become clearer as we consider various methods in turn. The first part of the
discussion which follows relates mainly to written data, followed by consideration of
some further issues raised by spoken data. Numerical data may also feature in many
research projects, and will be referred to at various points in this unit, and in more
detail towards the end.

A7.2 From 'closed' questionnaires to collections of written texts

If a study involves a survey comprising questions which require written responses (including ticks, crosses or even clicks on an on-screen image) from among pre-determined, limited choices, then the initial data analysis could in principle be done by a machine. Its job would be to identify and count each instance of the various categories of response to each question, and this would generate the initial 'results' of the study. Advances in technology (including free software for online surveys, such as GoogleForms and SurveyMonkey) make this process increasingly easy. Obviously the research would still require the interpretation of these statistics, but the analyst would have very few options about how to use the data from the questionnaires to arrive at some findings.

It is possible, of course, to carry out more sophisticated operations on data of this kind. For example, it may be relevant to do some 'cross-tabulation' – identifying respondents who gave ratings of '1' to each of several questions, and perhaps separating these into two further groups, of, say, older and younger speakers. What is clearly not possible, however, is to use data generated by this method to carry out discourse analysis. Similar considerations apply to the numerical outputs from an experiment measuring, say, response times to verbal or visual stimuli, or the spectrograms of specific sounds produced by informants reading aloud set lists of words. In other words, some choices of data collection method entail certain approaches to analysis and exclude others.

At the other end of the spectrum, if the data is a collection of texts which were originally written for some communicative purpose other than research, the potential approaches to analysis are much more varied, and the first stage of the process is therefore to refer back to the research questions and decide which analytical method(s) will best lead to useful answers. You may need to generate some quantitative results – about the frequency of particular lexical items, for example ('how many Xs?') – in which case, as for the questionnaires, a machine can assist with some of the work: this is partly what corpus tools have been developed for. If your questions are more qualitative ('what is X like?'), then you will need a different approach, although you may eventually want to explore how much or how many of the qualities you identify characterise your text(s).

In either case, you are likely to be looking for patterns in your data: to be transforming, and even reducing, in some meaningful way, the full set of material you began with to something which describes and/or explains it economically. There is a huge amount of literature on the analysis of discourse, to which scholars from several disciplines have contributed. It may be that you designed your project as an extension of something you studied earlier in your course, where you learned a particular approach to the analysis of written texts, so that you are reasonably well equipped to apply similar approaches to your larger data collection. On the other hand, this may be your first foray into analysing written text in any depth, but in either case you should by now have read fairly extensively about approaches to the analysis of discourse and have identified some 'probes' to make use of as you begin your analysis.

A range of these sources is included in the Further Reading section of this book, but below is a brief digest of the kinds of perspectives you could take to the analysis of written texts – always depending, of course, on what it is that you are trying to find out.

Research into language may be carried out to find out more about language itself, but it may also be done in order to find out about how language is used as an individual and social resource. This cannot be an absolute distinction, since language is a human product, and is always linked to human practice, but the emphasis in the questions posed, and thus in the analysis of the data, may be more social or more linguistic.

For example, Fairclough and like-minded critical discourse analysts advocate starting with 'a social problem which has a semiotic aspect', and investigating the problem using as data instances of the discourse (and other semiotic resources) associated with it (Fairclough 2001: 121). Such approaches take components of the social problem at the 'macro' level (social structures, institutionalised practices, genres), and explore how these are linked with microlinguistic features such as modality, nominalisations, and the grammatical representation of agency (active or passive clauses, patterns of transitivity). A detailed summary can also be found in Fairclough (2003: 190–4) of pointers for the critical discourse analyst.

While not completely divorced from social contexts, other, more linguistically oriented studies look at patterns internal to the language of the texts collected as data, such as, for example, the co-selection of particular nouns and modifiers, or representations of time through choice of tense in different kinds of narrative. If you think back to early courses you have taken in the description of language, you will probably remember becoming familiar with its various levels, from sounds, through morphemes, words, phrases and clauses to stretches of connected discourse – and each one of these can provide a perspective from which to approach your data analysis. Gee (1999) lists ways to conceptualise 'grammar in communication', elaborating on how clauses and participants realise what Halliday terms 'the **experiential function** of language' (p. 149); how grammatical relations realise 'the **interpersonal function**'; how the '**textual function**' is evident in choices about the ordering of elements in discourse; how 'the **logical function**' is expressed in the way clauses are related to each other; and he concludes by reviewing aspects of cohesion, advising that:

> in starting a discourse analysis, the analyst can ask questions like: How does cohesion work in this text to connect pieces of information and in what ways? How does this text fail to connect other pieces of information? What sort of sense are these connections making or failing to make and to what communicative ends?
>
> (Gee 1999: 161)

If you are unsure how to begin your discourse analysis, look at readings such as these and extract headings to use as a checklist for the contents of your analytical 'toolbox'. Identify which aspects of the particular texts which comprise your data are likely to be relevant, and select an appropriate 'tool' to begin with, such as patterns in modality, metaphor, clause type or cohesion – or whatever will give you an initial purchase on your texts – and work outwards from there.

Key Critic

A7.3 Analysing spoken data: first steps

If your data consists of recordings of spoken language, whether elicited or more spontaneously produced, the process of analysis begins at the transcription stage. As explained by several of the authors of the Further Reading texts, and discussed in C7 and Reading D7.1, the transformation of language from spoken to written data is an activity which is saturated with theory. Cameron (2001) discusses a range of relevant themes, including why a written record of spoken language is essential for analysis; why analysts should try to 'unlearn' the cultural bias which privileges writing above speech, characterising the latter as incoherent; why it is important to aim for faithful representations of what was said, and avoid the (sometimes unintended) tendency to 'tidy up' the data; how to decide which features to include and how to represent these with written symbols; how to decide on the amount of detail to include ('the trade-off between accuracy and detail on one hand, and clarity and readability on the other' p. 39); the surprisingly long time it takes to transcribe even short periods of recorded talk; options for representing speaker turns visually; options for representing (non-standard) pronunciation. In her summary of the issues on p. 43 she concludes, 'There is no "standard" way to transcribe talk', emphasising once again that your decisions about this are methodological – not just a simple technique, but a procedure linked with all the other dimensions of the research process.

Transcribed spoken data may, of course, take various forms. Cameron's (2001) concern is largely with unplanned speech, but projects may entail the analysis of elicited spoken data, such as interviews. The same considerations arise, but the decisions about how to transcribe may be different. A sociolinguistic interview, for example, aimed at encouraging the production of a particular phoneme, will involve a different approach to transcription from that appropriate for an interview about, say, informants' attitudes to accents.

A7.4 Identifying patterns

Assuming you have your data in written form, whether it was written or spoken when you first collected it, what will you do with it next? As you can no doubt anticipate, the answer will be 'it depends' – but, as with written data, you are likely to be looking for patterns. Do some similar themes emerge from several of your interviews, or in the open-ended, free text answers in your questionnaires? Does the production of a particular phoneme differ in a way which seems to correspond with some attribute of the speakers (such as their age or sex)? Is there a similar point in the elicited narratives at which several of your speakers switch from past to present tense? Are the modifiers for names of products in your set of adverts similar semantically (e.g. they are all words denoting size) or grammatically (e.g. there is a tendency for the modifiers to be nominal rather than adjectival)?

To some extent, the process of analysing your data is a continuation or extension of the identification of Xs and Ys which you have been doing since you began your project. If you are asking 'What is X like?', and X is in this case 'the "coming-out" narratives of young lesbians', for example, then, having collected your data set (several such narratives), your analysis entails identifying the sub-set of components, the Xs and Ys, if you like, which these narratives share – or, indeed, which some include while others don't. This process is similar to that suggested for qualitative sociological studies, but as a linguist you will be identifying not only themes ('anxieties about coming out to parents', say) but also linguistic features, such as how pronouns and grammatical realisations of agency are encoded in the telling of the narratives. There is more discussion and some examples in units B7 and C7 of identifying and coding themes and patterns.

A7.5 Identifying quantities

If your original research questions were of the type, 'How many Xs occur in the context of Y?', or 'Are Xs distributed differently in texts of type Y and those of type Z?', then you will need to do some counting and calculating. However, even if your original questions are more qualitative, you may well find that it will support your descriptions of what you have found to quantify in some way the characteristics you have identified. Be alert to this now, and again when you start to write up the project: if you find yourself claiming that X happens 'often' or 'more frequently' or that there is a 'tendency' for it to occur, then it may well be that you should be more precise, and should go back to the data and establish just how often, how many or how strong is the tendency.

In both cases – that is, whether you have begun with a quantitative inquiry or arrived at a point where your description and interpretation entail some quantification – you need to take account of some basic principles. This book is not an appropriate place to go into extensive detail about statistical procedures, and there are many textbooks you can consult which explain the theory and practice of quantitative research approaches (see Further Reading). However, you need to recognise the following:

1   Counting your Xs depends on having identified what the Xs are, so make sure you define your unit(s) of analysis.
2   Counting can only provide you with raw frequencies, so once you have these, you will need to convert them to figures which can legitimately be compared with each other (4 instances from a total of 8 potential instances is 50 per cent; 4 from a total of 100 is 4 per cent). The simplest way to establish relative frequency is to convert all your raw frequencies to percentages.
3   When you do this, be clear yourself, and make clear eventually to your readers, what is being presented as a percentage of what. Hudson (2004) provides an example, using the (h) variable in the speech of several informants. He does not specify the question that this study would have set out to answer, but it is something like, 'What are the differences among four different speakers in the use or non-use of /h/ in words where /h/ is possible?' The two variants are '(h): /h/ (/h/ present)' and '(h): 0 (/h/ absent)'. Hudson demonstrates how the data is displayed first as a frequency table (Table A7.5.1), and then as a percentage table (A7.5.2). 'The percentages you want', Hudson continues: 'are column percentages, showing

each variant, for each speaker, as a percentage of all the **tokens** of the same variable *for that speaker*. For example, speaker A produced a total of 63 tokens of the (h) variable, of which 35 were /h/; so 35/63 × 100 = 56% of A's tokens of (h) had the /h/ variant' (Hudson 2004).

Table A7.5.1 Frequencies for (h) (adapted from Hudson 2004)

Variant	Speaker A	Speaker B	Speaker C	Speaker D
/h/	35	23	37	6
0	28	37	15	45
Total	63	60	50	51

Table A7.5.2 Percentages for (h) (adapted from Hudson 2004)

Variant	Speaker A	Speaker B	Speaker C	Speaker D
/h/ (%)	56	38	74	12
N	63	60	50	51

Once you convert your raw figures to percentage values, you only need to report one of the two variables, as the other will be 100 minus that one. You should indicate, though, how many tokens you are dealing with, and the convention here is to label this number as 'N'. Thus, 'N' in Table A7.5.2 represents all the tokens of the (h) variable in each case.

4   While some kinds of analysis need do no more than identify this sort of pattern, it is likely that you would want to know whether differences in your results are statistically **significant**. This is the difference between a set of values which could well be attributable to chance, and one whose variations must be caused by something else. This calculation involves the concept of probability (conventionally labelled 'p') and a test such as the 'Chi-squared test of independence', which establishes the likelihood of the results being the product of chance.

5   Various kinds of software will do these calculations for you, and you can venture into much more complicated statistical operations if you have extensive quantitative data to analyse. However, do try, throughout the process, to be clear about what you are doing and why. The most sophisticated and detailed analysis of quantitative data is only as good as the basic information you have collected.

A7.6 Stages of analysis

The final point to note in this unit is that the analysis of your data may involve several stages. I have already observed that the process of transcribing speech to writing is in itself part of the analysis, but of course the analytical process does not end with the production of a transcript. Even with other kinds of data, it may be that your first step is to identify some patterns, and that these in turn raise questions which can only be answered by further analytical procedures. B7 provides some illustrations.

A8 WRITING AND REPORTING

There is no single best way to write because writing interacts with almost every other mental, physical and social activity. The path to successful writing involves understanding the many different ways that minds engage with the world to create text.

(Sharples 1999: xi)

As you will see from the readings in this strand, people who research students' writing note that it is common for both students and markers to concentrate on the 'skills' aspect of writing, whereas more recognition is gradually being given to the whole process, including the affective and political dimensions of writing for assessment in higher education. Starting with the former, this brief unit focuses on some basic issues of producing a written record of your research project, while other units in this strand explore what lies behind some of the expectations you are required to meet.

A8.1 The dissertation as a record of the research

Although the process of carrying out a piece of independent research is what underlies the dissertation, it is usually the text itself, the product of that process, which is assessed. There should of course be a close link between the two, but it is possible for an excellent study to fail to fulfil its promise as a written account of the research. On the other hand, an ill-conceived, poorly executed study can rarely be rescued by excellent writing. However, a project which didn't turn out as expected may well be the basis of a successful dissertation, so don't despair if your initial plans and your eventual findings don't match completely. One of the skills you are acquiring is that of demonstrating your understanding of the research process, including flaws and problems.

A8.2 Timing and planning

Another skill which this component of your studies is intended to develop is that of managing your time when more of it is under your control than is the case with taught courses and assignments. For your dissertation, you should have been working to an overall plan with the deadlines for submitting work in mind, and 'writing up' is a recognised stage. However, people approach this in a variety of ways, some drafting sections of the study as they go along, while others prefer to work from notes and begin the process of writing in detail only when they have all the component parts in place. Whichever suits you best, you will need to allow plenty of time for drafting the body of the text, editing it so that the optimum space is allocated to each component, proof-reading and producing a final printed copy. If this needs to be bound (check your institution's regulations), allow time for that too: it may take longer than you think.

A8.3 The dissertation as a text type

I suggest in several places in this book that by doing research you are, in effect, an apprentice in the discipline's 'community of practice', and the dissertation is an overt piece of evidence of this. As genre theorists have demonstrated, the forms which particular types of text take are closely associated with their function and value for various social groups, and novice members of those groups need to know what is expected if they are to produce acceptable texts of their own. There are perhaps three main ways of familiarising yourself with the overall look and feel of the dissertation as the text type you need to produce.

First, you may be able to access examples of previous students' dissertations, and this can be reassuring: if they can do it, so can you! On the other hand, I remember some second-year students attending a meeting where they had the opportunity to browse dissertations produced by others in their final year; one worried person exclaimed, 'I can't imagine being able to produce anything like that!' Of course eventually she did – and to a high standard, but it can be daunting, when you are at the very beginning of the process, to contemplate what is expected a year later. If your department doesn't routinely make previous work available, you could suggest that it would be helpful, and that there may be ways around the potential constraints of confidentiality, storage, and so on. The internet can also be a source of examples, but should obviously be used with care, as your particular department may expect something rather different from what you may find online.

Second, you should pay close attention to the guidance available from your tutors. Your department will almost certainly provide written support outlining the components which you are expected to include in the text, and your supervisor will also clarify details for you (though s/he will be more helpful if it is clear that you have consulted the available information first!). Students in my own department at the University of Birmingham are issued with an eight-page document, from which I include an extract from the section on potential structures of the 6,000 word dissertation. (They also have the option of writing a 12,000 word research project.)

Title page
Contents
Chapter 1: Introduction – statement of the research question and topic, and overview of the Dissertation; any general background (200–500 words)
Chapter 2: Background – review or discussion of relevant literature (1,500–2,500 words)
Chapter 3: Research method(s) – an account of how the research was carried out, and any issues arising, including methodological considerations (300–500 words)
Chapter 4: Analysis and results – discussion of the findings, including analysis of what has been observed (2,500–3,000 words)
Chapter 5: Conclusion – summary of what has been learned, and discussion of the implications (300–1,000 words)
Bibliography
Appendices

This skeleton model is preceded by the following text:

> The exact structure of a dissertation will depend on the topic and kind of research being undertaken, and supervisors will advise on what type of structure is appropriate for an individual's topic . . . The suggested word counts are entirely provisional, as chapter lengths will vary greatly according to topic and the nature of the data or theoretical models under investigation.

Whatever the length of the text you need to produce, it will help to break it down into sub-sections with an approximate word limit for each, as this reminds you that you have previously produced many assignments of an equivalent length; the dissertation is comparable to a set of shorter essays.

The third source of guidance is from the reading you have done of published studies. As text types, these are far from identical to student dissertations, but their overall structure is, as you will recognise, broadly similar to that outlined above, and if you read them at this stage with an eye to their genre rather than their content, you should be able to infer what the priorities are for scholars in your area of interest as they communicate their research to a wider readership. In particular, pay attention to how they condense an extended piece of research into the word-limited journal article; how they label figures (i.e. diagrams and the like) and tables (of statistical information); how content is distributed between running prose, statistical tables and appendices; and also note anything that, as a reader, you find unsatisfactory or obscure, so that your own text is more likely to be clear and complete.

A8.4 Style

Some aspects of the style you should adopt will be familiar to you from previous academic writing, and some may be spelt out in guidance from your tutors, while others are less tangible. Perhaps the biggest challenge is finding your own voice while still conforming to the expectations of the genre, which is linked to the problem of avoiding plagiarism while demonstrating familiarity with the relevant literature and concepts. As with other aspects of this stage of the process, you should refresh your acquaintance with all the relevant resources available in your institution, even returning to documentation issued when you began your studies, as this may well give you information and thus more confidence in the detail of how to present your work in the expected ways. Other ways of thinking about this issue are explored further in the other units in this strand.

A8.5 Presentation

If at all possible, it really helps to work to a private deadline which falls at least several days before the official one. If you can print out your work and leave it for a short time, you should then be able to do some final proof-reading and editing. This can catch trivial mistakes of the sort which, while they may not detract from the quality of the research, may be irritating to markers. Remember that they will be reading several texts like yours, and would prefer the punctuation to follow accepted conventions, the tenses used to be consistent, the contents page accurate and so on. It is very hard to see your own work with fresh eyes, especially when you have been so close to it for so long, but do try to empathise with the imagined reader and, especially if you have reorganised material in the course of writing it up, make sure that it is presented in a sequence which is accessible to someone who is not yet familiar with the details you may be taking for granted.

The observations above are primarily about the technical, procedural aspects of writing an extended text for assessment. You will find more discussion about these, and also the broader contexts in which they have developed, in units B8 and C8.

BEYOND THE DISSERTATION   A9

My discussion in this ninth strand of the book will be most relevant when you are getting towards the end of your project. This unit begins by asking you to reflect on what you have learned so far through the process of designing and carrying out a piece of independent research. It is hard, if not impossible, to do a project like this *without* adding to your knowledge. By the time you submit your work, you will have: read more than you had when you started; faced and solved challenges associated with clarifying a research idea and working out how to pursue it; inevitably had some false starts and setbacks, and overcome them; written a longer single text than you have probably ever done before. You should, of course, now know more about the topic you decided to research than you did when you chose it, but you will also know more about yourself and the kind of researcher you are.

In addition to adding to your knowledge, the process itself will have changed the person you are, even if only very slightly. You've had the space to 'stretch your wings', and discover whether the relative absence of constraints on this kind of assessed work makes you feel insecure or exhilarated. If you had a vocational goal before doing the research, what you've found out may have either weakened or strengthened your commitment to it, and if you were certain before that you either did or did not want to do any further studying, this experience may have confirmed or challenged this conviction. Your choices about what to do next will be influenced by many factors, only one of which is how you responded to doing independent research, but it is worth considering what your experience of researching English Language can tell you about the next steps to take.

To simplify the many possibilities facing you as you contemplate graduation, I have grouped them into just two main types: further academic study and paid employment which may or may not involve further formal education or training. Of course you might do neither of these things, and instead fund yourself by doing temporary jobs so as to gain experience as a volunteer, or travel round the world. And what you do immediately may not be what you do in the longer term. See Reading D9.2, for example, for reflections on the way applied linguists, in particular, often return to study their subject after sometimes lengthy periods of relevant paid employment; conversely, even if you stay within 'the academy' you will at some point become an employee rather than a student. How might your experiences as an English Language researcher prepare you for each of these pathways?

If you decide to apply for a postgraduate degree course, the work you did for your dissertation is very likely to be considered relevant by admissions tutors. There are potentially two routes into initial postgraduate study in the UK, the most common being a taught Masters degree, which usually involves a longer dissertation than at undergraduate level, and a Masters degree by research. The range of taught courses available, even within the UK, is extensive, including a variety of titles which reflect the different emphases in different departments. A useful website for all graduates is Prospects (www.prospects.ac.uk), which has extensive information about many kinds of opportunity, including those for further study. There are taught MAs in Linguistics, Applied Linguistics, English Language, English Language Teaching, Language Acquisition, Literary Linguistics – to name just some. Research degrees (often labelled as 'MPhil') give you an opportunity to do one extended piece of research and writing – typically a dissertation of around 40,000 words. Internationally, there are even more programmes open to English speakers, so you should do some investigating before you decide where to apply.

Institutions will differ in their requirements for entry to Masters programmes in these disciplines, but most will expect a good honours degree. Admissions tutors will want 'to ascertain', as one institution says on its website, 'your motivation and ability to engage with topics in applied linguistics [or any other MA subject] at postgraduate level' (Birkbeck, University of London 2009). Evidence of this motivation and ability is readily demonstrated by what you and your tutors can say about your experience of research and the outcome in the dissertation itself. Therefore, you could usefully think about not only the topic of your research project, but also the process you have been through and what it has taught you. In any application you make for further study, bear in mind that course selectors will be interested in what kind of a student you are likely to be – so if you can honestly say that you enjoyed tracking down hard-to-find sources, or conquering a software problem as you analysed your data, this will be at least as persuasive as indicating what your study was about.

The range of jobs in which you can draw on your experience of researching English Language is even more extensive. Below are some examples which identify aspects of the work involved and illustrate how your experience as an undergraduate researcher may be linked to what you would do.

❏   Jobs which involve working directly with texts include, for example:
    aspects of publishing:
        copy-editing, which involves taking material written by others (including
            sometimes by several authors) and checking it for both content and
            style (e.g. factual accuracy, consistency of terminology, house style)
        proof-reading, which involves doing quality checks on publications,
            including books, magazines and newspapers, websites, as well as
            publications aimed at a specialist audience, such as academic or
            business reports
    lexicography: contributing to the compilation of dictionaries
    journalism: researching and writing, usually to tight deadlines
❏   Jobs which involve working with spoken language include:
    speech and language therapy, which requires detailed knowledge of speech
    production and clinical problems experienced by adults and children.

Both of the above kinds of work also involve liaising and negotiating with other people, of course, while other careers span language and social interaction in yet further ways.

❏   You could work with language:
    in the context of contributing to the production of texts in various media as:
        an editorial assistant
        a researcher for film or television
    in jobs where your ability to communicate is critical, such as:
        teaching (at primary, secondary or tertiary level)
        public relations.

If you consider what is involved in careers such as these, it soon becomes apparent that the various stages of planning and carrying out your research project will have given you very valuable experience in directly relevant areas. In many cases, you will need to do some further study as well as gaining experience in the field, but this will no doubt build on the work you have done in the course of researching English Language as part of your degree.

Section B

DEVELOPMENT
THE HOW AND WHY
OF RESEARCHING
ENGLISH LANGUAGE

B1 THE HOW AND WHY OF GETTING STARTED AND CHOOSING A RESEARCH TOPIC

In A1 I note that there are two main kinds of reasons for doing research in English Language as part of an accredited programme of study. There are the obvious pragmatic reasons; that is, you may not be able to obtain your qualification if you do not demonstrate an ability to carry out a piece of independent research and report what you find out in an acceptable way. There are also less easily measurable considerations, connected with the attractions of scholarship as worthwhile in its own right, and the satisfaction of taking on a challenge and seeing it through.

Activity

> Make two lists of reasons for doing the research you are planning in some aspect of English Language, one identifying the requirements you need to fulfil for your institution, and the other explaining what you hope personally to gain from the experience. Is there any overlap between the two lists?

In the English university system, there is a requirement in each discipline to meet certain 'benchmarks'. Those for undergraduate qualifications in English explain that 'the key transferable and cognitive skills which English graduates should possess' include 'research skills, including the ability to gather, sift and organise material independently and critically, and evaluate its significance'. The authors of this policy document claim that such skills 'make them [English graduates] attractive to employers' (QAA 2007a: 5). There is a slightly longer list in the Linguistics benchmark statement, which says:

> Among the generic intellectual skills a linguistics degree can offer, the following abilities are of particular significance: . . . collecting, analysing and manipulating data of diverse kinds; using a variety of methods, and assessing the advantages and disadvantages of each method; writing . . . research reports using the appropriate register and style and with proper referencing; . . . using the necessary computational tools and software packages wherever appropriate for the analysis of data; considering the ethical issues involved in data collection and data storage.
>
> (QAA 2007b: 8)

How much do you know about *what* the requirements are of the degree programme you are studying, in terms of research experience, and about *why* they are there? It is likely that the component of your studies involving some independent research forms all or part of a course unit or module (terminology may differ between educational systems) and that the paperwork associated with this module specifies what students must do to be successful in it. This information should be helpful to you as you embark on the project, and it's worth familiarising yourself with it at the start, and returning to it from time to time – especially if at some point you feel that you have 'lost your way'. It is a very common experience for researchers at all levels to feel that their research is somehow running out of control. Reminders of the constraints and limited expectations associated with study at the level you are currently at can help to counter the sensation of being overwhelmed.

✪ Activity

Find out, if you don't already know, which benchmark statements apply to the subject(s) of your degree, if you are studying in an English university. If your university is governed by the regulations of another national system, what are those regulations? How much freedom, or how much tight specification, governs the decisions you and your tutors can make about the kind of research you can do/must do/may do?

Remember, though, that there are intrinsic reasons for embarking on a research project, beyond those specified in such rather dry statements of educational policy, which are often subject to repeated revisions as economic and political priorities change. As a student, you are presumably, by definition, a curious person, who wants to know more about and to understand better all sorts of things. Doing a dissertation or research project should indeed develop the skills identified above, and these skills will undoubtedly be valued by your prospective employers, but the most rewarding aspect of being a researcher is arguably that of learning some things you didn't know before, and, if you are really successful, making that knowledge available to others who share your interests.

Paradoxically, however, such genuine curiosity can be the source of some problems with small-scale, unfunded, individual research projects. This is because the things that may be the most fascinating may well also be the most difficult ones about which you can reach any substantial conclusions. Sebba (2000: 4) draws a distinction between 'eternal questions' and 'research questions'. In the former category are questions such as 'is there a common origin for all languages? Is thought possible without language?' These 'eternal questions', he continues, 'may be very interesting, but they make poor topics for research projects, especially small-scale ones. Even researchers expecting to devote years – perhaps a whole lifetime – to their researches would not try to answer questions like these. Nor should you'. We look further in B3 at the challenge of framing questions for your research, but for now it is worth noting that you will almost certainly need to rein in your curiosity and set limits on your ambitions, especially if this is your first piece of extended research.

So, overall, the goal is to find an area of interest that will sustain you for the lifetime of the project and that meets the requirements of any accreditation associated with it. Keep an open mind about what you will be able to do, and accept that throughout the project your perception of the boundaries of what you can achieve are very likely to both expand and shrink several times. Keep track of this process in the research project notebook that I recommended in A1.

Table B1.1.1 shows some extracts from various documents, including the note-book, produced by one student, Rosie, at the University of Birmingham, as she began to develop her initial ideas from a general area of interest towards a more focused project. Alongside each extract are some issues for you to con-sider. Reading and thinking about this example should give you some ideas for ways in which your own project may develop.

Table B1.1.1 Summary of some of Rosie's planning documents

Source of extract	Extract	Comments and questions
Initial proposal form (addressed to module convenor)	The language of insults and role of slang in youth culture Gender comparisons Insults in popular culture (music, TV, etc.) Perhaps comparisons American–British case studies/ dictionaries – language shift and change	Where do you think Rosie got this idea from (i.e. personal experience and observation, or previous study, or somewhere else)? Has this topic struck you as something of interest to investigate? If so, in what ways? What do you know about it already from any studies you have done? Do you foresee any problems for Rosie with this project?
Email to supervisor allocated on the basis of the proposal	As discussed, I would like to write an RP [research project] based on new slang formation, semantic change and new slang meanings for existing words, how new slang is added to modern dictionaries, and some dictionary studies. I am getting a bit worried that my ideas lack structure/focus and was wondering if I should have more defined ideas at this stage.	In what ways has Rosie clarified her ideas since identifying an initial area of interest? Has she made the task that she has set herself easier or not? How do you think her supervisor would have responded to the worry she expresses in her email?

Notes from notebook in the early stages of the project	*Slang and gender* Use of slang as a form of covert prestige Men using slang as a marker of in-group solidarity Masculine groups – slang becomes language of masculinity Looking at certain words – use frequency/context, e.g. all-female/mixed conversations by each sex – patterns	How does this entry differ from the previous thoughts Rosie has recorded? Does it constitute progress and, if so, in what ways?

Reflected in these extracts are concerns – likely to be shared by most people who are setting out on their first research project – about what it means to engage in this kind of activity. In effect, the process is a kind of apprenticeship, 'an induction into the world of academic enquiry, writing and ways of thinking' (Wallace and Poulson 2004: 5) and this includes critically reviewing the literature.

THE HOW AND WHY OF THE LITERATURE REVIEW: JOINING A 'COMMUNITY OF PRACTICE'

B2

While B1 suggests that all beginning researchers face some similar challenges, A2 includes some rather dry instructions about collecting details of all the sources you read. For some readers, these will seem like common sense, or possibly a reiteration of the demands associated with being a student with which they have become increasingly familiar since their school days. Others may respond with irritation, feeling perhaps that these rules and conventions are annoyances to be tolerated if you want a good mark, but of no real importance to the interesting aspects of doing research. A third reaction is more likely from readers who may feel marginalised by the predominant ethos of academic institutions. The conventions of reading, participating in seminars, and, especially, of writing 'like an academic' can be very alien and threatening for those to whom they are least familiar.

Applied linguistic researchers have explored these issues, and some of their work is presented in D8. It would be possible, of course, for you to consider some aspect of the reading and writing of academic English as a topic for your own research. (That's one of the attractions of working in our field – language data can be found in virtually all areas of human life and experience.) An influential idea developed by people researching literacy, including the advanced literacy involved in work at university level, is that of 'communities of practice'. As Hirst et al. (2004: 73) note, 'when we engage students in the practices of academic literacy, we are asking them not only to appropriate and develop new ways of thinking, but also to take on new ways of being'. Gee (1996: 45) makes a similar point: 'One always and only learns to interpret texts of a certain type in certain ways through having access to, and ample experience in, social settings where texts of that type are read in those ways. One is socialized or enculturated into a certain social practice'. As Gee stresses, this process is double-edged. It may be seen as conferring benefits on the students who participate in it: it is an 'apprenticeship' in academic practice, leading perhaps to privilege and quite possibly material rewards. At the same time, Gee wonders, 'are we endlessly trapped in replicating the given social status quo through enacting the social processes that instantiate it?'

The relevance of the community of practice idea for the housekeeping aspects of doing your own literature review is that, whatever the origins of – and power relations involved in – the bibliographic conventions you are expected to use, they represent one aspect of academic work as it is currently practised, at least in most English-speaking educational institutions. You may or may not find them oppressive, but observing them is one feature of participating in the processes of generating know-ledge and sharing understanding that characterises – or should characterise – 'the academy'.

Working academics are equally constrained by these conventions. If we submit articles to journals for publication, they are subject to a process known as 'peer review', whereby experts in the subjects of the particular kind of research reported read each article submitted to a journal and write a report on it. A typical example is the *Journal of Sociolinguistics*, which informs would-be authors, via its website, that, 'submissions will be peer-reviewed unless in the editors' opinion a paper falls out-side the journal's scope or is not of adequate scholarly standard'. Similarly, this is the process as summarised in the instructions to potential contributors to the *Journal of Child Language*:

> All submissions are read by a member of the editorial team to check whether, with regard to readability and content, they are appropriate to send to referees. All eli-gible manuscripts are then sent, anonymously, to two referees. When the referees' reports are received, each manuscript is evaluated by the editorial team, and the Editor informs the author of their decision.
>
> (Cambridge University Press 2008)

In A2 there is a demonstration of one of the shortcomings of relying on the entire unmediated resources of the internet to provide suggestions of what to read for research. In the course of your student career, you may have already discovered that this, including the use of Wikipedia, is frowned on by academics – and this is one of the reasons why. Although the aims of Wikipedia – to make available the knowledge of anyone who wishes to contribute – are not necessarily inconsistent with the search for knowledge associated with academic research, the peer review process described above does not apply to content posted there. As the site explains, '[v]isitors do not need specialized qualifications to contribute . . . Most of the articles can be edited by anyone with access to the Internet' (Wikipedia 2008). As a resource to provide you with a quick introduction to a concept it may be fine, but it is not a substitute for reading 'the literature' – partly because you do this to acquire more than simply information (see A2). For further discussion of reasons to be cautious about information from the internet, and a list of 'standards for believing web sites', see Fink (2005: 39).

It is not only the scholarly content of submitted articles that is scrutinised by other members of the academic community of practice. If you are familiar with the guidance from your institution on your own writing for assessment, you will recognise the genre of the following text, also taken from the advice to authors wishing to submit their articles for publication in the *Journal of Sociolinguistics*.

References

References should use the author/date system, e.g. (Hymes 1974). When the author's name appears in the text, use: Gumperz (1983) argues that . . . Page numbers appear after a colon (plus space) following the date: Labov (1972: 269–270). Do not use additional parentheses for the date of a reference contained in text that is already enclosed in parentheses. Use semicolons between a sequence of references by different authors. For works with three or more authors, either use all authors' names at each citation: Fishman, Ferguson and Das Gupta (1968); or use et al. after first mention: Fishman et al. (1968). All works cited must appear under the title REFERENCES following any notes and preceding any tables or figures. Start the references on a new page. Check **thoroughly** that all works cited in text and notes appear in the list of references, and that authors and dates match between citation and references.

(Wiley-Blackwell 2009)

Why such pernickety instructions to authors hoping to publish in academic journals? A cynical answer is that these arcane practices are part of the conspiracy to ensure that only the writing of a small elite gets published: anyone who fails to include every detail as instructed effectively 'fails' as a would-be author. An alternative answer would point to the process by which writers' work is evaluated, and its trustworthiness assessed. If you use evidence generated by others as support for your own claims, you owe it to your readers to give them all the information they need to allow them to consult that evidence for themselves, and to see whether your interpretation is convincing. That is why this community of practice insists on the provision of full bibliographic details for all works cited.

Activity

Consider, and preferably discuss with other students, the question Gee poses about the implications of conforming to the conventions of academic work – including the very basic and practical ones associated with documenting what you read in quite tightly prescribed ways. What is your own assessment of this requirement? Is it a necessary evil? Is it unobjectionable and unproblematic? Is it oppressive and the means by which those with power maintain their elite position and exclude everyone else? Or is it emancipatory, giving you access to a valuable set of skills that are inherently worthwhile? Whatever your initial reaction to these options, try to give each of these positions an airing, supported by argument and evidence.

The researchers who have studied academic literacy as a social practice have also noted that there is no absolute separation between the cognitive processes involved in learning and the affective and interactive dimensions of being a university student. You may yourself have experienced a disjuncture between the identity you felt you had before becoming an undergraduate and the one you have developed since. Perhaps members of your family and your pre-university friends have commented on how you've changed, or perhaps you are aware of making adjustments in how you behave and talk in the different contexts. It is from the perspective of learners as writers (see strand 8) that this has been most extensively investigated by researchers but reading, too, can change the way you see things, even to the extent of changing the way you see yourself and your situation in the world. Each text you read changes, albeit ever so slightly, the reader you are, and the knowledge and understanding that you bring to subsequent reading. Reading for your research project is thus an iterative process – that is, rather than seeing it as a closed step in the sequence of stages towards completing your dissertation, it is more helpful to recognise that you should continue to read even after you have compiled the notes towards a literature review chapter and planned and carried out your data collection. You may well bring new insights to what you read about another study once you have carried out your own – and, on the other hand, that study may have things to tell you to which you were not receptive before you had gained the experience of doing something equivalent yourself.

So, while it is important not to use the phase of preparing and reading as a means of endlessly deferring the subsequent stages of carrying out your research, it is sensible to keep reading even as you move on to identify your questions and how you propose to answer them.

THE HOW AND WHY OF CLARIFYING RESEARCH QUESTIONS   B3

B3.1 Research studies without explicit questions

Does your study need research questions? It is possible to produce a successful dissertation that does not include explicit research questions, and there are certainly articles published in learned journals that do not state the questions – if any – that underpinned the research reported. As an example, below is an extract from an article published in *Discourse and Society* (Cook et al. 2004). It is about a funded project that was concerned with the language used by different kinds of people (particularly scientists and non-expert members of the public) to talk about a specific issue – the genetic modification of crops and food. The article is structured in a fairly conventional way, beginning with some background to the topic, including summaries of previous relevant research. The article then 'reports on a case study investigating how one community of GM scientists engage with the variety of voices and issues in the debate' (p. 435). Before presenting their findings, these authors, in a section headed 'The project', summarise what they were hoping to find out in their research. Look closely at the language in which they do this, and note how there are questions implied in this passage, even though they are not phrased as interrogatives. How might you rephrase these statements of aims and interests as questions?

> Our project aimed to investigate the views of GM scientists within one academic institution. We sought to understand their perceptions of non-expert knowledge and views, their explanations of opposition to GM, and their ideas about how best to present and justify their research to non-specialists. In addition we wanted to see how these perceptions are reflected in argumentation strategies and language use, and the actual effect of these choices upon non-experts.
>
> (Cook et al. 2004: 435)

The article then presents what the researchers found out about these issues, explaining as it does so how they collected data and analysed it in various ways.

'Models' from published studies such as this example – and you may well find similar ones in your own reading of the literature – may lead you to question the necessity of spending time and effort in framing and revising your own research questions. My advice would be that, while it may not be crucial to do so, you are much less likely, as an inexperienced researcher, to be able to focus your investigation clearly unless you do. 'Underneath' the article by Cook et al. lies the extensive experience of a team of researchers whose work was facilitated by a research grant, which was only awarded when a detailed proposal had been carefully reviewed by other experienced academics (rather as journal articles are peer reviewed – see B2). The reviewers of the proposal and the article, respectively, were able to judge whether the findings presented contributed answers to the questions implied by the account of the study, and by previous research. Until you have experience that comes close to this, it is advisable to submit to the discipline of stating as clearly as you can what it is that you intend to find out.

B3.2 Refining your questions

Blaikie (2000) has advice on the process of drafting and redrafting questions. He suggests starting by:

1   brainstorming all the questions you can think of about your topic, without worrying about how sensible, practical or answerable they may be.

Only at the second stage should you:

2   rule out the most difficult or outrageous ones, and those that do not really interest you.

He then advises:

3   grouping the remainder thematically, a process that 'will make it possible to eliminate some and to consolidate others' (p. 66).

His next stage involves:

4   separating 'what', 'why' and 'how' questions

and I pursue this in more detail below.

Next, Blaikie advises:

5   exposing assumptions and presuppositions embedded in any of the questions – and your expertise as an English Language student, especially with (critical) discourse analysis, should support you in this.

The remaining stages help you to:

6   narrow your scope, separating major and subsidiary questions and checking whether each one is necessary for – and achievable within – your particular project.

 Activity

> Try Blaikie's procedure in relation to your own research topic (or topics, if you are still uncertain about which to choose). It may well help to do this with one or more other people, as they may generate questions that you haven't thought of and, even if you reject them, this will help you to firm up what you do want to investigate.

B3.3 Appropriate questions for empirical research

Let us look in a little more detail at the forms questions can take, and the implications of different kinds of questions for the answers likely to be generated. At the most general level, language topics for beginning researchers lend themselves to questions whose answers reveal (a) what something is like, (b) how much of something occurs in some specified context, or (and this is more challenging) (c) why something is the case. Some questions, those usually described as 'closed' and 'polar' are effectively (d) yes/no questions, although in practice most studies will discover something more than whether something is or is not the case. In practice, the questions devised for any given study will need to be much more precisely specified. Also, this underlying typology will not necessarily be visible in the wording of the question.

Activity

For each of the research questions in Table B3.3.1, taken from published reports of language-related research, identify whether it is of type (a), (b), (c) or (d) above. That is, is each question of the type (a) 'What is X like?', (b) 'How much of X is found in Y?', (c) 'Why X?' or (d) 'Is X the case or not?'? (Some questions may combine more than one type.)

Table B3.3.1 Examples of research questions in various kinds of language study

Topic of study	Question
'Measures of linguistic accuracy in second language writing research' (Polio 1997). This is a survey of ways in which researchers have attempted to measure accuracy in L2 writing.	1 What measures of linguistic accuracy are used in L2 writing research?
	2 Can **intra-** and **inter-rater reliability*** be obtained on the various measures?
'Methodological problems in the analysis of metaphors in a corpus of conversations about cancer' (Semino et al. 2004). This is a methodological paper discussing the challenges of trying to do this kind of analysis.	3 How is cancer talked about and conceptualised via metaphor in our data?
	4 What are the dominant conventional metaphors?

Topic of study	Question
	5 Are different metaphors used by different categories of people in different contexts?
'Epistemic modality markers in research articles: a cross-linguistic and cross-disciplinary study' (Vold 2006)	6 Does disciplinary affiliation influence the frequency of epistemic modality markers used?
	7 Does the frequency of epistemic modality markers vary across languages? If so, what are the explanations for this?
	8 Are there differences between male and female authors when it comes to the use of epistemic modality markers?

* Intra-rater reliability is high if the same analyst is consistent in the way s/he rates data across many instances; inter-rater reliability is high if different analysts are consistent in the way they rate the same data.

Comments

1   I would classify Q1 as of type (a). The answer to this question will tell us about the characteristics of X – in this case, the kinds of measures of linguistic accuracy that L2 writing researchers use.

2   Q2 is a closed, polar question, so it is type (d). However, as an experienced reader of research articles, I would expect the author to tell me more than either 'yes they can' or 'no they can't'. I would also anticipate some kind of grading of the different measures, as there is an implicit assumption in this question that reliability across different raters is a desirable thing. In fact, the author finds a lot of variation in how the literature reports on this aspect of measuring writers' accuracy, and concludes, 'studies should more consistently report interrater reliability' (Polio 1997: 130).

3   Q3 is type (a), directed at establishing the nature of the metaphors used in talking about cancer. Note that, although this question begins with 'how', it is still a question about what something (in this case, metaphors for cancer talk) is like.

4   Q4 is a subtle combination of (a) and (b). One aim of this study, as the previous question demonstrates, is to find out which metaphors are used, but addressed here is the question of which ones are 'dominant'. Thus, despite the absence of 'counting' words ('how many?', 'how often?' 'with what frequency?'), this question is concerned with establishing which kinds of X are more prevalent in this data set.

5   Q5 is, superficially again, of type (d), but I would expect information to be reported that would be of type (a): not just whether different speakers use

different metaphors, but which ones in which contexts. The authors have been cautious, though, in not assuming in advance that there will be patterned differences.

6   Q6 is of type (d), but, once more, I would expect the article to answer the further question that is easily inferred from the one given, namely 'and, if so, in what ways/how?'

7   Q7 is another one formulated as type (d), but it also implies a quantification of type (b), since we cannot know whether one thing is more frequent than another unless we know the frequencies of both. The supplementary question to Q7 is the first example in this set of type (c), in that it seeks 'explanation' – that is, it is concerned with reasons or causes, answers to the question 'why?'

8   Like Q6, Q8 seems to be type (d), but implicitly entails a question of type (a) or (b) or both, since, if there are differences, they will presumably be in either the kind of X to be found in the data (here, markers of epistemic modality) or in the comparative frequencies of occurrence of X in different contexts (here, the writing of women and of men respectively).

Implicit in the questions asked by all these scholars – and indeed in any account of a research project – are theories about the nature of the world and how things work. When we ask and try to answer any question about what something is like, this entails some sort of assumption about the characteristics and boundaries of that 'something' (which I refer to as 'X'). Most of the time, we need not be concerned with these rather philosophical questions: for practical purposes, we can get on in everyday life without worrying too much about what is meant by 'discourse' or 'language impairment' or 'the English language'. However, if we want to investigate any of these areas of language and communication seriously, we shall need to think more carefully about what such labels mean. The same applies to measurement. There is a difference between a casual observation about how widespread English is becoming and a research project seeking to establish how many speakers of English there are worldwide. How can this be measured? What counts as evidence of any individual's ability to speak a language? Most challenging of all are questions about causality. Questions about *why* things happen have occupied philosophers since time immemorial and, although there is no consensus about this, one conclusion that seems fairly clear is that we can rarely observe causation directly. You may, for example, direct heat underneath a pan of water and witness the water bubbling and turning to steam, but how exactly can you establish what is causing this process that you observe? Similar problems bedevil studies that try to establish the effectiveness of educational initiatives, including approaches in language teaching. How can we be sure, even if students taught using a particular method do well, that the method itself is the only, or even the main, *cause* of their success? Such examples involve some additional problems, too. The water can be expected to boil fairly reliably, regardless of who lights the gas, or where in the world they do this (although the temperature at which it happens will vary – predictably – with variations in height above sea level and atmospheric pressure). It is much less likely that the teaching method will work for all learners, in all classrooms, everywhere in the world. These are some of the reasons why I counsel caution in incorporating 'why' questions into your research design.

Activity

*Music +
Lyrics
c.
Influence* (handwritten note)

One student chose as his topic 'the impact of hip hop and rap on the English language – particularly focusing on lexis'. At the planning stage, his research questions were:

1   Which lexical items have transferred from hip hop and rap music/culture into (mainstream) English?

2   How have these lexical items become part of mainstream language?

3   Is there a widespread understanding/appreciation of what these words mean?

❑   Classify these questions using the typology suggested above (a, b, c or d).

❑   Do any items in the wording of these questions seem potentially problematic? If so, which ones and why?

❑   Which entities (Xs) are presupposed in these questions, and do they need definitions before data collection and analysis can begin?

❑   What kinds of data collection and analysis are implied by these questions?

❑   What advice would you give this student about these questions?

Now look back at the questions you devised in relation to your own research and see whether you can refine the wording further to be even more clear and specific about what you hope to find out. If not, don't be disheartened – and do read on! Consideration of the data you need and how to obtain it is another way in to clarifying your research questions.

B4   **THE HOW AND WHY OF CHOOSING RESEARCH METHODS**

I don't know where we picked up the habit of referring to everything we do as 'methodology'. I do think I know *why* we do it. It makes our humble methods seem more high-falutin'.

(Wolcott 2001: 93–4)

B4.1 Methods and methodology

As with other aspects of doing your research project, the choice of research methods can be approached in light of both practical and more theoretical considerations. You are bound to be influenced by the culture in your own department and institution, maybe your supervisor's experience, the resources available, and so on, as well as your own preferences, so that extrovert students may enjoy setting up interviews with people they hardly know more than shy students will, for example. From a more academic point of view, research **methods** are – or at least should be – closely linked with a research **methodology**. Many students (and not a few academics) conflate the two, so that 'methodology' is used as a sub-heading or chapter title to introduce nothing more than a descriptive account of the methods used in the study. The distinction between the two terms is important, though, because the '-[o]logy' suffix is not redundant; it denotes that methodology is the science of method. As Olsen and Morgan (2005: 262) put it, 'a method is narrower than a methodology. A methodology is a combination of techniques, the practices we conform to when we apply them and our interpretation of what we are doing when we do so'. Now you do not need to be intimidated by this, nor to become a student of the philosophy of science before you can get on with planning your research project. But you should be aware that many scholars, for many centuries, have thought hard about the very challenging problem of how we can gain knowledge about the world (or indeed the universe) and what it contains, and that the various methods that have become established for researchers to use are products partly of the conclusions such scholars have come to.

If all this seems rather abstract, it can easily be illustrated with an obvious example. Suppose, as part of a larger project, you wanted to know how often the contemporary children's author, Philip Pullman, uses the word 'dust' in the trilogy of novels, *His Dark Materials*. For simplicity, let us restrict your choice of methods to just two: you could arrange to go and interview the author, or you could use an electronic version of the text and an automated search tool. It may be obvious which of these would be a more appropriate *method*, but influencing your decision are *methodological* theories, even if you haven't made them explicit. Pointing them out involves an even greater statement of the obvious, but learning to use similar lines of thought when the issues are not so apparent requires more work.

Your question, 'How often does *dust* occur in these texts?' is an empirical one, and it is of the quantitative kind ('How many Xs are found in Y?'). It presupposes a number of things that, again, seem hardly to need saying. One such presupposition is that there are such things in the world as 'words', and that *dust* is one of them. Remember, though, that there are competing theories in linguistics about the definition of 'word', and the designers of any software intended to search for and count 'words', just like those using the manual procedures that preceded them, have to make decisions about what 'words' are (e.g. is 'don't' one word or two? are punctuation marks counted in the text's statistics, or are they something different from a 'word'? what about the spaces between words? and so on).

Moving from the nature of the question to the choice of method, I am assuming that you rejected the option of the interview with the author, and not merely because this would be difficult to arrange. So why is this method not a particularly appropriate one for answering this kind of question? If you were researching Pullman's opinions about religion, for example, you might well want to ask him some direct questions. Yet you probably think that his opinion about how often he included a particular word in his novels is less reliable as evidence than the output of a frequency count on the text itself – even though he is the author of the text. You might even anticipate that he would not necessarily welcome such a question, whereas you, as an analyst of his novels, which you perhaps conceive of as forming part of a particular genre, believe you have very good reasons for wanting to know this statistic.

If any of this reflects your reasoning, it is because, quite legitimately, you already have some ideas about different kinds of knowledge, about knowledge of different kinds of things, and about how these can be accessed. One of the reasons that these more abstract, methodological, considerations often become conflated with issues of method, even in the published literature, is that they can seem so obvious as not to be worth discussing. Also, when research traditions have become well established, the methodological considerations that underpin decisions about methods can be obscured, and choices are made more out of habit than through careful reflection. In my view, however, both beginning and more experienced researchers are well advised to make their decisions about methods in light of methodological concerns.

B4.2 Choice of method in (English) language research

The point of doing research is surely to find out something more than what is readily apparent from everyday experience and common sense. This leads us to concepts such as **reliable** evidence, **valid** conclusions, **representative** samples and generalisable findings. In relation to the Pullman example above, I suggested that his opinion about word frequencies in his novels was less 'reliable' than a machine-assisted count would be. What about using the method of establishing the frequencies of items such as 'dust' as a means of exploring religious ideas in these texts: is it a 'valid' one? In other words, does the method used to answer a particular research question actually generate evidence that can be used to answer it? If you decided to look at the frequency and uses of particular words in only one or two chapters of the text, would this give you 'representative' data, or not? Suppose this hypothetical research project included data only from Pullman's novels: how 'generalisable' would any conclusions drawn be to contemporary fiction for children?

In the next section, we take just some of the methods frequently used in (English) language research to consider such questions. It has to be recognised that entire books have been written on all of the topics touched on here, from many different perspectives, so this section can do no more than raise some issues for you to think about and to bear in mind as you plan and carry out your research. You are unlikely to be able to resolve the sometimes conflicting ideas about the issues, but your project will be more successful if you have developed the habit of evaluating the suitability of the method(s) you use for the kind of knowledge you are seeking. As space is limited, I look here at just three kinds of research method, although some of the points made are relevant to other types, and more methods are considered, at greater length, in strands 5 and 6.

B4.3 Interviews in language research: how and why?

Interviews, like all acts of communication, are potentially linguistic data, regardless of what they are about. It is possible to analyse almost anything an interviewee says from a linguistic point of view: that is, to identify the sounds, words and grammatical structures that occur in the speech of the interviewee.

Typical of this kind of interview in our field is the variationist, sociolinguistic interview pioneered by Labov. He incorporated the telling of personal narratives into his interviews, because 'narratives consistently show a shift towards the vernacular – that is, towards the first-learned style of speech that is used in every-day communication with friends and family' (Labov 2004: 31). This illustrates attention to validity: if the analyst has identified 'the vernacular' as the 'X' of interest, the research method required must generate data of that kind and not something else (such as careful speech that perhaps accommodates towards the accent or dialect of the interviewer). There is debate in the sociolinguistic literature about the **sample**s used in traditional dialectology studies. Some scholars have been critical of the convention of selecting as informants mainly older men in rural areas, who were thought most likely to produce speech representative of the 'true', 'pure' version of the variety. Looked at from another angle, the speech of a particular location or community would be better 'represented' by a cross-section of inhabitants.

A rather different kind of interview is used to find out about particular people's attitudes, experiences or beliefs. How useful it would be for researchers if they could ask people about these things and be given totally *reliable* information in reply! Unfortunately, language researchers are as well aware as anyone that all acts of communication have a social dimension (what Halliday refers to as the '**interpersonal metafunction**') and that human communication is not the same as punching numbers into a calculator and being provided with a mathematically indisputable answer. As we know from the extensive literature on discourse, interlocutors make myriad 'online' judgements about each other and the situation, about what is meant in relation to what is actually said, about what can be regarded as 'shared' and what needs to be explained and negotiated, and so on.

 Activity

Think of a situation in which you have been an interviewee.

❏ What was the context and what was your relationship with the interviewer: job applicant/potential employer; witness to an incident/police officer; student/university admissions tutor; activist/journalist – or some other combination?

❏ Did you do any preparation for the interview, and, if so, how? Did you plan how to present yourself visually (clothes, hair, make-up/shave) and, if so, what influenced your decisions? Did you plan what to say? In how much detail?

❏ Did you make any effort to include or exclude topics or details during the interview? On what basis did you make any such choices?

❏ If your interviewer had had different characteristics from those s/he actually had (older/younger; the other sex; more/less friendly/intimidating), might it have influenced what you said?

> ❏ How close to the 'truth' about the topic of the interview was the account you gave?
> ❏ If you were interviewed in exactly the same situation again, would your utterances be identical to what you said in the first interview? If not, what are the implications for the validity of interview data?

If you use interviews as a method, anyone you interview will inevitably make similar calculations to those you made, even if there is less at stake for them as your research informant than there may have been for you as, say, a job applicant. And of course, if you are researching, say, the language women use when they are in single-sex friendship groups, your informants may be less forthcoming in interviews with you if you are an unfamiliar man!

So it is a mistake to rely on interviews as an unproblematically 'valid' means of access to every kind of knowledge held by informants: they are social situations, and interviewees will shape their responses in various ways. Furthermore, even an interviewee who chooses to be as open, honest and accurate as possible may not know, or be able to remember, as much as you would like. These considerations are well summarised by the authors of Reading D4.2, Barton and Hamilton (1998: 65):

> Interview data is essentially self-report and it is important to be clear about the status of this material and that it needs to be complemented or triangulated* with data from other sources, such as observations. An interview offers the researcher one participant's reporting of events, what they think it appropriate or comfortable to tell us or can remember, what they define as [the topic of the research] and what they think the interviewer is interested in hearing about.

*'**Triangulation**' is the use of more than one approach to a research problem, including using several research methods or instruments to investigate the same thing, so as to corroborate findings and minimise the possibility of a method distorting the evidence.

None of this discussion of interviews is intended to suggest that you should not use them – and we return to other aspects of the method elsewhere in this book. It is simply to alert you to some methodological considerations to bear in mind if you do.

B4.4 Selecting textual data in language research: how and why?

The large number of books on discourse analysis is an indication of how extensive the field is. Even if we restrict attention to the analysis of written texts produced without the intention of their being used for research, there are many ways to go about this, and many contrasting positions from which researchers approach their analyses – even within language studies (as opposed to other kinds of social research which make use of texts of many kinds as data).

This section, therefore, will limit its focus to issues of **sampling**, **representativeness** and **reliability**. Although I have narrowed the discussion to written texts, some of it has implications for other methods – though people, who may also be 'sampled' as research subjects, are in many ways quite different from written artefacts.

Whether selecting informants to participate in an experiment, survey or focus group, or selecting texts to include in a data set to analyse, researchers need to consider which people or texts can 'stand in for' or *represent* the whole population of people or texts that could have been included. 'Sample' is another term that has both an everyday and a more specialised meaning. For researchers, there are theoretical assumptions underpinning the concept of 'sample', including the idea that sub-sets of an entire 'population' (whether people, bacteria, texts, plants, or any other kind of X) have certain characteristics in common. A *sample* of this whole population should mirror, but on a smaller scale, the population at large, and have similarly distributed sets of characteristics.

This does present researchers with some methodological challenges, and these are less of an issue if no claims are made about the texts (or the interviewees, or the subjects in an experiment or observation) 'representing' any larger set. If, for example, you decide to investigate the stylistic patterns in one long text, or perhaps several shorter ones, and you report your findings as not *generalisable* to any other texts at all, then you should not claim to have selected a 'sample' and should not imply that your findings are applicable to any texts other than those you analysed. Indeed, there are some research traditions of textual analysis that set comparatively little store by 'representativeness'. The authors of a study of student writing in higher education (Lea and Street 1998: 160) state quite clearly that 'Our research . . . was not based on a representative sample from which generalisations could be drawn but rather was conceived as providing case studies that enabled us to explore theoretical issues and generate questions for further systematic study'.

Different perspectives on this issue can be illustrated by the fairly extensive debate between some practitioners of Critical Discourse Analysis (CDA) and their critics. Stubbs (1997) discusses whether, if the texts analysed by CDA analysts are restricted to fragments, the conclusions can be considered *reliable*: if they had chosen different texts or different fragments to analyse, would they have found the same Xs (here, ideological assumptions and presuppositions)? Stubbs highlights those values in academic research that he finds wanting in many CDA studies, including 'the *replicability* of methods of analysis and the *reliability* of results (such that different analysts would produce the same analysis), *comprehensive coverage* of data, and *representativeness* of data' (p. 103, emphases added).

Stubbs is a corpus linguist, and designs his own studies in light of a methodological orientation which he aims to make explicit, emphasising, for example, that 'one of the most important implications of corpus study [is] that the data of linguistics becomes publicly accessible' (Stubbs 1996: 234). Nevertheless, just as interview data cannot give the researcher unmediated access to the interviewees' knowledge, so corpus data is never a transparent window to 'facts about the language'. Corpora are constructed by people, and software is designed by people, so a lot of theory is involved in any corpus linguistic study. For Stubbs, this is all the more reason why researchers should be explicit about the decisions they make and the methods they use, and why it is an advantage if any study can be *replicated* by others.

A very large corpus may aim to be 'representative' of the language as a whole

– but is there really such an entity, and can it truly be 'sampled'? How many words in English were uttered and written by its speakers across the world even in the time it has taken you to read this page, so how could you sample even that output? The point about the **replication** of studies of similar issues by different analysts using different corpora is that if these consistently corroborate each other (produce similar findings) it is increasingly less likely that the results were an outcome of the particular corpus (sample of 'the language') that happened to be chosen for the original study.

A further point to bear in mind when selecting data for textual analysis is that, once again, your research questions should indicate what an appropriate 'sample' may be. This applies to decisions about how much of any given text to include, which is 'but one of the many methodological considerations that must be addressed before one begins collecting data for inclusion in a corpus' (Meyer 2002: 30). Is your question a grammatical one? If so, text excerpts may be adequate. Biber and Finegan (1991: 213) state that '1000 word samples reliably represent at least certain linguistic characteristics of a text, even when considerable internal variation is anticipated'. However, if you are interested in, say, the differing distribution of items as a particular type of text unfolds, then clearly you need to construct your corpus to include whole texts. (Stubbs 2001, for example, includes an analysis of a single short story with graphs indicating the relative frequencies of a character's name at different points within it.)

Although several of the points made here derive from corpus analysis, which has come to be virtually synonymous with a computer-assisted analysis of electronically stored texts, similar considerations apply to other methods of text analysis, including those that do not use computers at all.

Activity

> A student has decided to investigate the discourse of film reviews, and two of his research questions are: 'What are the similarities and variations in the discourse of film reviews?' and 'How constant are these across reviews of different genres of film?'
>
> ❏   What does this student need to consider in respect of selecting a 'sample' of film reviews so that his study will produce:
>   reliable results?
>   generalisable findings?
> ❏   What advice would you give him about his questions and about the data he needs to select?

B4.5 Controlling variables in experiments: how and why?

The white coat worn by the stereotypical researcher in a laboratory is not entirely a fiction. It symbolises one of the values of experimental research – the importance of not introducing into the procedure anything that might 'contaminate' it and lead to false or misleading results. Consider the report on a potential treatment for asthma that was investigated first with laboratory animals, cited in C3 (Ziegelbauer et al. 2005). The methods used in this study are described with repeated reference to 'standard conditions' and clear indications that all the tests were carried out in comparable ways. As you could predict, the quantities of the compound given to the animals, and the way it was administered, as well as the way results were measured were all standardised and equivalent. It is fairly obvious why research like this aims to vary only the X under scrutiny and keep everything else constant: if some mice were well fed and others given short rations, or if they were all given differing doses of the treatment, then conclusions about its effectiveness could be quite erroneous, influenced by misleading factors or 'variables'.

These methodological considerations do not always transfer well to human social research problems, as we shall see, but experiments are sometimes used in language research. If you decide that your question (or perhaps **hypothesis**) is suited to an experimental method, then you need to be clear about what this entails. Methods textbooks routinely explain the difference between the **independent variable**, which is the entity or phenomenon thought to be potentially responsible for some specified outcome, and the **dependent variable**, the X to be tested. The data you collect are likely to need analysing in particular ways too, so that any correlations you find are 'significant'. This is another everyday term that has a much more precise meaning in academic research.

An experimental study by language researchers that can be used to illustrate this is one concerned with stuttering (Hubbard and Prins 1994). The researchers wanted to know, among other things, whether unfamiliar words caused more problems for stutterers than high frequency words, and designed an experiment 'using specially designed sentences read orally by 10 adult stutterers and 10 adult nonstutterers' (p. 564). Note that this, like many experiments, is driven by a 'why' question. Here, the independent variable is words' degree of familiarity and the dependent variable, the X to be tested, is stutterers' production of the word. The study found that '[s]ignificantly more stutter events occurred on sentences containing less familiar words' (p. 569). Note, however, that the study involved extensive measurement and counting, with statistical procedures used to establish a 'significant rank order correlation between stutterers' word recognition vocabulary scores and amount of stuttering on sentences with high versus low frequency words' (p. 564). In this kind of research, it is not enough to present raw figures that seem to you to be 'significant': well established calculations must be used that demonstrate that differences between your Xs and Ys are not due merely to chance.

Studies of language learning also sometimes try to emulate laboratory experiments, with 'Teaching Method A' as the independent variable and 'Learners' Progress' as the dependent variable. It is customary to include a 'control group' of learners to monitor alongside the 'experimental group', with the aim of establishing whether 'Teaching Method A' leads to different results from the conventional teaching method in the dependent variable ('Learners' Progress'). (The project done by Enam, outlined in A4, is an example of this approach.) Many such studies, however, report on the problems of the **confounding variables**, where it proves impossible to manage and control everything that *might* have an effect on the outcomes.

The kind of study in this methodological tradition that you are likely to be able to carry out is probably on a small scale and one with tightly limited objectives.

Activity

> Suppose your interest is in the writing process, that you want to know more about the discourse contexts within which writers are most likely to pause when typing at a computer keyboard, and that you have decided to gain experience in using experimental methods.
>
> ❑ Specify a question about this area of interest that can be answered using an experimental method.
> ❑ Identify the variables you will explore, being clear about which are the independent and dependent variables, respectively, and what might act as confounding variables.

B5 THE HOW AND WHY OF SORTING OUT THE DETAILS

As suggested in A5, whatever method(s) you decide to use in your study, it helps to be well prepared for the realities of collecting language data, which usually means being realistic about human beings and the ways we interact with each other. Such realities can be messy, unpredictable and sometimes problematic. A number of established researchers in Applied Linguistics, as well as less seasoned students undertaking their first projects, have been kind enough to share some of their recollections of experiences 'in the field', and I draw on these in this unit. The activity which follows shortly invites you to think in some detail about some specific cases of the ways in which research plans can go awry, but I begin with some snapshots taken from the contributions of a wide range of researchers. The extracts are adapted from examples supplied to me, usually by email.

B5.1 What can go wrong with research?

1   Noise: house renovation (BANG BANG BANG through a whole tape – drives a transcriber mad)/TV left on all the time/visitors arriving.
2   The context was a project on the language of the classroom in the early 1990s. After lengthy negotiations with the local education authority and the Inspector of Modern Languages, permission was received to record three different classes over four days. This involved some 90 pupils and 11 teachers. When the day came, so did a flu epidemic and only 14 pupils and two teachers were present.
3   I originally wanted to do parent–child interaction in my own thesis, but, to a

woman [i.e. 'in all cases'], the mothers saw me as a really useful babysitter and did other things while I played with their children.

4   A colleague working on learner–learner discourse set a small group of adult learners a learning task and left them to it. As he left the room, he switched on a hidden tape recorder. Returning 20 minutes later, he triumphantly produced the recorder, proposing to listen to the recording with his learners – who were extremely embarrassed, refused the activity, made excuses and left. It transpired that they had spent the whole 20 minutes discussing the teacher's shortcomings, including his personality, methodology, looks, etc.

5   A postgraduate student studying early bilingualism circulated a letter to parents of a primary school asking for permission to include their children 'in a research project'. The request was almost unanimously rejected and several parents pro-tested to the school head and the local authority. It appeared that for them, a 'research programme' necessarily involved intervention with drugs, machinery, etc., and they weren't having any of it.

6   On a number of occasions, I have known projects fall through because:
     questionnaires were too long
     people who had agreed to be interviewed suddenly back-pedalled when they
         realised they would be recorded
     permission had not been sought from the interviewee's hierarchical superior.

 Activity

Consider the following questions in relation to each of the mini accounts that follow.

❏   Could the researcher have done anything to prevent the problem from arising in the first place and, if so, what?
❏   Once the problem had arisen, what do you think the researcher should have done?
❏   How, if at all, do the issues raised by the account relate – even indirectly – to the kind of research you are planning to do?
❏   How would you summarise the 'moral' of each cautionary tale?

B5.2 Relationships with people

Account 1

Some of the guidelines and safeguards described in A5 have been developed as poten-tial pitfalls have become better known and understood. As Coates (1996) observes in Reading D5.1, ethics committees were not well established when she began record-ing her women friends' discussions in the early 1980s. The following incident took place around the same time, and it perhaps illustrates, as does Coates' account, some of the reasoning behind the tighter regulations which have developed in the interven-ing period.

     A PhD student was collecting child language data. He visited children in their homes at three-weekly intervals to make audio-recordings and administer a language test. In all cases except for the one described here, at least one of the parents was present or within earshot for the whole visit. The student had just set up his recording equipment when the mother of Child X suddenly said she had to go down to the shops and would be back before he had finished. To the researcher's horror she had disappeared and shut the front door behind her before he could protest. Child X was always a challenge, being quite uncooperative at times and this occasion was no exception. He ran round the house, turning electrical appliances on and off, going in the fridge, opening cupboards. The student had no idea what the child was usually allowed to do and what was forbidden. He had very little control over him, if any, though he did manage to collect some data. Fortunately, the child's mother returned fairly soon.

The student was in an exposed situation and was therefore glad to be protected by the fact that the tape recorder had been recording everything that happened. At the time, he was concerned about breakages and injury, and was most worried by the fact that he couldn't control an energetic 3-year-old!

Account 2

A researcher at the start of her career prepared carefully to conduct her first ever focus group to gather data about the discourse associated with a particular issue. She was to work with a group who were already established, being involved in the area in which the researcher was interested. She had prepared some stimulus material and a set of questions in case the discussion got stuck. Unbeknown to her, one of the group members was an MA student of linguistics, who responded to her first question by challenging her methods of data collection. She managed to deflect that criticism at the time, thanking the group member for her input and offering to discuss the issue after the focus group meeting.

This experience led the researcher to be more aware of the lines of work or education her informants are in – and to avoid linguists or other social scientists!

Account 3

A research student who was interested in how the redrafting process affected language learners' writing sought access to the initial attempts produced for assessment by international student writers on a university course. She was hoping to analyse first drafts of MA dissertations, then second and third drafts, and so on. She encountered two problems. First, students were generally unwilling to hand drafts over. To get any at all she had to form personal friendships with the students concerned, which she did by offering free English language help in return for the drafts. However, this was very time-consuming, which reduced the number of student dissertations she ended up being able to use. In addition, she found that students were very unwilling to give her the real first draft. The students with whom she had formed a good rapport wanted to 'please' or 'impress' her so they wanted to make sure their drafts were 'good' *before* they handed them over. From her point of view, the less good the first drafts were, and the more they changed before the final draft, the better. So, in spite of working extremely hard to collect data, she ended up with less than was ideal for her project.

B5.3 Contexts: times, places and circumstances

Account 4

A postgraduate researcher planned to collect data from the participants in an online course organised in the UK university where she worked, for students in another country. Setting this up involved the co-operation of the tutors running the course, who were based in a foreign language department in the researcher's university, the ethics committee in that institution, the postgraduate's supervisor, who was based in yet another institution, as well as the overseas students. The courses in question were sponsored by the other country and, as the researcher had been assured that a new cohort would be enrolling at the usual time in the coming year, she waited for confirmation that the course was about to start so that she could recruit participants for her study, meanwhile producing and piloting research tools. As time wore on, the language department contacted the foreign institution, at first receiving no reply but eventually discovering that the person who arranged these courses was on indefinite sick-leave. It gradually became clear that no one had taken over her role in organising any courses and that this course would not run in the foreseeable future. The research student had, in effect, lost ten months working on her thesis and was obliged to find a completely new source of data.

Account 5

An undergraduate student was researching the dialect of her own local area, and was investigating in particular lexical erosion, that is, whether there were any changes in the use of locality-specific vocabulary. She prepared a questionnaire which asked informants to 'define [various] words to the best of your knowledge . . . and [indicate] how regularly you use them in your everyday speech'. Her preliminary study involved asking six participants (of varying age ranges) to complete this questionnaire, in order to establish whether they understood many of the old dialectal forms of this local variety.

As it happened, four of these participants were together in the same room while completing the questionnaire, and began to discuss it openly. The result was four questionnaires with the same answers, because between them the participants belonged to every age-group whose usage was being probed by the questionnaire. As this student reflected later, 'Disaster! Not only did I not have six different question-naires, but the diversity that I was expecting to see between the ages was lost – the older participants (70+) were informing the younger ones of the "answers", and vice versa'. There was little this student could do except regard this as a pilot and not repeat the approach in the actual study.

B5.4 Concepts

Account 6

This research project involved a group of teachers who had a high percentage of second generation immigrant children in their primary school, and who were con-vinced that the poor performances of these children was the result of 'linguistic poverty' manifested as a lack of fluency, poor vocabulary, etc. These teachers were asked to record their classes, which they did and then teachers and researchers sat down together to listen to the tapes. But when the researchers asked the teachers to identify the voices as 'immigrants' or 'French', they were completely unable to do so. Only when they could see the children could they hear the difference.

Commentary

I expect you will have decided that there are different degrees, in these accounts, to which the problem can be explained by bad planning on the researcher's part. Some of the examples would be much less likely to happen now, as research training and guidelines have become more established. In some cases, however, the problems are simply a function of the way the world works and the way human beings are. As suggested in strand 4, I believe that good social research takes into account the 'properties' of people, philosophically speaking, including a recognition of what makes them distinct from other kinds of entities, such as plants, isolated chemicals, electrons and even other animals.

Human beings are unique in their ability to use language, a capacity which makes possible the exchange of ideas, values and attitudes, and all the elements of the culture which provides a context for our interactions. A particular challenge for researchers who are interested in the social and educational aspects of language is the way in which existing cultural and social arrangements mean that people are routinely assumed to belong to various groups – according to their sex (or gender), their age, their social background or their 'ethnicity', which is a notoriously problematic social category, and one which proves impossible to define consistently.

Researchers whose interest is in human language are thus dealing with something that is more complex than many of the things that are the focus of research in other disciplines. This can be dispiriting and daunting, but it can also be exciting. If your own data turns out to be different from what you expect, or even messy and lacking an obvious pattern, this may be because you failed to plan thoroughly or because you are new to this kind of enterprise. But it may also be because you are discovering empirically something which is supported by several theories about the subject – that people and their uses of language demand approaches to research which are different from those appropriate for other kinds of things in the world. As one professor wrote when she sent me her contribution for this section, 'One thing our students worry about is messy data – I think it is important to stress that real data will be messy'.

THE HOW AND WHY OF DATA COLLECTION   B6

> It is impossible to present a set of invariant rules about data collection (how much
> data, what kind of data, obtained through what method or in what situation),
> because choices have to be made in the light of the investigator's goals.
>
> (Cameron 2001: 29)

B6.1 What kind of data?

Descriptions of the research process sometimes make it seem tidier and more linear
than it really is. It could seem as though the question, 'What kind of data do I need?'
almost answers itself once some substantial reading has been done and some research
questions have been identified: if you want to know more about X, you need examples of X to investigate. In reality, as has been noted, students often revisit and revise
their questions as their research progresses, including as they come to recognise practical constraints on what is feasible. Planned sources of data may prove unreliable in
the event. A line of enquiry originally envisaged as peripheral may become the main
focus of the study and the parameters of the data are changed accordingly. So it is that
the process of collecting data is not always a separate stage in the research, located
after framing a question and unchanged once it begins.

Nevertheless, at the planning stage, some decisions will always need to be taken
about where to begin with data collection. Table B6.2.1 suggests the kind of data likely
to be required for investigation into various topics in English Language research,
together with some issues raised in each case. None of these sets of suggestions is
exhaustive: there are other topic areas, other kinds of data and other issues that could
be raised. The summary is, however, indicative of the things you are likely to need to
consider.

B6.2 Where will the data come from?

If you need 'human subjects' for your data, the most obvious starting point is people
you know, including relatives, friends and perhaps workmates. Often, some individuals from this pool of potentially willing subjects will be suitable sources of data, but not
always. For example, if you are interested in international students learning English, or
in how children in primary schools develop certain aspects of written language, you
may need to approach people you don't already know to arrange contact with potential
participants. Even if you do have enough people to call on from your existing circle,
they may not be the best people for your project. There is always a relationship between
a researcher and the people s/he is researching, and existing relationships (based on
knowing people as friends, siblings, colleagues, and so on) may cut across the sharing of information or behaviour that is your priority in this context. This is related to

the phenomenon of the 'strangers on the train', or hairdressers and their clients, where, paradoxically, some people feel able to be more open with someone they hardly know. Informants who have an established relationship with you may feel constrained about what they say or how they behave if they are aware of wanting to maintain that relationship after the data collection is over.

Another disadvantage of staying within your existing group of contacts is that it may lead to a reinforcement of your existing ideas about, for example, how male friends of your age-group behave. Recruiting some informants from a different social circle could help to widen your appreciation of the influence of gender on friends' interactions. An existing interest in the language of young children will be developed more if you collect data from several unfamiliar toddlers than if you concentrate exclusively on your little brother, with whose language patterns you are already well acquainted.

On the other hand, recruiting and building relationships for your study may be difficult and time-consuming. The chattering 3-year-old you are introduced to in the nursery may clam up entirely when you, an unfamiliar adult, arrive to collect data. Friends are more likely to be available when you need them and, especially if they too are involved in doing research for their studies, they will understand your situation and your need for their co-operation. Whatever the pool from which you draw your participants, remember that they are, effectively, making you a gift of something you really need: acknowledge this thoroughly, by expressing both informal and formal thanks (at the end of your questionnaire, by card or letter after the interview, in the acknowledgements page of your dissertation).

As noted before, written texts are a different proposition, usually presenting fewer challenges, since they do not have priorities or feelings of their own, and will stay where you leave them and be available at any time for you to resume your collection and analysis. One of the issues you may face, in the increasingly multimodal world of communications we inhabit, is how to determine what exactly constitutes your data. Just as transcriptions of spoken language are not the speech itself (see Reading D7.1), so texts such as brochures, leaflets, advertisements, web pages, and so on, comprise much more than the grammar and vocabulary used in the language. While it may be relatively easy to 'grab' the text from a web page and save it as a text-only file for corpus analysis, the decision to do so assumes several things about the nature of texts, and these assumptions are potentially controversial.

As with all other aspects of data collection, it pays to think carefully about such matters, and about the pros and cons of different approaches, making explicit, at least for yourself, in your project notebook, the reasons for the decisions you take. At the same time, do not allow yourself to become paralysed by the range of options, and your recognition of some disadvantages to each. At some point you will need to start collecting your data and to see where this leads you (Table B6.2.1).

Table B6.2.1 Examples of kinds of data relevant for various language study topics

Topic	Potential data	Issues to consider
Accents and dialects	Speech produced by people from specific speech communities	How are the speakers to be selected? (See C6)
Acquisition of English as a second language	Speech or writing produced by learners	Which learners, at what stage of their learning?
Bilingualism and code-switching	Speech produced by people with particular language backgrounds	Does the researcher need to be a speaker of both varieties?
Development of English as a first language	Young children's talk	Is there time for a longitudinal study? What can feasibly be investigated if not?
Discourse of advertising	Advertisements – from billboards, magazines, television, the internet, fliers, etc.	Is there a homogeneous 'discourse of advertising'? How do you deal with the multimodal elements of advertisements (music, pictures, cartoons, etc.)?
Forensic linguistics	Transcripts of court testimony, legislative texts, legal contracts, witness statements	Can you obtain access both to the texts you need and to the background information associated with them?
Language and gender	Same-sex interactions, mixed-sex interactions, discourse aimed primarily at one gender or the other, questionnaires	How can you know in advance that the speakers' gender will be significant in these interactions? Is it possible to generalise from small amounts of data about men/women in general?
Language and power	Workplace interactions, political interviews, political speeches	How can you know in advance that power will feature in these interactions? Does this matter?
Language and the media	Texts from certain kinds of sources – radio, newspapers, television, the internet, audience responses to media texts	If the texts you are interested in contain images, including moving images, and/or sounds other than spoken language, how will you record and transcribe these elements?

Table B6.2.1 (continued)

Topic	Potential data	Issues to consider
Language attitudes	Elicited responses from informants to speech of different kinds, questionnaires, maybe interviews	Will informants be truthful in their responses? What stimulus will you present to your informants?
New technologies	Text messages, emails, online chat, gameworlds	Can you be sure that the authors of these texts are who they say they are? (How much) does this matter?
Pragmatics	Greetings, apologies, compliments, jokes; leave-takings, etc.	How can you collect authentic data when the kind of speech act you need is fairly unpredictable?
Stylistics	Written texts	How accessible are the texts (in electronic form)?
Text types and genres	A range of texts in certain categories – of form or function	How do you avoid the circularity problem: defining a genre by certain characteristics and then using your data to illustrate the same features?

B6.3 How much data?

Students who have reached the stage of deciding on their questions and general approach, and have identified the kind of data they need, often put to their supervisor a question about how much data they should collect. The reply is likely to be frustrating, or at least not definitive, along the lines of a rejoining question of the 'how long is a piece of string?' type. There are always several considerations, some practical and others more methodological; also, there is usually a trade-off between depth and breadth.

Activity

Three small-scale projects of 3,000 words (pre-dissertation) from students I have recently supervised provide illustrations. Table B6.3.1 summarises their respective areas of interest, types of data and initial research questions. What advice would you give them about how much data they should collect, or include in their analysis?

Table B6.3.1 Examples of student projects

Topic	Data	Questions	How much data?
A Varieties of English used abroad	T-shirts seen in Japan featuring printed slogans in a non-standard variety of English	How does the language of these texts differ from standard English?	How many slogans?
B The double layer of humour in comic poems for children	Roald Dahl's poetry	How does the language of these poems provide humour that appeals simultaneously – but differently – to children and adults?	How many poems?
C Persuasive language in literature designed to recruit the armed forces	Army recruitment texts	How do these texts use metaphors as a persuasive device?	How many texts? How much of the total material in each text? How many metaphors?

Commentary

Let's start with the potential 'universe' of all the data that could be included, if there were no limits to these students' time and resources. The most clear-cut calculation would be for project B: once the researcher has decided to narrow her focus from 'comic poems for children' to just those written by Dahl, she is constrained by what he has published, so her potential data set is all of these poems. Project C is a little less obvious, in that there are various texts associated with the function the student has identified, including some available in hard copy and others on the internet. Such texts change over time, so a decision needs to be made about which ones may be legitimately excluded if the project is to focus only on current material. The boundaries of data for Project A are the hardest to specify: how could anyone be sure that all instances of the category (T-shirts found in Japan bearing slogans in non-standard English) have been observed and recorded? In practice, as the student was obliged to collect her data via the internet, this potential data set is reduced to those examples that are photographed and published online.

Sometimes, this process of identifying the potential data set leads fairly quickly to the specification of a smaller amount of data to answer the research questions you have in mind. The bigger your 'universe' of potential data, the more important it may become to clarify which small area of it you will choose to investigate. Thus, 'humour in children's literature' becomes 'humour in selected poems of Roald Dahl'. Similarly, since you cannot possibly analyse all the lonely hearts ads ever printed, you might narrow your data set to those published in a particular type of larger text (two contrasting types of magazine aimed at women readers, perhaps) during a particular period. In relation to the 'How much data?' question, Wray and Bloomer (2006: 140) note that:

> If you want to know how the word *the* is pronounced in continuous speech, you won't need more than a few minutes worth, because *the* is such a common word. But, if you are interested in how topics are linked together in debates, you will need enough material for sufficient topic changes to occur.

Another stage in a research project which often answers the 'How much data?' question is the time it takes to process and analyse the data, as well as the proportion of your word limit which is used up as you do. Students typically over-estimate how much data they can handle, and under-estimate what they will find out and want to report. It is very often the case, therefore, that the final project focuses on a more limited set of data than was originally envisaged. For their 3,000 word independent studies, the students referred to above eventually analysed, respectively, 22 T-shirts, three poems by Dahl and a single brochure produced by the army. Once it becomes clear that only some of the potential data that exists, even with a narrower focus than you started with, can be included in your investigation, you are then faced with the challenge of selecting which part(s) to include.

B6.4 Which data to include?

Wray and Bloomer (2006) advise collecting more data than you think you will need, if, for example, your interest is in accent, and it is important to have several examples of a particular phoneme. You may not need to transcribe everything you record, but you will need plenty of examples of spoken language from your informants from which to select.

In a sense, the process of narrowing down your data from all the potential data that exists to a sub-set which you can manage in a small project is the process of 'constructing' your Xs and Ys. B4 includes a discussion about issues of sampling, which are linked to the idea of generalisability. Try to make sure that you are clear about these issues in your own mind. Use one or more criteria, which you can make explicit, to select your data, and then draw conclusions only about what you have investigated, rather than claiming, or suggesting, that these conclusions will apply to all other language from a similar source.

One principle here, especially if your study involves some kind of measurement (a 'How much?' or 'How many?' question), is to use a process of selection of data, from everything available, that is *not* derived from the X you are investigating. In other words, if you have planned to find out whether texts of type A use a particular linguistic feature more frequently than texts of type B do, you should sample texts of each type by some criterion other than the target feature, and not choose to look only at those which you have already noticed include lots of examples for you to analyse.

For example, suppose you suspect that, in lonely hearts ads, women highlight their personalities, while men emphasise their activities and interests. You collect some 'men seeking women' and 'women seeking men' sections of the lonely hearts pages from a specified source (perhaps a newspaper that is aimed equally at male and female readers) and find that you have far too many ads to analyse them all. When you narrow down your data selection, you should *not* do so by including those which confirm your predictions and excluding those which challenge them. Instead, you might take the first ten from each section, or every fifth one, or all the ads which fall between a certain number of words in length, or use some other criterion which is unconnected to your research focus.

Activity

A student has identified the language of product packaging as his area of interest. In particular, he has begun to focus on the 'blurb' in the packaging of many products; that is, the text additional to the product's name, logo, list of ingredients, and so on. He has noticed that this blurb often seems to contain both informative and persuasive language, and wants to investigate the properties of this discourse. He has approximately three months to work on this study, alongside other modules on his course, and must write a report of 6000 words on his research.

❏ What is the smallest number of package labels he could include in his study and still be able to come to some valid conclusions about this kind of discourse?
❏ What is the largest number of examples he could include and have a manageable set of data to investigate in the time available?
❏ What criteria could he use to select packages to include in his data set? Are there criteria he could use to *exclude* certain items, or kinds of item?
❏ If he comes across items which seem to have no blurb on their packaging at all, should he exclude these from his study or not? Why?
❏ If he notices items where the language looks to be immediately interesting, in terms of its persuasive-informative characteristics, should he make sure to include these in his study, or not? Why?

Commentary

As indicated at the start of this section, there is no definitive answer to the question of 'How much data?' However, as I hope you have found in thinking (and perhaps talking with others) about these questions, it is possible to make explicit for yourself some of the reasoning behind taking such decisions. One aspect of the process will sometimes be that, as you begin your analysis, you encounter diminishing returns beyond a certain point. In other words, having found a range of types of language feature across, say, 20 separate texts, you realise that the subsequent items you look at are not providing you with any new features, but rather with further examples of the same kinds of things you have already identified. If the question was of the 'What is X like?' type, as in this study, it would in that case be fairly safe to stop at 20 items. However, suppose the question was 'Does the packaging on organic food products use more persuasive language than that on non-organic food products?' or 'Is the language on the packaging of cosmetic products aimed at women different from that of cosmetics aimed at men?' In this case, it may be that there should be 20 texts from each sub-group in the data set, to be more certain that the contrasting features in each sub-set (if there are any) have been robustly established, because this question is of the type 'How many Xs and how many Ys are there in texts of Types A and B respectively?' This is related to the issue of sampling, which is touched on elsewhere (B4). If you are comparing two kinds of things (an X and a Y) you need adequate examples of each, which may mean you need twice as much data as you would if you had only an X to investigate. More dimensions means more 'cells', as Figures B6.4.1 and B6.4.2 illustrate.

In the first case, the aim of the study is to compare the language of persuasion across a number of advertisements, considering how the different kinds of target audience may influence the language used, including two kinds of advertisement (for material products and for job recruitment), and just two further attributes of the potential audience – general type of occupation and two broad age groups. Many more attributes could be included, but even these rather broad and crude subdivisions of a potential data set generate eight 'cells' to be filled, and each one would need a number of texts to be sure that it was in some way representative of the type of text the researcher intended. The same is true of the second hypothetical study, which this time focuses on dialect, and the vocabulary used by people in different categories: I have used similar ones to keep the discussion simple. Again, you would need informants from each of these cells, and enough of each to give your findings validity.

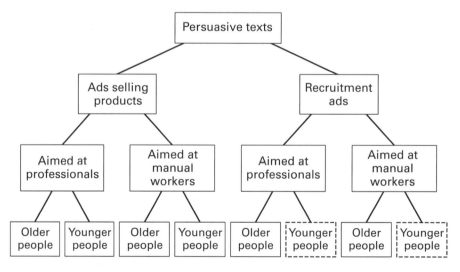

Figure B6.4.1 The effect of including texts with a wide range of attributes in a data set

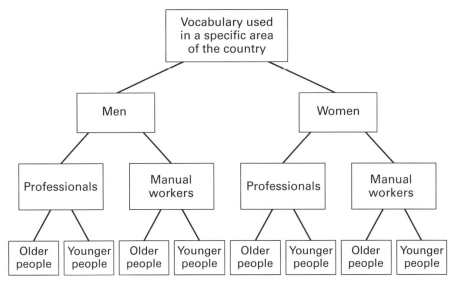

Figure B6.4.2 The effect of including in a study speakers with a wide range of attributes

I would not recommend that a limited study of the kind most undergraduates are likely to be attempting should tackle as many variations as this. There will be too much data, and the permutations are likely to become unwieldy. On the other hand, you could draw up a similar kind of table, thinking about the various dimensions that could characterise the data in which you are interested, and use this to filter your potential texts so that you have a clearly specified sub-set on which to concentrate in your analysis. Thus, you might compare advertisements aimed at recruiting relatively unqualified school-leavers and recent graduates, groups which would correspond with the cells indicated by broken lines in Figure B6.4.1. This process can help you to sharpen your focus for data collection, and indirectly contribute an answer to the question 'How much data?'

THE HOW AND WHY OF DATA ANALYSIS   B7

In this unit, several different levels of language, from sounds to discourse, provide an organisational framework within which to consider how different kinds of research project deal with the analysis of data.

As you read each example:

❏ Think about how you would analyse the data generated in order to answer the research questions posed in the study.
❏ Try to identify in each case what the researchers' Xs and Ys were, and the extent to which their research design involved direct intervention in the production of their data (see units A4 and A7).
❏ In light of those decisions, consider how much flexibility the researchers had in each study, in their approach to data analysis.

Also, in each case, consider, and preferably discuss with other students, the following questions:

❏ Which types of data lend themselves to analytical procedures like those in the example and which do not? Why?
❏ Can you think of any ways to improve on the data analysis in the study? (You should read it in full if so, as you have access only to a brief summary here.)
❏ Are there other ways to generate and analyse data which could shed light on the same issues as those addressed in the study? If so, what would they be?

B7.1 Data analysis example 1: sounds

In forensic linguistics, the accurate identification of a speaker by his or her voice can be extremely important; for example, does the voice on the tape of the police interview with a suspect match that on the recording of the threatening telephone call which s/he is accused of making? Experts in voice recognition can use various resources to establish speaker identity, but sometimes the only witness to the call is the victim, who may be asked to participate in the aural equivalent of a visual identity parade, and pick out a suspect on the basis of samples of phone calls made by different speakers. Noting that this can be quite difficult, despite the common perception that speaker recognition is simple and straightforward, Foulkes and Barron (2000) devised an experiment to test the abilities of ten young male friends to distinguish each other's voices as heard in a recorded phone message which each of them made, from a prepared script. Each was asked to listen once to each recorded message and note the names of each speaker they thought they had heard, in the order they heard them.

> ⭐ **Activity**
>
> ### Questions to consider
> ❏ If you had conducted this experiment, what would your data set be?
> ❏ How would you analyse this data?
> ❏ Would you anticipate more than one stage of analysis and, if so, what do you think would be involved at each stage?

Analysis

The first calculations that Foulkes and Barron did were of the actual success rate of each subject, which they turned into percentages (see A7). Their article provides tables and detailed descriptions indicating (a) which subjects identified which voices correctly, and (b) which voices were identified correctly more often. These results raised some further issues which they investigated in a different way. Remember that the researchers were interested in how both experts and naïve listeners perform in speech recognition (SR), so they used both interviews with some of the participants, about their perceptions of the task, and 'close auditory analysis of the samples to identify the most salient phonetic characteristics of each voice' (Foulkes and Barron 2000: 189). The latter analyses established that 'some of the problems and errors that occurred in the SR test' could be explained by 'the general segmental and supra-segmental characteristics of the voices' (p. 189). Several of the voices sounded very similar to the participants, despite displaying distinguishing cues which the research-ers, as phoneticians, could perceive. Next they did yet another stage of analysis, using specialised software to identify and compare each speaker's fundamental frequency (or 'F0', an acoustic term referring to the number of pulses in the auditory signal). For each speaker, as well as determining his average F0, they also used the statistical calculation of '**standard deviation**' to determine how widely his voice ranged away from its average value – '[m]ore monotonous voices', as they explain, 'are reflected by a lower standard deviation' (p. 191). At this point, as they report in their article, they noticed that the speakers most likely to be correctly identified were those who had 'very high or very low F0' and 'very high or very low standard deviations (indicating a wide pitch range or a monotonous voice respectively)' (p. 194). But would a more precise statistical test show that these things (ease of identification and these aspects of voice quality) were actually correlated, as opposed to being only an apparent ten-dency, which could have occurred by chance? To find out, they used a one-tailed Pearson product moment correlation test. Although this is a daunting term, you can easily become familiar with what it means if you read a little about simple statistics for quantitative research. In this example, the test supported the authors' interpretation of the patterns in their data, giving them greater confidence in their conclusion that 'average pitch is a robust diagnostic of speaker identity, not only for forensic phoneti-cians, but also for naïve listeners' (p. 180).

One final point to note is that they also acknowledge the small size of their sample, and identify the areas where further research is needed.

B7.2 Data analysis example 2: words

My colleague, Paul Thompson, and I had a grant to investigate how primary school children might learn about the English language using corpus-based methods. (The project, 'An investigation into corpus-based learning about language in the primary school' was funded by the Economic and Social Research Council (R000223900).) From the BNC (British National Corpus), we constructed a corpus of fiction aimed at young readers and, in one part of the study, we compared this with a corpus of fiction written for adults, in order to answer the research question, 'Does writing for children demonstrate different linguistic properties from writing for adults?' This question was broken down into various sub-questions, one of which was, 'Are there differences between the child and adult fiction corpora in the uses of particular lexical items?'

In an article reporting on this part of the study (Thompson and Sealey 2007), we explain the various ways in which we calculated the relative frequencies of lexical items in the two corpora – as well as in a third corpus of news texts, which contrasted much more clearly with both the fiction corpora than these two sets of fiction texts did with each other. As was the case in example 1, above, our findings from the first stage of analysis, when we compared the three corpora from a purely numerical point of view, led to a further stage of analysis. We used the semantic categorisation program, WMatrix (Rayson 2008), to identify broad areas of experience represented in the two fiction corpora, and our article displays the numerical contrasts, calculated as 'log likelihood' scores by the software (again, you can explore this concept in most introductory texts on statistics). The semantic domain which WMatrix identifies as 'Living creatures generally' was top of the list for the child fiction corpus, whereas for the adult fiction corpus it was 'Relationship: intimate/sexual', and there were several other differences.

This approach to analysis allowed us to present a table of the figures for each corpus, whose significance we summarised as follows:

> The world as construed in literature written for a child audience appears to be highly distinctive in the importance of animals generally (living creatures), food and plants. Communication stands out too, with . . . a high degree of direct speech and also of speech acts. It is a world of bravery and fear, where movement and speed are important, a world of objects, and a world in which sight and size are emphasised. The world of adult fiction, on the other hand, is distinguished by intimacy and sexuality, and is a world in which beliefs and broad questions about life predominate, and is a world of social laws.
>
> (Thompson and Sealey 2007: 15)

The third stage of analysis was to look in detail at some specific instances of particular words, and this was done by comparing concordance lines containing the same **node words** in each of the two fiction corpora. Because of our interest in potential differences in the way children and adults are depicted as perceiving the world, we explored expressions relating to both time and space, and one expression that we analysed in each corpus was *in time*. We classified each instance according to whether the meaning, in context, was more literal or more figurative. As this is a matter of interpretation, we included the concordance lines in our article, so that readers can decide whether they agree with our categories. We summarised our interpretation as follows:

> In the majority of the [children's fiction corpus] examples, *in time* refers to the meeting of a deadline, the accomplishment of an action that must be completed before a penalty or some other unwanted outcome should occur. In the [adult fiction] corpus, *in time* can be used to refer to the same local sense of time . . . but in other lines time is invoked on a larger scale, either in the sense of the centuries passing (. . . 'Everything would change in time') or in terms of a gradual unfolding of events (. . . 'in time we should be able to . . .').
>
> (Thompson and Sealey 2007: 19)

In summary, then, we approached the analysis of our data – one child fiction and one adult fiction corpus – in order to answer our research question about differences between the two in the uses of particular lexical items by:

1   using corpus-analytic software to calculate relative frequencies of words and types of word (including by part-of-speech categories, though I have not summarised that aspect here),
2   using different software to compare semantic domains in the two corpora, and
3   generating concordance lines so as to compare particular expressions in context in each corpus.

B7.3 Data analysis example 3: clauses

There are many approaches to the study of words in combination, and the example I have chosen is arguably at the interface between grammar and semantics. It is a study of one causal conjunction, namely *seeing as though*, which was investigated in depth by Taylor and Pang (2008). Their article reports how this expression came to their attention in a brief email correspondence between a student and tutor, where they note that it 'served as a subordinating conjunction, with roughly the same value as more common alternatives such as *since* and *seeing that*' (pp. 103–4). Having been struck by how it had been used in these emails, the researchers went on to read about this expression and equivalent conjunctions (or 'causal connectives'), and to evaluate various possible sources of data, before themselves collecting 50 examples, using the internet, and analysing them from various perspectives. They realised that, in order to identify what was peculiar to *seeing as though*, it would be useful to compare it with *since* and *seeing that*, so the analysis developed into a comparison of these three expressions.

Their reading, and further exploration of the issues raised, led them to focus on the topics of each of the two clauses connected by such conjunctions, contrasting those which were about the speaker ('subjective') with those which were about 'third parties or descriptions of "objective" states of affairs' (p. 116). To establish the patterning of *seeing as though* in comparison with similar expressions, they identified the grammatical subjects of the clauses, and categorised these into 'first person (*I* or *we*), second person, or, if third person, whether human or other (animate or abstract)' (p. 116). What they found was that, '[o]n this measure, *seeing as though* constructions turn out to be more speaker-centred than the other types' (p. 117).

A subsequent passage in their article is quite informative about how data analysis may proceed, including slight shifts of approach like those which have been noted in the previous examples in this unit:

> Initially, we had intended to classify the contents of the reason clauses according to their information status, whether common ground or newly asserted. We quickly discovered that decisions in this regard were often variable and unstable. We therefore turned to more 'objective' criteria of analysis.
>
> First, we identified those reason clauses whose content pertains to some aspect of the speaker herself, such as her mental or physical state, her recent experiences, or her past history. Although the content of such clauses might well constitute 'new' information to the hearer (the hearer might be ignorant of the speaker's age or of her activities in the recent past), the information is, for the speaker, irrefutable; as such, it is able to constitute an unassailable basis for the content of the main clause.
>
> (Taylor and Pang 2008: 117)

Throughout the report, the authors provide both numerical data ('About one-third of the *seeing as though* clauses . . . fell into the speaker-centred category', p. 117) and examples of the sentences they are analysing, which allows the reader to evaluate their classifications. Tables are provided with the precise figures, and tests of significance have also been carried out (as explained in example 1, above, and in A7).

The analysis continues with classification of the grammatical subject in the second ('consequent') clause, and then the researchers explore 'the "locus" of the causal relation, that is, the agent who is responsible for establishing the relation between the two clauses, whether the speaker, a protagonist other than the speaking subject, or a generic, unnamed third party' (p. 123). Their results, again presented in tabular form, revealed that:

> *Seeing as though* is used almost exclusively to express a relation established by the speaker, only rarely to state an 'objective' relation attributable to a generic third party . . . or to report a relation established by a third-person protagonist.
>
> (Taylor and Pang 2008: 123)

> **Question to consider**
> These researchers took some further approaches to the analysis of this expression in comparison with the others they selected; without reading ahead, can you predict what these were?

The next phase of analysis was speaker stance, as expressed both overtly (*I think, it seems to me*), and 'other stance expressions, such as *presumably, probably, really,* and the like'. They also included 'epistemic uses of modals such as *must, can't,* and *will*' (Taylor and Pang 2008: 124). They then looked at the sequence of clauses, finding that the reason clause tended to occur before the consequent clause. The analysis was linked as well to a discussion of the metaphorical qualities of the expression, where 'knowing is seeing', before the researchers turned their attention to the internal grammatical properties of the construction, concluding from this that '*seeing as though* is a compound expression, which cannot be analysed as a compositional function of its parts' (p. 127). This claim is supported by a comparison of *as though* and *as if,* which led to the collection of further data, as often happens in the course of studies of this kind.

B7.4 Data analysis example 4: discourse

As with the other levels of language analysis, there are countless examples which could have been selected to illustrate the process of analysing data which consists of extended stretches of discourse. On the other hand, there is an extensive range of sources which you can read to learn about how to do discourse analysis (see Further Reading).

The study I have chosen concerns interactions between international teaching assistants (ITAs) and American college students (ACSs), and had as its 'primary purpose ... to find out whether mutual understanding may be achieved in ITA–ACS interactions' (Chiang and Mi 2008: 272). More specifically, the researchers wanted to find out:

1   Under what specific circumstances does understanding uncertainty arise in the ITA–ACS office hour interaction?
2   In what specific ways is understanding uncertainty displayed and managed in the ITA–ACS office hour interaction?

(Chiang and Mi 2008: 273)

The ten participants in the study were five postgraduate students of economics, originally from China, with an obligation to teach some undergraduate classes at their university in the USA, and five native speakers of English, who, as students in these ITAs' classes, visited them during their office hours for assistance with their homework or to prepare for an exam. The data for the study was audio-recordings of the interactions between them, which were transcribed in the detail recommended for Conversation Analysis, because of the need to 'capture most paralinguistic features such as vocal inflections, intonation, overlaps, and pauses, all of which are crucial for locating understanding uncertainty' (p. 273). Chiang and Mi go on to explain how they carried out the analysis of their data:

These office hour interactions were examined for understanding uncertainty in two steps. First, the interactions were reviewed turn by turn by two instructors of communication. The reviewers compiled a list of moments in the exchanges that brought to light linguistic deficiencies and resulting confusion. The list was used as a guide for the subsequent playback sessions with the participants. Second, all five interaction sequences were reviewed turn by turn with each participant individually. Each was asked to comment on any moment during the exchange in which confusion was experienced. The playback session also was audio-taped.

(Chiang and Mi 2008: 273)

This analytical procedure, like all the others presented in this unit, led to the identification of some recurrent patterns. The researchers found that various kinds of misunderstanding occurred, but that these were handled by the participants by reformulations of what was said, which allowed them to proceed with the necessary communication. Unlike my previous examples, this approach did not make use of quantification, but it did identify several types of reformulation, and each one is illustrated with extracts from the data. The analysis here is clearly qualitative, and a fine-grained commentary is supplied to explain how each data extract has been interpreted. There is not space here to reproduce an example in its entirety, but an extract will be illustrative. The topic of the exchange is the student's (Frank) need to understand a concept from the economics class which Ms Cai is teaching.

```
112   Cai:     Yeah, and (0.2) and this price, (0.5) the quantity demanded will be
113            higher than the quantity supplied.
114            (2.0)
115   Frank:   quantity demanded will be higher
116   Cai:     Right?
117   Frank:   well
118   Cai:     mm
119   Frank:   I don't u:::m,
```

(Chiang and Mi 2008: 278)

This is how the researchers interpret this part of the longer exchange:

Frank seemed to experience uncertainty as shown in the long pause in Line 114 and he subsequently repeated a part of Ms Cai's statement in Line 115. Ms Cai seemed to notice his confusion since she made a comprehension check in Line 116. Frank did not provide a simple yes-or-no answer, but 'Well' in Line 117, which conventionally indicates hesitation. Frank's uncertainty was more clearly displayed in his unfinished utterance in Line 119 where he attempted to say something to follow up his 'Well' in Line 117.

(Chiang and Mi 2008: 278)

B7.5 Data analysis examples: summary

These four examples are very different, spanning the levels of language from sounds to discourse, and using data from both spontaneous and scripted speech, through informal electronic communications, to published writing. I hope you can see how the various approaches to analysis correspond with the questions that the researchers had posed, and thus how you might match your analytical approach to your own research questions. (This, too, is an aspect of *methodology* – see B4). You may also be encouraged to note that the researchers in each example decided on some of the steps in their analysis only after they had undertaken some initial analytical work: it is not always possible to plan every aspect of this in advance (though you should certainly not wander into the analysis stage with no idea at all about how you will do it – see C3). Some of the research summarised here used counting and statistical tests of significance; other aspects are much more a matter of interpretation. However, each example demonstrates the researchers making available a 'warrant' for what is claimed, whether that is a recognised quantitative procedure or an extended extract from the data which readers can evaluate for themselves. As you read published studies in your particular area of interest, try to take note of these aspects as a guide to making decisions about your own approach to data analysis.

THE HOW AND WHY OF WRITING UP YOUR PROJECT   B8

> [. . .] student academic writing constitutes a very particular kind of literacy practice which is bound up with the workings of a particular social institution.
>
> (Lillis 2001: 39)

In my experience, students are well aware that there are 'literacy practices' in which they must engage in particular ways if they are to obtain the reward of good marks and qualifications. In strand 2, I discuss the conventions expected of researchers when they cite other texts, and how these are linked to practices which may be perceived as favouring certain people's interests at the expense of others. These practices extend to the whole process of writing up a research project for accreditation, and A8 specifies the basic elements likely to be relevant. One source of potential problems is the interpretation of these conventions and expectations and, as Lea and Street point out in Reading D8.1, both students and tutors can sometimes misidentify the source of such problems, locating them at the surface level of writing rather than in the less obvious underpinnings of the enterprise. In this unit, I take just two frequently asked questions as a starting point from which to consider potential answers from the perspectives of both skills and social practices.

B8.1 Writing: the how and why of style

Q: Am I allowed to use first person pronouns when writing up my research?

A1: One answer to this question is to check whether there is a policy on this in your department: you don't want to be penalised for contravening local guidance. Personally, I advise my students that it is permissible, but to use it sparingly. The convolutions necessary to avoid saying 'I did this' are often awkward, and referring to themselves as 'the researcher' instead can be ambiguous. I also explain that the proscription is partly due to the value placed in academic writing on demonstrable, shared knowledge in preference to subjective personal opinion and anecdote, which is why an over-use of 'I' in such texts may be suspect.

A2: A slightly more detailed answer is indicated by debates you will find in places such as the website associated with the American Psychological Association, which produces a very extensive guide covering probably every aspect of stylistic choice you can think of. The guide is aimed at academic authors and is also the basis for the style and editorial policies for many journals in the social sciences. First person pronouns are associated with the active rather than passive voice, and advice on this has changed with revisions in recent editions of the *APA Publication Manual*. Whereas once it was reasoned that the passive should be used so as to focus readers' attention on the topic of the research rather than on the authors of the text, the fashion has shifted so that the authors of the sixth (2010) edition of the *Manual* now say:

> Verbs are vigorous, direct communicators. Use the active rather than the passive voice, and select tense or mood carefully.
> * Preferred:
>   We conducted the survey in a controlled setting.
> * Nonpreferred:
>   The survey was conducted in a controlled setting.
> (American Psychological Association 2009)

A3: The first layer of response to the question of using 'I', then, is from the perspective of knowing a local rule and following it, without too much regard for where it comes from or whether it is justified. The second layer provides a justification: the *APA Manual* claims that 'rules of style' have been developed to 'achieve . . . clarity of communication'; '[t]hese rules are designed to ensure clear and consistent presentation of written material'. Contemporary research in literacy as a social practice adds a third layer to the discussion, pointing out that achieving such 'clarity' is less straightforward than it may seem. The concept of dialogism associated with Bakhtin, for example, challenges the notion that meaning resides unproblematically within the text, as indicated in this passage cited by Lillis (2001: 42):

> Language is not a neutral medium that passes freely and easily into the private property of the speaker's intentions; it is populated – overpopulated – with the intentions of others. Expropriating it, forcing it to submit to one's own intentions and accents, is a difficult and complicated process.
> (Bakhtin 1981: 294)

If you feel unsure about such an apparently trivial matter as whether to write 'I did this' or 'this was done' or 'the researcher did this', it may well be because of the factors so graphically described in the preceding passage. Cameron (1995) speculates further on the tussles over clarity and standardisation in published writing. She reports on the monetary value of the expertise held by people whose jobs involve monitoring and enforcing the house styles of publishing enterprises, and explains why 'the principles of linguistic standardization [are carried] to excessive and apparently pointless lengths' (p. 39). While she does not reject 'the particular qualities that present-day users of English have learned to take as virtues – for instance, clarity, consistency, precision and plainness', she does try 'to show that the arguments used to justify particular ideas about style are historically variable and contingent, and that they have frequently served vested interests – class, professional and ideological' (p. 76).

⭐ **Activity**

Try to do this in collaboration with fellow students, if possible.

❏ Starting with the use of 'I + active verb' (e.g. 'I investigated . . .'; 'I collected . . .'), make a list of the stylistic prescriptions and proscriptions which concern you, in relation to how you should express yourself in reporting your research. Some further examples I routinely come across include 'What should go into appendices?' 'Should I use headings for subsections in the writing?' 'Can I include my own opinions and argument or must I stick to reporting evidence?' Also of concern to students and their tutors are issues such as the accepted ('correct') use of apostrophes, commas and semi-colons, frequently 'confused' words (such as 'affect' and 'effect'), 'academic-ese', when novice writers forsake clear expression to aim for a style with more polysyllabic vocabulary and grammatically complex writing, and so on. Many style guides give advice on all of these topics (see Further Reading).

❏ Find out, if you do not know already, whether there is a policy or guidance in your department or institution on each of the items on your list and, if so, what it is. Is there an explanation of the origin of the guidance, and/or a rationale? If so, how persuasive do you find it?

❏ Identify examples of writing, from the literature you have consulted for your study, of the use or avoidance of items on your list, and see whether you can identify a pattern in how published scholars deal with these. In each case, consider the effect on your understanding of the text.

❏ Take two paragraphs representing contrasting examples of academic writing style in your field of study and use your discourse analytic skills to identify the linguistic features of each. What implications can you draw for your own writing style?

B8.2 Writing: the how and why of managing the writing process

Q: I've begun to write my dissertation and now I'm stuck. It's running away with me and I don't know how to regain control of all my ideas: what can I do?

A1: There are numerous guides available to help students with academic writing (see Further Reading), and it may help to stem the panic if you consult one or two of these to be reminded of the sensible advice which you probably know but can easily forget. There is more space in such dedicated texts to go into detail about the processes which can help, but advice tends to be along the following lines.

The sense of being overwhelmed is often reduced by breaking the enterprise down into more manageable pieces, and relating the time you have left to the various tasks remaining. Go back to your plan for the text as a whole, and identify which parts you have done, which you have begun but not finished, and which you have yet to start. Allocate a realistic amount of time to each one, and try to forget about the others while you concentrate on one achievable small goal which can, in a short space of time, be moved from your 'to do' to your 'done' list. If all your notes and materials have sprawled into one confusing pile, take time out from writing to do some house-keeping, sorting components into potential groups associated with different chapters or sections. Look back at your initial outline or proposal and remind yourself how you envisaged turning this into a feasible study: you will almost certainly see that you have made a lot of progress since then. Divide not only the tasks but also the time available into smaller units, maybe setting a timer to tell you when you have spent 20 minutes, say, concentrating on your writing, or reward yourself with a short break when you have written 100 words. Make use of (temporary) colour coding to identify for yourself passages you should return to for rewriting or inserting the details you do not have to hand.

A2: As indicated in the quotation from Bakhtin above, the process of writing very often feels 'difficult and complicated'. You invest a lot in your degree as a whole, and your independent research project is likely to be the single assignment which carries the most marks. As also discussed above, you find yourself expected to conform to institutional literacy practices, and yet you must still produce an original piece of writing. Not only technical skills, but cultural, political and emotional factors contribute to the challenge. Some or all of these considerations may lead to procrastination ('I know I should be working but I just can't make myself do it') or panic ('I'm fighting a losing battle with control of my dissertation'). Howard Becker is an eminent sociologist with countless publications to his name. In his book of advice on academic writing (1986), he reflects on his own experience: 'I don't know about other people, but beginning a new paper gives me anxiety's classical physical symptoms: dizziness, a sinking feeling in the pit of the stomach, a chill, maybe even a cold sweat' (p. 134). In his case, these feelings are caused by '[t]he dual possibilities, one as bad as the other, that the world has no real order or that, if it does, I can't find it'. His advice is consistent with that of many other people:

> Relax and *do it!*. You cannot overcome the fear without doing the thing you are afraid of and finding out that it is not as dangerous as you imagined. So the solution for writing something that will not fully, logically, and completely master the chaos is to write it anyway and discover that the world will not end when you do.
> (Becker 1986: 134)

One of his own 'tricks' is to imagine that the text is 'unimportant and makes no difference – a letter to an old friend, perhaps' (Becker 1986: 134), but as he says, 'I know how to trick myself, but I don't know how others can trick themselves. So here is where the advice stops. You can't start swimming until you get in the water'.

Just as there is no one set of guidelines about the text itself which will invariably lead to a 'good' piece of writing, there is no recipe for being the kind of person who is always a 'good' writer. Nevertheless, it may be helpful to reflect on the kind of writer you are.

While the typical textbook sequence suggests that 'writing up' is the final stage of a research project, some types of research, in particular, lend themselves to writing as you go along. Alvermann et al. (1996) report on a 'discussion' among themselves about writing as part of the research process, to which O'Brien contributed this observation:

> Now I . . . write early – I write as soon as I find something interesting to say. If I am not writing, I don't have anything interesting to say and I think about why. As I write to shape various representations of a study, I can see ultimately how the pieces fit together, but I keep changing them.
>
> (Alvermann et al. 1996: 119)

A related contrast is associated with different kinds of writer: 'those who write as a way of finding out what they want to say' and 'those who write to record or communicate what they have already prepared'. Sharples (1999: 112) attributes to the poet Stephen Spender the identification of these two archetypes, with their labels as 'Beethovians' and 'Mozartians' respectively. He develops this idea into that of two approaches, the 'Discoverer' and the 'Planner', the former 'driven by engagement with the text' and the latter 'driven by reflection'.

 ✪ **Activity**

Try to do this in collaboration with fellow students, if possible. Reflect on your answers to the following questions, keeping a record of anything useful for supporting you in the final stages of writing your dissertation.

❏ From your vantage point as a more experienced student, what hints and tips would you give undergraduates in their first year about coping with the demands of academic writing?

❏ How do you organise yourself when you sit down to do some writing, and what practical resources do you use (filing systems, colour-coding, online journals)?

❏ Would you say your research design is better suited to a final 'writing up' phase, or to writing as you go along?

❏ Based on the academic writing you have done in the past, decide whether, on balance, your approach is typically to 'discover' or to 'plan'. Do you like to get lots of material together first, or to write and redraft from near the start of a project? If you have tried both, which approach has worked better for you?

❏ Do you have any ways of 'tricking yourself' to lessen the anxieties associated with needing to write? If so, what are they and how successful have you found them in the past?

B9 **THE HOW AND WHY OF TAKING IT FURTHER**

This unit begins by considering how various organisations report their perspectives on the links between undergraduate work and paid employment. It goes on to encourage you to think about some specific directions in which your achievements as a researcher in English Language may lead you.

B1 contains a list, published by the Quality Assurance Agency, of 'the generic intellectual skills a linguistics degree can offer'. Other related subjects identify similar ones. As you approach the point where you put your research project behind you, you may want to reflect on how these skills have featured in your experience of doing it – and how these may prove useful to you in the future:

- collecting, analysing and manipulating data of diverse kinds
- using a variety of methods, and assessing the advantages and disadvantages of each method
- writing research reports using the appropriate register and style and with proper referencing
- using the necessary computational tools and software packages wherever appropriate for the analysis of data
- considering the ethical issues involved in data collection and data storage.
(adapted from QAA 2007b: 8)

The links between your undergraduate experience and your potential as an employee are also considered in an 'employability profile' for English graduates (English Subject Centre 2004), which lists the qualities identified by employer members of the Policy Forum of the Council for Industry and Higher Education. Among these are: 'the ability to identify and solve problems; work with information and handle a mass of diverse data'; 'the ability and desire to learn for oneself'; 'to be a self starter (creativity, decisiveness, initiative) and to finish the job (flexibility, adaptability, tolerance to stress)' (p. 34). This publication goes on to encourage students to reflect on their experiences in relation to these qualities. One means of doing this is to answer some questions which it poses – some of which are similar to those you have been asked elsewhere in this book. For example, under the heading of 'analysis', glossed as 'relat[ing] and compar[ing] data from different sources, identifying issues, securing relevant information and identifying relationships', students are asked questions such as:

- When you have to analyse information and make a recommendation, what kind of thought process do you go through? What is your reasoning behind your decision?
- How do you deal with data from a variety of sources, to identify the key information?
- How would you identify appropriate data sources to inform your decisions?

- How do you distinguish between different types of information provided to inform your conclusions?

(English Subject Centre 2004: 35)

The experiences and skills you have gained in doing your research project are thus clearly valued by both employers and the tutors who welcome postgraduate students onto their courses. However, this could be seen as a fairly instrumental view of the gains you have made and the uses to which you can continue to put them. In C1, I suggest that one motivation for research is to produce something of benefit to others, and that students with a strong commitment to social justice often choose topics where language issues are interwoven with inequalities of various kinds.

Activity

> You have already considered the skills associated with doing research and how these may be identified in your own CV and recognised by potential employers or tutors. Consider now how you may bring a heightened aware-ness of language and how it is used to contexts you will find yourself in as you move into the next stage of your life. If possible, discuss with fellow stu-dents the challenges or dilemmas raised in the following scenarios:
>
> ❏ You are socialising with friends from a range of backgrounds. One per-son, who has a strong regional accent, seems uncomfortable about being routinely mocked by one of the others, and told to 'talk properly'. How might you draw on your specialist knowledge about English Language to offer some support for the 'victim' in an effective way?
> ❏ As a parent of a young child, you decide to stand as a governor at the school s/he attends. How could you make use in this role of the know-ledge about language developed in your degree in general and your research in particular?
> ❏ During team meetings at work, you notice that different people con-tribute in very different ways, some team members apparently making it hard for others to get their opinions heard. Can your linguistic aware-ness help you to take a role in improving this situation?
> ❏ You become part of a campaigning group on an issue about which you feel strongly. How can you draw on what you have learned through carrying out your English Language research project to make your con-tribution more effective?

Section C

EXPLORATION
ISSUES AND DEBATES IN RESEARCHING ENGLISH LANGUAGE

LANGUAGE RESEARCH TOPICS

Researchers who are concerned with how different people learn additional languages have identified various kinds of motivation. In units A1 and B1 I have alluded to these, encouraging you to consider planning your research project from the perspective of different kinds of benefit to you. This unit explores these ideas a little further, and also suggests other kinds of potential benefits of doing research in English Language.

Broadly speaking, one kind of motivation could be labelled 'instrumental', where you engage with the work required because doing so will bring you something else that you want, such as a qualification, and another as 'intrinsic', where you obtain enjoyment and satisfaction directly from doing the work itself. Ideally, your research project will bring you both kinds of reward, but it is worth recognising which kind of potential benefits motivate you more, as this may help you to decide on both topic and method as you plan the research. For example, if you plan to work in a particular kind of job, you may want to gain some experience while still a student that will help you to secure your first post, in which case you may be prepared to tailor what you do in accordance with what you would like to be able to put on your CV. You may by contrast be the kind of person who can apply yourself properly to studying only if you find the work inherently stimulating, in which case the deferred satisfaction of some potential future relevance will be less important. A third kind of spur may be a commitment to 'making a difference'. Some researchers – and students – put a strong emphasis on knowledge as a resource in the conflicts between those with power and those with less. For them, the most important criterion for choice of topic may be that the findings are of potential benefit to disadvantaged groups. In the language field, Critical Discourse Analysis is the most obvious example of this research orientation, and an example is provided by a student of mine with a keen interest in the experiences of British Muslims. She used a CDA approach to investigate changing uses of labels for the perceived 'problem' of conflict among people of different backgrounds in the UK, focusing on the transition from 'multiculturalism' to 'community cohesion' in official policy statements.

C1.1 Projecting towards the future: the benefits of students' research skills to employers

Depending on where in the world you live, as a student of English Language or Linguistics the 'real-world' relevance of your course may seem more or less obvious. There is a perception in some quarters that English, unlike, say, chemistry or engineering, is a 'soft' subject with no real utility, whereas, especially in parts of the world where English is not the most widely spoken language, it is seen as a valuable asset, worth studying because it is associated with economic prosperity. Sometimes the arts, humanities and social sciences generally come under attack because they are perceived as an indulgence at a time when government spending on education should be directed towards obvious economic benefits to society.

In the UK, each academic discipline taught at universities is linked with one of the various 'Subject Centres'. Perhaps as a corrective to the stereotypes of arts graduates as ill-equipped to make useful contributions to the community, some research was funded by the Higher Education Academy, involving the Subject Centres for several humanities subjects (Languages, Linguistics and Area Studies, History, Classics and Archaeology and English). The study used in-depth interviews with humanities graduates from the 1970s onwards to find out how their university experience related to the work they eventually went on to do. The link between the two is perhaps less obvious with non-vocational subjects than those which are designed with a specific career in view, but research (Allan 2001) argues that this may be an advantage, as it gives humanities students a wider range of options. In relation to doing independent research, interviewees provided various examples of how their experience at university was useful in their work.

'We get lots of reports and documentation and I need to write lots of reports, pulling together information from different sources, so my experience in drafting assignments and asking questions of the material that I was reading, that kind of skill was developed at A Level but certainly built on at degree level and is something that I use on a daily basis here' (Caroline, American Studies, 1998).

Another commented:

'I generally use a lot of research skills as I compile reports on different titles and for different markets' (Lucy, History and English, 1999).

Not only did the graduates speak about developing this skill in general but they suggested that during their degrees they had developed ways of being able to synthesise information more effectively. Taking notes and skim reading were mentioned by one participant as techniques he developed to aid his study which have proved important in later life (John, French Language and Literature, 1987).

(Allan 2001: 19)

Activity

Sit quietly for a few minutes and visualise yourself as the person you hope to be in five years time. What would you most like to be doing? What kinds of activities fill your working days? You may be very certain of the career you're aiming for, and what it entails, or you may have no idea yet how you will earn a living – though it's likely you can identify a preference for the characteristics of some kinds of job over others. Even if you hope to have married a millionaire or won the lottery, you will need to spend your time doing something. What will it be? You may already know, especially if you have attended any careers advice sessions, perhaps including aptitude and personality tests, whether, for example, you prefer being in situations involving lots of social interaction or working alone. Now ask yourself whether the work you envis-age yourself doing links in any obvious – or perhaps not so obvious – ways with the opportunity you have now to plan a research project. For example, would it help to be able to describe in a job interview how you organised and carried out a series of interviews with adolescents as part of your study on teenagers' discourse styles; or if you were able to cite the analysis of some statistics on phonological variation as an example of your ability to manage and process data?

Do you relish the prospect of bringing home armfuls of books from the library and reading about a new topic in depth, or would you rather be out 'in the field', conducting interviews or participating as a kind of ethnogra-pher in interactions that will become data for your study? Do you see this experience as primarily a requirement of your programme of study, or as a contribution to knowledge? Are 'contributions to knowledge' value-free and intrinsically worthwhile, or should they bring practical benefits to society? If the latter, which people's interests should be served by research?

Depending on your answers to these questions – and you may think of other similar ones – you should be in the position to sketch out, just for yourself, a mini profile of the kind of researcher you are, and therefore to identify the kind of study that will bring you some intrinsic satisfaction.

C1.2 Identifying what interests you

Another way of approaching the challenge of getting started with your research pro-ject is suggested by Cameron (2001). She emphasises the importance of becoming familiar with what has been established – or at least claimed – by previous research-ers, and strand 2 considers the practice of conducting a review of the existing litera-ture, which should underpin your decisions. In the light of what you find published by other researchers, Cameron suggests, you can generate a study of your own in one of a number of ways.

The first of these is to replicate. 'You ask the same question(s) and use the same methods as a researcher whose work you have read, but you collect your own data: your question is whether your findings will resemble the original findings' (Cameron 2001: 182).

The second approach suggested by Cameron is to 'compare and contrast'. Many studies of discourse genres concern the linguistic features of different kinds of text. Cameron's examples are all from spoken language, as that is the focus of her book, but similar approaches are used with written language, and of course there is increas-ing interest in the 'hybrid' modes of computer-mediated communication. Ling and Baron (2007), for example, collected examples, produced by American college stu-dents, of both instant messages sent via computers and text messages sent by mobile phones. They compared the length of the messages, the use of emoticons, and the specific linguistic features of lexical shortenings and sentential punctuation. Another example of comparative data is provided by a student of mine who compared a

replicate data {

corpus of text messages sent by females with an equivalent one of messages from males.

Another starting point may be to 'take issue with a previous claim' (Cameron 2001: 184). There is a fairly extensive body of language-related research which could seem to perpetuate various social stereotypes – despite the fact that it is one of the 'values' of academic work to strive for **objectivity** and evidence rather than accept everyday, commonsense assumptions. (I discuss what is meant by 'objectivity' elsewhere in this book.) I have sometimes encountered both male and female students who feel dissatisfied with what is reported in the research literature about men's and women's styles of speaking, and who feel intuitively, as Cameron (2001: 184) also reports, that there are 'unwarranted stereotypes of men's talk' – and indeed of women's talk – to be challenged. My students, predominantly in their early twenties, often wonder whether times – and language usage patterns – are changing, and thus undermining the findings produced by researchers from previous decades. One group project I know of explored the extent to which the attitude judgement techniques used in some of the classical sociolinguistic studies such as Giles and Powesland (1975) were still applicable in contemporary British society, with its heightened sensitivity about social stereotypes. They wondered whether people like themselves, that is, young people who had experienced a liberal education, and been alerted to the hazards associated with reaching unsupported conclusions about people just from the way they speak, would provide the kind of data required in studies like this. Another student had a 'hunch' that younger people would be less divided along gender lines in their use of prestige forms, or their acceptance of taboo expressions, than is suggested by some earlier studies (e.g. Trudgill 1983; see McEnery 2005 for a discussion of the changing trends in research on gender and swearing).

The final suggestion made by Cameron in her list of approaches is to 'describe something new' (Cameron 2001: 184). This is an attractive option, because it clearly meets the assessment criterion of 'originality' for your research. It may be more difficult than you anticipate, however, to find a variety of language that has never been studied. This is where a thorough search of the literature is vital, as someone, somewhere, may well have had a similar idea to yours. Moreover, if you do identify something completely original, it may be difficult to find previous work on which to draw to support you with your own study. More likely are compromises, where you follow some existing type of inquiry, but using data from new discourse varieties such as recently emerged media texts (cult television programmes that have intriguing features, for example) or trends (again, quite likely among younger people) in culturally significant ways of speaking, texting or writing that signal knowledge or membership of current fashions. If you live in or have access to a 'discourse community' where an under-documented variety is used, you could make that the focus of your research, exploring, for example, whether patterns and trends reported in respect of English Language data from the 'inner circle' countries (Kachru 1992a) are also found here.

Whatever focus you choose, it will be instructive, as you become a member of this 'community of practice', to read accounts of others' experiences – both of doing research, and, from a slightly different perspective, of becoming researchers.

THE LITERATURE REVIEW

There is plenty of material in research methods textbooks that will tell you how to go about doing a literature review, together with explanations of why it matters so much to do this and to do it in particular ways. At the same time, the readings in D2 provide examples of the writing produced by researchers once they have done their reviews of the literature that pertains to their own areas of interest. It is much rarer though to find published accounts of the processes by which researchers decided which sources to look at, their note-taking routines, the criteria for making decisions about which details to include in the final version of their articles, and so on. In this section, I aim to bring together these two perspectives – the process and the product of the literature review – with examples from English Language research projects, to help you explore how reading about other people's research is an integral component of doing your own.

C2.1 Organising and structuring a literature review

Many research articles begin with a brief review of the existing studies on which the authors plan to build, so we shall start here with an example. This author, Paul Simpson, is making a contribution to the extensive work on the discourse of advertising. So much has been written on this, from so many different perspectives, that he could not possibly summarise everything relevant to his area of research. Instead, he uses his opening paragraphs to demonstrate his awareness of some key texts already published in this field:

> There has over the last two decades been an enormous upsurge of interest in the linguistic and discoursal characteristics of advertising. Introductory book-length treatments of the subject have tended to concentrate on the major levels of language organisation in advertisements, including phonology, graphology, lexis and syntax (Vestergaard and Schrøder 1985; Cook 1992; Myers 1994). More specialist studies of advertising have highlighted, variously, its cognitive features (Pateman 1983; Redfern 1982; Harris 1983), its cultural and anthropological dimensions (Aman 1982; Goldman 1992; Schmidt et al. 1994; O'Barr 1994; Ohmann 1996) and its status as a genre or register of discourse (Toolan 1988; Bex 1993). Working within the tradition of critical discourse analysis, other analysts have explored the political and ideological significance of advertising discourse (Williamson 1978; Kress 1987; Kress and van Leeuwen 1990) and from this perspective special attention has been given to the representation of gender in ads (Goffman 1976; Barthel 1988; Thornborrow 1994). Finally, given the interactive and dynamic properties of advertising, and the importance of contextual factors on the processing and interpreting of ads, it is not surprising that this type of discourse has been investigated within the parameters of models in linguistic pragmatics (Lakoff 1982; Geis 1982; Coleman 1983, 1990; Tanaka 1994; Short and Hu 1997).
>
> (Simpson 2001: 589–90)

Note the way Simpson groups together the authors he cites – not in order of name or date (although each sub-list is presented chronologically), but thematically, according to the different ways in which they have written about the subject of language in advertising. This is quite a short paragraph, only about 200 words, but behind it lies a prodigious amount of reading, which demonstrates an almost paradoxical aspect of this kind of writing: the more you have read, the more concise you may need to be in condensing your discussion of it; a corollary of this is that students who write a lot about not very many sources are likely to achieve a lower grade for their literature review because they simply cannot demonstrate the range of knowledge of the field that should underpin a new study. In addition to this, Simpson's summary also man-ages to demonstrate relevance: although the range of sources cited is extensive, it is not so broad as to leave the reader wondering what his own article is concerned with. It would not be difficult to construct a visual 'map' of the literature on the discourse of advertising, using the sources Simpson cites as landmarks on the terrain. Figure C2.1.1 is my attempt to represent his list in a visual way. Note as well that any reader who consults the sources included in his list of references can decide whether they agree with his characterisation of them.

This is how Simpson continues his introduction, contrasting the studies he has cited with the objective he has set himself:

> Although several of the areas outlined above will be touched upon in the analysis that follows, it is the last of these – the pragmatically orientated study of advertis-ing discourse – that forms the principal remit of the present study.
>
> (Simpson 2001: 590)

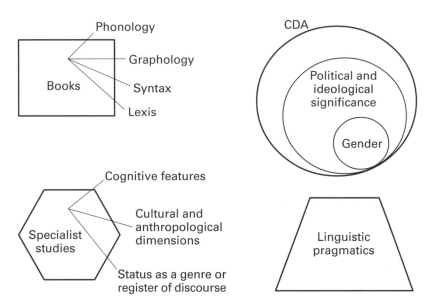

Figure C2.1.1 Diagrammatic representation of the various sources summarised in Simpson (2001)

So now we see that his ordering of sub-topics was carefully chosen, leading to the area most nearly matching his own at the end of a list, from the most general to the most specific. As this article is published in the *Journal of Pragmatics*, it is not surprising that he narrows his review down to the pragmatic aspects of the topic, and the last part of this extract makes a neat link between these existing publications and his own contribution:

> The present analysis differs from other pragmatic explorations of advertising discourse largely in terms of the position it occupies relative to the object of study.
>
> (Simpson 2001: 590)

Activity ✪

If we look closely at the previous research summarised in any article that presents some new research findings, we can 'back construct', so to speak, the work that must have gone into reading about the topic to enable the author to summarise existing studies as the context for the new one. The example I have chosen for this activity (see Table C2.1.1) is from a study of code-switching (abbreviated to CS) among Spanish-speaking school-children who have immigrated to the USA (Reyes 2004). I have no 'insider knowledge' about this; all that is available to me, like any other reader, is the published account, but I can draw some inferences and hazard some guesses about the process, and I invite you to do the same, using the prompts that are presented alongside the text.

Table C2.1.1 Extract from a literature review passage, with questions to consider

Segment number	Published text	To consider/discuss
1	'This study presents data on the discourse characteristics of children's code switching, and the functions that Spanish and English have according to context. In addition, the data are described in relation to children's language competence and preference. The study found that code switching occurred both within and across turns. The older children's switches were more frequent and were deployed for a wider variety of functions than the younger children's.' (From the abstract, Reyes 2004: 77)	Which areas of research literature is the author likely to have consulted so as to be well prepared for her own study? Formulate the questions she would have tried to answer from her reading before designing her own empirical study to answer new questions.

Segment number	Published text	To consider/discuss
2	Most of the early research on CS has looked at adult–adult interaction (e.g. Clyne 1967; Gumperz 1967, 1973; Weinreich 1953).	If the author's own study is to be about children's code-switching, why does she mention this research about 'adult–adult interaction'? Why does she reference studies from such a long time ago?
3	However, the early 1980s witnessed increased interest in studying children's CS (Álvarez 1979; Genishi 1976; Zentella 1982, 1997). These studies have shed some light on how bilingual children use different languages according to addressee and context.	Why mention these studies at this point?
4	However, these studies do not describe how children develop CS over the years, and how CS is used to extend communicative competence for achieving conversational goals during peer interaction.	Why does the author draw attention to what these studies failed to do?
5	In the classic CS study by Poplack (1980) with Puerto Rican American bilinguals, she analysed adults' conversations in natural settings and speech during a sociolinguistic interview to learn about bilinguals' linguistic competence and their use of CS. Poplack's findings pointed out that CS was used by those individuals whose language skills in both languages were balanced.	Can you infer the most relevant research question that Reyes suggests Poplack was trying to answer in her 1980 study?
6	While CS might be an indicator of bilingual ability in adults (Poplack, 1980), it might indicate development of bilingual communicative competence in children who are still learning a second language (L2) (Reyes 2001).	How does this claim link the summary of previous findings with the author's own research interests?

Suggested responses

My own thoughts about these questions are as follows; you may have noticed other things, of course.

1   From what she says in her abstract, I would expect the author to be familiar with both the general theories and findings about CS and with specific studies about children's CS. She will also need to have knowledge of theories and findings about first and second language acquisition, with particular reference to CS. Questions that can be answered from a library search, without necessarily embarking on new empirical work, include, 'What do we know already about how and why bilingual speakers code switch?' 'What do we know about CS as a developmental process?'

2   It is typical of the process of narrowing down a general topic into something more specific to refer to the broad context first. Knowledge of the history of a field helps to identify how current research priorities have developed.

3   These studies are part of the context for the present research, and it is important to be aware of them.

4   It is reasonable to point out aspects of the topic that previous studies did not explore – while recognising that it is quite legitimate for other researchers to have different priorities.

5   The question underlying Poplack's research, as it relates to Reyes' concerns, would be something like, 'How are CS and linguistic competence inter-related?'

6   The summary of previous studies is now leading towards a gap in the existing literature – one which the present study will seek to help fill.

C2.2 Reading for different purposes

Reading the literature associated with your research topic, as I have noted, not only helps you to learn what knowledge already exists, but can also give you ideas about questions to ask in your own study and about appropriate kinds of data and methods.

Activity

Choose an article or chapter that seems particularly central to your own topic. Then read it several times to practise the different kinds of reading you need to make use of when reviewing the literature for a research project:

❏   By skimming to get an overall idea of the piece, and scanning for key terms, read in order to make some brief notes that effectively 'tag' this text, notes of the kind that will help you to keep track of it among the range of sources you read.

❏   Scan the text to see whether it makes explicit the research question(s) that the study was aiming to answer. Make a note of these questions.

❏   By reading in a little more depth, identify the main findings of the study. Decide whether it did actually answer the questions set out above.

❏   Scan the text again to find any sections that explain what kind of data
    was collected and why it was chosen. Consider whether you are con-
    vinced by this process.
❏   Finally, scan the text for any sections that describe and justify the meth-
    ods used for (a) data collection and (b) data analysis. Again, consider
    whether these sections are persuasive.

C2.3 Reading critically

If you train yourself to read the existing literature in these different ways, you will
begin to bridge the gap between 'passive' and 'critical' ways of reading. That is, schooling, especially in some contexts and traditions, can give the impression that the
printed word, especially in texts that are academically prestigious, is to be relied on as
authoritative; a more critical approach to reading is demanded of those who participate in the academic community of practice. Novice researchers are positioned somewhere between the two, and it is a challenge to negotiate ways of reading – and of
reporting on the reading that you do – in ways that both demonstrate respect for conventions and hard-earned academic authority, while at the same time being sceptical
and developing independent responses to reading.

However, if your area of interest is some aspect of English Language studies, you
may have an advantage in this respect, since you may well have studied, as a component of your taught courses, how it is that the way texts are constructed relates to
issues of power and contested meaning. That is, if you have learned about Critical Discourse Analysis, and read work by authors such as Fairclough, Kress, Fowler, Gee, or
the genre analysts such as Martin, Christie and their associates, as well as analysts of
evaluative stance encoded in texts (Hunston, Thompson) you may well have thought
before about how linguistic choices can be shown to incorporate social and political
stances and values. The functional grammar developed by Michael Halliday underlies
much of this research, and Halliday has written about the meanings of literacy, how
students learn scepticism, and the part played by the language itself in the reproduction of ideologies.

> [W]hat is it that sanctifies the written text? It is not simply the high status that is
> accorded to the social contexts of writing; it is equally the written words them-
> selves, and, most of all, perhaps, the interaction between the two. In other words,
> the authority of the text rests ultimately on the perceived resonance of form and
> function: the 'fit' between its linguistic properties (especially its lexicogrammar
> and discourse semantics) and the sociocultural processes by which its value and
> scope of action are defined.
>
> (Halliday 1996: 366)

Many textbooks addressed to postgraduate researchers recommend looking closely at
the wording of texts read in the context of the literature review, suggesting in particular that readers should be alert for metaphors, for evaluative labels given to

phenomena, for passive constructions that conceal processes and agency, and so on. As a student of English Language, these are skills that you should already have developed, so you can apply them to the reading you do for your literature review if you see good reasons for doing so.

C3 RESEARCH QUESTIONS

> The biggest single error made by individual researchers is not thinking about what the results will look like until they have them.
>
> (Wray and Bloomer 2006: 12)

In other units in this strand I encourage you to anticipate the directions in which your provisional research questions may lead you. In this unit, I want to clarify further what this anticipation means – and does not mean – in practice, and why I believe these considerations are important.

C3.1 Predicting what your study will involve

There are two senses in which you may be involved in predicting the outcomes of your research. The first is the one I have encouraged you to do – to ask, in relation to potential research questions, meta-questions that clarify what these questions would entail, in terms of the data needed to answer them, potential methods of analysis, and so on. The main prediction of this type answers the question, 'What could the answer to my research question look like?'

Example

Here is an example of a published study to illustrate the projection from research question to study design. Pancsofar and Vernon-Feagans (2006) compared the talk of mothers and fathers to their 2-year-old children. Their investigation had several aims, but just one is the focus here. One of the research questions was, 'How does the language input of fathers differ from that of mothers during triadic free play sessions in the home when their children were 24 months old?' ('Triadic' means 'three-way': participants were the mother, father and child.) You may have noticed that this question is of the type 'What is X like?', with the additional component of 'And how does X differ from Y?' It may also have struck you that the wording of the question is very precise: an earlier version of this question might have been, '(How) do mothers and fathers talk differently to their young children?' and perhaps you can explain why greater specificity is required. The authors of this study will have needed to predict what would be involved in producing an answer to this question. Based on their retrospective account of the findings published in the article, I would list the following:

- [ ] access to a sample of families large enough to draw meaningful comparisons,
- [ ] ethical approval and consent to record the triadic interactions (see strand 5),
- [ ] access to knowledge of various features of the families' lives, so that differences in talk to the child linked with the parent's gender could be isolated for the comparison,
- [ ] the equipment and expertise to record all the necessary aspects of the interactions (which were, in fact, videotaped),
- [ ] the means (and time) to transcribe the talk recorded,
- [ ] measures for making the comparisons (those they used were 'output, vocabulary, complexity, questions, and pragmatics', p. 578), and
- [ ] a means of calculating the significance of differences found between mothers' and fathers' talk to the children (a statistical procedure known as a MANOVA test was used).

Again, this may seem rather daunting, but it is better to do this kind of prediction early on, and scale down your ambitions if necessary, rather than to realise much later that finding out what you want to know would involve challenges you cannot meet. An unfunded, time-limited beginning researcher could not hope to replicate a whole study like this, but what you could do is record some interactions in one or two families (provided you have the requisite ethical approval and consent) and ask a question along the lines of 'Are there differences in the talk of these particular mothers and fathers to their children and, if so, how far are these differences similar to those identified by Pancsofar and Vernon-Feagans (2006) and other previous research?' Note that such a study cannot tell you *why* such differences occur (or fail to do so), but, as I suggest elsewhere in the book, this kind of explanation is rarely available from empirical research alone.

C3.2 Predicting the outcomes of your study

The second kind of prediction is slightly more risky, because it is less about planning the process and more about anticipating the results. This begins to take us into territory where there is not full consensus about the research enterprise in the academic community of practice itself. You may already have noticed differences of emphasis and of advice in your reading of both published studies and research methods textbooks, and even your tutors may imply slightly different priorities when they talk to you about research. While this may be unsettling, it should not alarm you too much, as another convention in the code of academic practice is respect for work that is consistent and true to its own methods – even if readers do not subscribe to all aspects of the approach themselves.

So, on the one hand, it is obviously sensible to have some idea in advance about what you are going to be looking for, while, on the other, it is not a good idea to be too certain before you start about what you will find. The point of research is to learn something that was not known before, not to look selectively for evidence that will confirm an existing prejudice. 'Seeing what is before your eyes is not easy', writes Fisher (1988: 125), 'particularly when your head is full of ideas about what ought to be there'. Some supervisors even counsel their students *not* to read too much in advance of collecting their own data, so as to avoid finding only what they expected to.

The position I suggest you adopt requires a fine balance between being properly informed about previous research and, at least to some extent, the theories underpinning it, while at the same time being genuinely open-minded and willing to analyse and interpret the evidence you generate. This leads us to a third kind of prediction – the research **hypothesis**.

C3.3 The role of the hypothesis

As I have indicated, planning a research study involves articulating clearly what you hope to find out. Identifying the questions you can answer is difficult, and these may well be revised in the light of doing the study (as was the case for the researchers in Reading D3.1). Another way of approaching this is to express what you hope to find out as a hypothesis to be tested. One reason for caution here is that 'hypothesis', along with various other terms, has a more specialised meaning in academic disciplines than in everyday usage. You may well have a hunch or intuition about what you're likely to find from your research, but it is inadvisable to declare this as a hypothesis. By all means include a statement along the lines of, 'From evidence produced in previous research, I predict that . . .'. Wray and Bloomer (2006: 8) say that 'in an observation study, your hypothesis might be that a child will interact differently with adults from the way it does with other children'. In my view, while this is a reasonable position to adopt, it is a prediction rather than a hypothesis, for reasons I explain below.

A second reason for caution about using hypotheses is that, while you may be able to modify your questions as the study progresses, it is much less acceptable to change your hypothesis part way through a study. This is because the whole study would be structured to try and establish as definitively as you can whether your hypothesis is supported by the evidence. (In fact, in very strict interpretations of this approach to research, the scientist attempts to *dis*prove the hypothesis.) It is then not good academic practice to modify the stated hypothesis in the light of the results; this is akin to 'moving the goalposts' when the favoured team look likely to lose the game.

A third point to note is that 'the formulation of good hypotheses requires a great deal of theoretical work' (Blaikie 2000: 27). The role of a properly constituted hypothesis is, very often, to test the relationship between two things, between X and Y, say, which entails having very clear ideas in advance about the nature of both X and Y and about how to establish what their relationship is. In the natural and physical sciences, it is often appropriate – and practical – to set up an experiment, which the researcher is able to control very closely, and to manipulate X and Y in well established ways to see how they interact.

To illustrate this, I have chosen an example from the natural sciences, where this approach is entirely appropriate. You may question its relevance to this book, but I use it to make clear the important contrast between different kinds of entities that exist in the world. In this brief example, the things under investigation are the workings of the pulmonary system and chemical compounds, with the research designed to test whether the latter works on the former in predictable ways. The things that you, as an English Language researcher, will probably be investigating are likely to be of very different kinds – and that's the point. People using language to interact and communicate are not, I would argue, equivalent to laboratory mice subjected to chemical treatments. Neither, in many ways, are the products of these acts of language use – written texts, electronic corpora, transcripts of conversations. Furthermore, the theories about how language 'works' in actual interactions are different sorts of theories from those underpinning theories about biochemical processes, and are therefore less susceptible to devising useful hypotheses to test.

In an exploration of possible treatments for illness (e.g. asthma), pharmacology researchers (Ziegelbauer et al. 2005) studied the results of previous work and noted that particular substances (glucocorticoids, or 'GCs') have a very good record in treating the symptoms – but that they don't work for all patients. The researchers speculated that there could be alternative ways to produce the same effects as GCs, and designed experiments to test their hypothesis. Here is how an early trial of their idea, with laboratory animals, was reported in the *British Journal of Pharmacology*:

> GCs inhibit airway inflammation by directly interacting with and inhibiting the activity of the transcription factors NF-*k*B and AP-1 (De Bosscher et al. 2003; Leung & Bloom 2003). Thus, inhibition of NF-*k*B activation should result in an anti-inflammatory effect similar to or superior to that of steroids. First experimental data support this hypothesis and demonstrate that COMPOUND A is efficacious in reducing airway inflammation in animal models of asthma.
> (Ziegelbauer et al. 2005: 189)

You may not understand all these technical terms and concepts, but you can, I hope, recognise the kind of process involved in this testing of a hypothesis. Now, as Long (1993: 235) warns in relation to the study of second language acquisition (SLA), it is important 'to be aware of the dangers inherent in importing criteria from the natural to the social sciences, since we are dealing with people, who can affect the systems and processes SLA theories seek to explain in ways physicists, for example, need not worry about'. These ideas are developed further in other units, but for now we should consider some exceptions to the points made so far in this section.

There are some topics in English Language that have some elements in common with those of the pharmacologists looking for treatments for asthma. For example, the physical apparatus with which we process speech has come to be understood through the sciences of biology and physiology. A significant branch of linguistics, too, is concerned with the workings of the brain, and both these areas of the subject involve researchers whose interests are in clinical aspects of speech and language processing, which overlap extensively with research approaches familiar in the biological sciences.

If you have taken courses in areas such as these, and if you have learned about the conventions associated with these research traditions, it may be appropriate to devise a hypothesis that can be tested.

An example of such a study from the clinical field is published in Shriberg et al. (2005). They explain in their abstract that, '[c]onverging evidence supports the hypothesis that the most common subtype of childhood speech sound disorder (SSD) of currently unknown origin is genetically transmitted' (p. 834). Notice that the hypothesis cited here is a causal one: 'the cause of X (certain kinds of childhood speech sound disorder) is Y (genetic transmission)'. Their investigation involved identifying a group of children who both had SSD themselves and also had two or more close biological relatives with speech-language disorder. This group was compared on various measures with another group of children who had SSD but did not have relatives with speech-language disorder. Because they found that there was a strong correlation between a particular kind of SSD and being in the first category (relatives with speech-language disorder), they conclude that this supports the hypothesis about genetic transmission.

C3.4 Summary: kinds of question

So how do you know whether you should include predictions or hypotheses in your own research design? There are two ways to answer this, one pragmatic and one more intellectual, but they are likely to be related. The pragmatic consideration relates to your institution and supervising tutors, who can advise you on their expectations for research design. If you are told to learn and practise the procedures involved in drafting and refining research hypotheses, then of course you will need to do this. And if you are, it is likely to be because the academic context within which you are undertaking your research project is one which both values and is appropriate for these methods of investigation. Otherwise, it is probably best to avoid trying to devise testable hypotheses, especially if you are investigating entities and processes that are not susceptible to being empirically researched in this way.

In discussing the process of drafting and refining questions to underpin your research, I have advocated clarifying

❏   the kind of question you propose to ask (see B3)
❏   the nature of the entities or phenomena you propose to investigate. In my discussion, I have used Xs and Ys to represent the foci of various studies, and these might, depending on the particular project, stand for such things as 'the speech fathers use when talking to their 2-year-old children', 'adverbs ending in -*wise*', 'childhood speech sound disorder of unknown origin', 'metaphors in conversations about cancer', 'epistemic modality markers', etc.
❏   the extent to which you can and should predict what you will find, including predictions about how Xs and Ys are related to each other.

★ Activity

Using the extracts from the two studies below, identify the following in each case. Ideally, you should discuss this with other students, considering the implications for the research context in which you are working, and the local expectations about what constitutes appropriate research practice in English Language studies.

❏ What kinds of question (a, b, c or d) did the researchers pose to investigate their areas of interest further?
❏ What sort of entities or phenomena were they interested in? (i.e. what are the Xs and Ys in the study?)
❏ In what ways, if at all, did the researchers make predictions or devise hypotheses to steer their investigations?
❏ Based on the extracts reproduced here, can you project forward, so to speak, and work out the implications for research design of the researchers' questions?
❏ In your opinion, how appropriate are the questions/hypotheses for each kind of study and why?

Study 1

A study by Feist and Gentner (2007) was designed to investigate a version of the linguistic relativity hypothesis also known as the Sapir-Whorf hypothesis. This is a weak version, associated with Slobin (1996, 2003), and known as the '*thinking-for-speaking* hypothesis, which states that linguistic influences occur when language is used during a task' (Feist and Gentner 2007: 283). The researchers were interested in whether people's 'encoding and memory of pictorial scenes' would be influenced by 'the presence of spatial language – specifically, English spatial prepositions'.

> In answering this question, we sought evidence bearing on two questions: (1) whether participants' memories showed language-related alterations (Experiments 1 and 2), and (2) whether these alterations resulted from an active comparison of language and the picture in pursuit of a common construal of the two, a process we refer to as *interactive encoding* (Experiment 3).
>
> (Feist and Gentner 2007: 284)

> Across [the] three experiments, we varied the input conditions and asked under what conditions participants would show this effect. If we were to see language effects only when the participants were provided with language at encoding, this would provide support for a *thinking-for-language* hypothesis – a generalization of Slobin's thinking-for-speaking hypothesis to encompass comprehending as well as producing language. If, on the other hand, we were to see spatial category effects even without the presentation of language at encoding, this would support the possibility that language influences cognition in a more far-reaching manner.
>
> (Feist and Gentner 2007: 284)

Study 2

Baker et al. (2008) were interested in a very different kind of English Language issue, and their study is a combination of a methodological suggestion and a substantive example – 'discourses of refugees and asylum seekers in the UK press'. The methodological dimension is concerned with 'the extent to which methods normally associated with corpus linguistics can be effectively used by critical discourse analysts'. The example they used to illustrate this is 'a 140-million-word corpus of British news articles about refugees, asylum seekers, immigrants and migrants'.

> The project aims were related to both subject matter and methodology. In terms of the former, the project set out to examine the discursive presentation of refugees and asylum seekers, as well as immigrants and migrants in the British press over a ten-year period (1996–2005). For reasons of economy, refugees and asylum seekers will be referred to by the acronym RAS, and immigrants and migrants by the acronym IM, whereas all four groups together will be referred to as RASIM. The analysis was concerned with both synchronic and diachronic aspects, while also contrasting the discourse used by broadsheets versus tabloids and national versus regional newspapers. The main research questions addressed were:
>
> - In what ways are RASIM linguistically defined and constructed?
> - What are the frequent topics of, or issues discussed in, articles relating to RASIM?
> - What attitudes towards RASIM emerge from the body of UK newspapers seen as a whole?
> - Are conventional distinctions between broadsheets and tabloids reflected in their stance towards (issues relating to) RASIM?'
>
> (Baker et al. 2008: 276)

One final example to consider here is from a second language acquisition researcher, Cook (1986: 19). He discusses the narrowing down of a potential research question, from 'Is speech more important than writing?' through eight redraftings, to its final form: 'Are the scores on the EPVT of a group of educated French adult learners of English in technical schools in France who are taught orally significantly better than those of an otherwise identical group who are taught through writing?'

As you go on to plan your own work in greater detail, you can continue to return to these units about research questions, and perhaps find reassurance in the recognition that none of the published examples I have used, I believe, is likely to have arisen fully formed in the researchers' minds. Good research questions are the product of (often invisible) academic work.

RESEARCH METHODS

C4

> The value of empirical research ultimately depends on the quality of conceptual analysis that defines the objects of enquiry.
>
> (Widdowson 1990: 25)

C4.1 Finding your way around different methodologies

'English Language studies' spans a wide range of topics and interests, and is influenced by a number of research traditions and conventions. On top of that, there are some areas of strong disagreement between researchers even within many of these sub-fields. This may be rather worrying news for you as an apprentice researcher aiming for a good grade from your tutors. How do you know which research conventions to adhere to?

There are several sources of reassurance. Firstly, your tutors and supervisors will guide you in the conventions associated most closely with the research you are expected to do. Furthermore, students' earliest experiences of planning and carrying out research projects cannot be expected to resolve the problems that continue to challenge seasoned practitioners, so you should not be afraid to document honestly any conflicts of approach that you encounter. Secondly, while academics do sometimes disagree, they rightly respect sincere efforts to meet the challenges of seeking new knowledge, so if you adhere consistently to a particular methodology, even if it is not universally embraced (and few are), then you should be able to meet your assessment criteria. Thirdly, and this is an aim for this unit, the more you understand the thinking behind relevant methodological positions, the more secure you will be in the decisions you make.

We start by probing yet further into the nature of the potential Xs and Ys that (English) language research may seek to know more about, while examples of published studies give you the opportunity to practise making explicit the methodological considerations underpinning various choices of research method.

In A4, I suggest that the various kinds of research that make use of language as data can be thought of as located along a continuum. At one end are already existing texts, produced with no awareness (since texts do not have consciousness) of their subsequent status as evidence in a research project. Towards the other end are very carefully controlled experiments, where the researcher aims to exclude everything other than the phenomenon under investigation. I shall start this section at this latter end, exploring why some scholars think such tight control is important – and why others disagree! This will take us to the other end of the continuum, where participant observation increases authenticity – but at the expense of researcher control.

Before exploring this issue, it is relevant to note that an important aspect of some research methodologies, especially experimental approaches, is the concept of **random** sampling. 'Random', like several other terms mentioned in this book, has a specialised meaning in academic research. Usually it is completely impractical to investigate every member of the whole population in which you are interested – such as every language learner currently learning English, or every dating ad ever printed, or every mother of a 2-year-old child. Therefore, you select a 'sample' to represent the total population of people, or texts, or any other source of evidence. The disadvantage of this is that the very act of making the selection may distort what can be found, because the 'sample' is not truly representative of the total population in every respect. This would be the case, for example, if only mothers with a particular educational background were included, or dating ads from only some kinds of magazines. The idea of a 'random' sample is that, while it can contain only a sub-set of the total population of interest, that sub-set is not selected by any criteria which could skew the sample. For example, to study the discourse structure of newspaper stories, even in one publication at one time, you would need to select which texts to include in your corpus. Bell (1991) explains how a sample made up of daily newspapers published every nth day (but not every 7th day, because of the weekly cycle pattern of many newspapers) could produce a less biased corpus than if the researcher chooses which issues to include on a less 'random' basis.

C4.2 Experimental studies in second language acquisition: advocates and critics

Hulstijn (1997: 134) explains why laboratory studies are chosen by some researchers in second language acquisition (often abbreviated to 'SLA'): 'in order to have complete control of exposure to input and instruction, thereby eliminating potentially confounding variables present under normal language learning conditions, in or outside teacher-guided language courses'.

Although the X of interest to SLA research is some aspect of the acquisition of a language variety that people are already learning, some studies involve teaching an artificial language so that the language-learning process can be focused on with no 'interference' from any other additional language learning experience. An example of this approach is an experiment by Yang and Givón (1997). This was the method they used:

> Twenty-nine monolingual English-speaking undergraduates spent 50 hours over the course of a 5-week period learning a specially constructed miniature artificial language, Keki. These paid volunteers were randomly divided into two experimental groups. One group (the pidgin group) received pidgin input initially for 20 hours of instruction and then fully grammatical input for the remainder of the instructional period. The other group (the grammar group) was introduced to the grammar via fully grammatical input right from the start. Besides this single manipulation of the input, all other aspects of instruction and testing were identical.
>
> (Yang and Givón 1997: 176)

Consider the following questions, discussing them with other students if you can.

❏ What are the objects of research in this study (the Xs and Ys)?
❏ What were the variables (independent and dependent)?
❏ Why were the learners 'randomly' divided into two groups, and how might the experimenters do a 'random' division?
❏ What do you understand by 'identical' instruction here? How literally is the reader to take this?
❏ Why do you think the researchers chose to compare the use of 'pidgin' and 'fully grammatical' input?
❏ Can you see any reason why some scholars would not be convinced about this research approach?
❏ I imagine that it is quite unlikely that you would be in a position to replicate a study like this, for reasons that are fairly obvious – though it might be useful for you to set out what these are. However, if you were to attempt a scaled-down version of this research, which aspects would you need to retain, and which would be dispensable?

Some researchers respond quite differently to the issue of **extraneous variables** in SLA research; like confounding variables, these are variations that could prevent researchers from having confidence that they have demonstrated an unambiguous relationship between X and Y. Block (1996: 74) suggests that trying to control for extraneous variables 'is difficult at best, and probably not even desirable'. His argument is that language learning actually involves many of the things that experimenters classify as 'extraneous', and so studies should actively investigate these, rather than try to exclude them. He has in mind, for example, the 'environment' where the learning takes place and 'people issues (such as individuals' perceptions and expectations about the study affecting their performance)'. Block quotes Prabhu (1992: 230), who observes:

A classroom lesson is . . . an arena of human interactions – not the pedagogic interactions desired or elicited as a part of teaching strategy (which may or may not occur as expected) but the more elemental, inevitable interactions which occur simply because human beings, with all their complexity, are involved.

An implication for researchers who see things this way is, as Block (1996: 74) suggests, that what some would see as 'extraneous variables' are 'possibly the most interesting part of a study'. So from this kind of perspective, an appropriate method to research second language learning is one that, far from excluding as much as possible, embraces and explores learners' personalities, interactions with each other and with the teacher and methods used, and their values, aspirations and experiences beyond the classroom. Therefore, in complete contrast to experimental approaches, some scholars choose ethnographic methods for research into SLA.

One such is Canagarajah (1993), who advocates taking a 'closer look at the day-to-day functioning of the classroom and the lived culture of the students' (p. 603). His choice of method was influenced by his belief that '[t]he methodological orientation and fieldwork techniques developed by ethnography enable us to systematically study the students' own point of view of English language teaching in its natural context' (p. 603). Canagarajah's method was to carry out 'an intensive participant observation' (p. 606) of the ESOL class he taught for six hours per week during an academic year, collecting 'naturalistic data' (which included, for example, jottings the students made in the margins of the textbook), as well as conducting interviews with them and asking them to complete questionnaires.

Activity

As before, consider the following questions, discussing them with other students if you can.

❏ What problems may there be for a researcher who is both teacher and observer in his own classroom?

❏ How could practitioners of this kind of research answer the criticisms of experimenters who would be concerned about the problems of confounding or extraneous variables?

❏ The contrasting positions between these two sets of researchers arise partly, of course, because there are some differences in interpretation of what the Xs and Ys are – and should be – in SLA research. How much do you think Canagarajah's Xs and Ys have in common with those being investigated by Yang and Givón, in the previous study? If they are similar, where is the overlap? If not, what are the differences?

❏ I imagine that it is quite unlikely that you would be in a position to replicate a study like this, for reasons that are fairly obvious – though it might be useful for you to set out what these are. However, if you were to attempt a scaled-down version of this research, which aspects would you need to retain, and which would be dispensable?

C4.3 Recognising and naming Xs and Ys

What was your conclusion about the overlap between the objects of study in these two examples (Canagarajah 1993; Yang and Givón 1997)? Both were trying to find out more about how people learn an additional language, and to some extent, therefore, both incorporated causal questions: how does X (teaching method or learning experience) lead to Y (successful learning of the language variety)? We have to consider the possibility that, even if there is a superficial similarity between the Xs and Ys examined in these two studies, the terms used to label them may mean different things.

Such issues are of particular interest in English Language research because they arise partly from debates in social research about language itself, and particularly about how naming things may influence how we think about them, dating back to the Sapir-Whorf or 'linguistic relativity' hypothesis – although the true philosophical origins of this question go back much further than this. All the studies I have used as examples in this book must, to be comprehensible by readers, refer to the things they report on by using labels to name them.

This applies particularly to naming categories of people, although even types of text can cause definitional problems. On what grounds do you decide whether a text such as Pullman's *His Dark Materials* trilogy (see B4) qualifies as 'children's literature'? What qualifies an informant in your study to be classified as 'a native speaker of English' or as 'bilingual in Welsh and English'? Some researchers might observe speakers from Wales in conversation, switching between the two varieties, in order to answer the question, 'How are these two varieties used by these speakers in particular contexts?' In other words, 'What is X [here, the use of Welsh and English by these speakers in these contexts] like?' – a qualitative kind of question (see Garrett et al. 2003). Others might count up the instances of certain linguistic features occurring in the same conversation to investigate how often, say, the clauses in which code-switching occurred had either Welsh or English as the 'matrix' language governing the grammatical structure of the clause (see Deuchar 2006). In other words, the question is of the type 'How many Xs are there compared with Ys?' In either case, though, the researcher has to work with, and perhaps explore, concepts including what is to count as 'a bilingual Welsh-English speaker': this, like many examples in the social world, is not a transparent, undisputed category.

What are the consequences for research if the labels used by analysts misleadingly name things that should more properly be called something else? Critical discourse analysts, for example, as well as other researchers in the 'social constructionist' tradition, point out that the terms we routinely use for people and processes are far from transparent and may very well be ideologically loaded.

For instance, in their introduction to a book whose title is *Discourse Analysis: investigating processes of social construction* (Phillips and Hardy 2002), the series editors (van Maanen, Manning and Miller) pose the following questions:

> How do our notions of a 'nation', the 'individual', or even the 'social' come about, solidify, shift, reemerge, and guide our thought and action? How do such taken-for-granted ideas concerning work, family, freedom, and authority become seemingly natural, objective, autonomous features of the world? How do these presuppositions influence, for example, the way we judge refugees as attractive and welcome or disruptive and dangerous? Or more critically, what is a refugee anyway? What constitutes the definitional character of such a label, and when do we apply it to specific people and groups? What are the consequences of our talk and application?
>
> (Phillips and Hardy 2002: iv; series editors' words)

Their concerns here are with how discourse analysis can explore such issues in the context of social action and communication about it, but the implications for researchers are equally serious. Even apparently simple labels may be evidence of suppositions and theories, so researchers need to make these explicit – to define their terms. This is another illustration of the distinction between 'method' and 'methodology': depending on what kind of an entity or phenomenon you think is denoted by the label associated with it, the means by which you choose to investigate it may well be different.

Look again at any drafts or plans you have for your own research design, and consider your answers to the following questions:

❏   What exactly are the Xs and Ys that you want to find out more about?
❏   Can you research them all or, as is much more likely, can you only include a sub-set in your data?
❏   If you can only investigate a sub-set from the whole 'population' of Xs in which you are interested, how will you select your sample?
❏   Do restrictions in the samples available to you affect the accuracy of any of the labels you are using? If so, should you change the label to make it a more accurate term for what you are actually able to research?

C4.4 Theory and methodology

The questions we have been exploring here involve quite challenging philosophical ideas. When doing research, it can sometimes feel as though the things you are dealing with, which seemed initially to be solid and well-defined, start to become blurred, insubstantial and perhaps nothing more than illusions created by the language used to name them. Often, especially when time and other resources are limited, the way to deal with feelings of insecurity such as these is simply to continue with the practical aspects of your research, rather than allowing yourself to wander too far into this difficult theoretical terrain. Alternatively, you may find it helpful to think in a little more depth about what it is that researchers (including you) *can* find out, and *how* they can do so, about: the social world; the multiple ways in which human beings process language; how they use it to get things done; and how they make discursive and textual products as they do so.

Below are three 'position statements' summarising in a rather simplified way some perspectives taken in the debates in English Language research literature on what we can know and how we can know it. (Although these include quotations from other authors, some parts are in my own words, which may differ in the detail from claims these authors would make themselves.) If you can, discuss these positions with fellow students and decide which of the three you find most convincing. As you read further around your own topic, and as you continue planning your own research, keep alert for indications of these different theoretical orientations – and their methodological implications.

Position statement 1

Research into language-related phenomena, like research into anything else, including in the natural and physical worlds, involves breaking the phenomenon of interest down into its constituents, in order to understand it and analyse it effectively. Researchers have a responsibility to conduct experiments that can be replicated by others, thus making their claims available for others to test and refine.

> An experimental approach starts from the realization that the real world is a complex bundle of many things; it focuses on a single aspect at a time in order to establish its nature; it brings everything down to a single, precise question. Having posed the question, it looks for evidence that is explicit and objective. From this evidence it argues its way back to the original issue.
>
> (Cook 1986: 13)

Position statement 2

Research about language recognises that language is itself a symbolic system, and is not 'real' in the way that stones or atoms are real.

> When we speak, we do not refer to a discourse-external reality but to what has been said before. When we negotiate the meaning of a text segment, we do this within the discourse, not outside or on top of it.
>
> (Teubert 2005: 7)

Things that exist in the social world are, by definition, 'social constructs', so the methods for researching them need to be sensitive to this.

> Reality enters into human practices by way of the categories and descriptions that are part of those practices. The world is not ready categorized by God or nature in ways that we are all forced to accept. It is *constituted* in one way or another as people talk it, write it and argue it.
>
> (Potter 1996: 98)

Research is not about counting or measuring things that are external to language, but about exploring how language brings things into being through discourse. In relation to research, different people's interpretations will inevitably co-exist and the researcher does not evaluate these in relation to any external reality.

Position statement 3

There is a reality that exists independently of our linguistic descriptions of it. Some of the causes of actual events cannot be seen empirically, nor predicted with absolute regularity. This is because the social world is a complex and open system, made by people with interests and goals, and, as some of these people died a long time ago, aspects of social life need to be thought about on different timescales. 'We might acknowledge tendencies or patterns, but resist claiming applicability for our applied linguistics findings beyond specific times and places' (Larsen-Freeman and Cameron 2008: 235).

There is no point trying to break complex things down to find out about them, since they are what they are by virtue of the inter-relationships between the parts. External reality includes various institutions such as schools and universities – and many other sites where language is taught, learned and used to get things done. Individuals may interpret in many different ways the values and traditions associated with such structured social arrangements, and may even challenge or seek to undermine them, but they cannot simply talk them out of existence. Although human beings must use available discourses and descriptions to communicate, nevertheless, there *are* non-discursive things to be described, and research can help us to know which descriptions are better than others.

> [T]here are always various factors in assessing whether concrete events change the world and how, and language is only one of them. And the fact that certain ways of using language **may** have certain effects does not mean that they always or regularly **do**, it depends on other factors.
>
> (Fairclough 2009: 518–19, emphasis in original)

C5 DETAILS

One of the principles I hope you will take from this book is that it pays to be as clear as you are able (and this may only come from experience, of course) about both the practicalities and the theoretical ideas relevant to the kind of research you hope to do. I also believe that these are not two separate dimensions of the research process, but that the latter (theory) underpins the former (practice), and that if the theory is not sound, then neither will the practice be. This is what the discussion of 'methodology' as distinct from 'method' in B4 aimed to highlight.

Let us explore this with some further examples. One which will be familiar to anyone who has studied sociolinguistics is the 'observer's paradox' identified by Labov (see A4). Having identified what s/he wants to know more about, namely how people speak when they are not being observed, the **method** will inevitably involve making some recordings of people speaking. The **methodological** challenge is how to get to this practical procedure in such a way as to minimise the paradox (that the very act of observing people causes them to behave differently). Labov's solution was, as you probably know, to elicit narratives of near-death experiences, although many other aspects of the social interaction, and his negotiation of relationships with informants, the locations, and so on, also come into the decisions about how to collect the most useful data.

I have already referred several times to the different properties of written texts and social interactions respectively as sources of language research data. I suggested in A6 that the former are more stable and less susceptible to problems such as the observer's paradox – since a text has no consciousness and will not change its language because it is aware that you are reading it! (I suppose this may change as technology and interactive media develop, but the claim still stands for most written texts.) However, this does not of course mean that approaches to the research of written language are atheoretical, or do not need to engage with methodological issues.

Consider a research project concerned with discourse patterns in texts aimed at improving people's health by encouraging them to change their lifestyles – by taking more exercise, eating more healthily, giving up smoking and reducing their intake of alcohol. The researcher may decide that the identification of such patterns will be facilitated by using a corpus approach: this is both a practical and a methodological decision.

The practical, technical aspects relate to matters such as accessing the texts you need, converting them to an appropriate digital format, stripping or inserting various kinds of data other than the words of the texts themselves, and so on – see A6. Even some of these practical aspects are underpinned by theories: some corpus linguists value detailed annotation while others emphasise the advantages of deriving categories from the data, rather than imposing labels in advance.

A further methodological challenge, though, is to justify the use of this approach rather than, say, a close interpretive reading of a selection of the kinds of text in which you are interested. What sort of knowledge is likely to result from each kind of analysis? Which approach is more likely to answer your research questions – and why? Sinclair (2004) draws a distinction between a text and a corpus:

> Considering a short stretch of language as part of a text is to examine its particular contribution to the meaning of the text, including its position in the text and the details of meaning that come from this unique event. If the same stretch of language is considered as part of a corpus, the focus is on its contribution to the generalisations that illuminate the nature and structure of the language [or language variety] as a whole, far removed from the individuality of utterance.
>
> (Sinclair 2004)

Methodologically, then, the two approaches are associated with different perspectives, and to some extent with different theories (or at least different emphases) relating to what language is like and how we can find out more about it.

Consider the following potential projects and research techniques. Try to identify:

❏ any practical problems and potential pitfalls which could arise with such a study,
❏ the theoretical assumptions which underlie the proposed research, and thus
❏ the methodological challenges presented by it.

(1) Many of my students are fascinated by questions about men's and women's language, and the many research studies which have highlighted differences between their ways of talking – in both single-sex and mixed-sex contexts. An initial proposal might include a research question framed along the following lines: 'In mixed company, do women swear less than men do?'

Commentary

You should by now recognise that, in order to collect data to answer such a question, you would need access to a much larger number of people who belong to the categories 'men' and 'women' than is likely to be practical, otherwise your study can only realistically claim to tell you something about the particular men and women you recorded. This is a practical problem. In addition to this, though, did you spot the theoretical assumptions underpinning the question?

Unless the researcher gives some thought to these assumptions, and avoids conflating 'method' and 'methodology', the practical challenges of the study may be outweighed by its theoretical problems. The *method* may be impeccable: carefully chosen, willing participants, ethically approved procedures, reliable recording equipment, and a thoroughly piloted set of instructions to get informants talking such that taboo language is likely to occur among those speakers who feel comfortable using it.

Methodologically, though, the study draws, however implicitly, on a network of ideas, including some assumptions about people and how they act, which warrant further questioning. The most obvious of these is something we often take for granted because ideas about sex and gender are so deep-rooted in human culture (albeit in different forms at different times and in different places). It is that there are two categories of human being, and that these categories are 'male' and 'female'. There is quite a lot of research now which questions these binary categories, and suggests that:

1 biological sexual characteristics are less rigidly and permanently distributed than many people assume (so that there is a sizable proportion of the human population which is neither 'male' or 'female' in any absolute way; this includes transsexuals and people born with ambiguous genitalia, and so on)

2 the 'gendered' ways in which people are socialised to behave are more complicated than was once assumed, so not only can we not presume that being biologically male equates with being 'gendered' to behave in a 'masculine' way, the

norms associated with behaving that way are very varied in different social contexts, and often implicit.

The researcher may not explicitly subscribe to the next part of the underlying assumption, but it is there in the question as posed, and it is that the attributes of 'maleness' or 'femaleness' override any other social or cultural influences on the way people use taboo language. This suggestion may not be intentional, but what if you accept that some men, in some circumstances (perhaps male tutors in a department staff meeting), will swear less than some women (say young women attending a hen party)? In that case, the question as posed is theoretically flawed, because it fails to allow for heterogeneity among the people to be studied. Thinking this through should lead to the conclusion that *methodologically* it would be inappropriate to find a few men and a similar number of women and proceed to make recordings of their interactions. No amount of technical improvements to the *method* can compensate for the presuppositions about how and why people with different characteristics, in different circumstances, will use language in different ways.

Activity

(2) Moving on from the framing of questions, the choice of approach to the collection of data can also illustrate the way in which practical and theoretical issues are linked. Consider, for example, if you decide to use an interview method to ask people about some aspect of their language experiences, attitudes or practices. What practical, theoretical and methodological problems may arise?

Commentary

A5 and B5 outline some of the practical issues to consider when planning and arranging interviews (time and place, acoustics and background noise, equipment, the presence of people other than your informants, and so on).

The main theoretical issue concerns the extent to which you believe that people are capable (quite apart from their willingness to tell the truth) of articulating their knowledge and understanding of the issue in which you are interested – and the basis for your belief. Methodological issues underlying the practical method of interviews include theories about how well social actors (by which I mean people who perform actions in the social world, not those who act in drama) are able to understand their placement in that world, and the influences which affect what they do. This is not to imply that people are stupid, just that there are often forces acting upon us of which we are only dimly, if at all, aware.

Consider the sociolinguistic concept of 'covert prestige'. Trudgill (1972) found that certain speakers *reported* that they used the prestigious forms of particular sounds (such as the yod /j/ in 'tune'-words) *more* than was actually the case when he analysed their speech, while for others the reverse was the case: they *used* prestigious forms *more* than they *reported* that they did. (This finding is controversial when tied in to the debates about gender differences in language, but that is not so significant here, when the focus of the argument is the research method.) The 'covert prestige' explanation rests on the plausible belief that speakers are likely to report themselves as using the form which has positive connotations for them, the form which they wish to produce. The discrepancy between use and report needs an analyst's interpretation – and we can debate whether Trudgill's explanation convinces us or not. The methodological point is that there are good reasons for doubting that you can gather data about such topics merely by asking people about them. At the more visible level of *method*, you can plan carefully, interview skilfully and collate your findings accurately – but it remains likely that the study will not tell you what you want to know. And this will be because of its theoretical, not practical, shortcomings.

Activity

If you are still with me at this point, and are not yet put off by the myriad considerations which necessarily beset researchers grappling with the realities of people and their language, then you may want to see how far the issues raised in this and the other units in strand 5 apply to your proposed research project. To this end, you could review the checklist of questions below, annotating a copy of it with the aspects to which you are likely to need to pay the most attention in your own work. If it is practical, doing this in pairs is likely to prove more useful than trying to think it all through on your own.

People
- ❏ Who will you need to negotiate with to be able to do your project?
- ❏ Do you have contact details for them and information about their availability?
- ❏ Are you well prepared to explain to them exactly what you need from them?
- ❏ Have you checked the procedures in your institution relating to ethics and informed consent?
- ❏ Do you need ethical approval for what you plan to do?
- ❏ Have you prepared an appropriate information and consent form, and had it checked by the relevant person in your institution?
- ❏ Will you need to have a Criminal Records Bureau check (or equivalent) before you can gain the access you need and if so have you found out what you need to do to acquire this?
- ❏ When you anticipate the context where you will be working, who will you come into contact with in addition to your main informants, and what kinds of relationships may you need to negotiate?

Equipment
- ❏ Make a list of the equipment you need, to be able to do your research. Do you have ready access to all of this and, if not, (how) can you obtain it?
- ❏ Are you familiar with how it all works and, if not, can you arrange training, or at least a demonstration?

- ❏ How will you transport what you need to the place(s) where you will need it?
- ❏ Is your computer equipment reliable, and how are you backing up copies of important files (both data and written drafts of your study)?

Other resources

- ❏ Have you drawn up a bibliography of the reading you need to do?
- ❏ Are all the sources available to you and, if not, how can you obtain copies?
- ❏ If you will be away from your main institution at points when you need library access, can you arrange temporary access at a different institution?
- ❏ Will you need help with processing your data and, if so, do you know how to access it?
- ❏ Will you be handling statistics and, if so, do you have the necessary expertise, or have you consulted the relevant support unit in your institution?

Time

- ❏ What is the final deadline for handing in your project?
- ❏ Have you made a time-line of the whole project, with leeway built in to take account of the unexpected?
- ❏ Have you checked that the plans you have made will work for the other people you hope to involve, such as your informants?
- ❏ Do you know when your tutor(s) will be accessible, how long they expect between receiving material from you (such as a draft section of your work) and providing you with a response?

Ideas

This is a much more difficult area to handle via a checklist, but consider the following. What assumptions about each of these areas underlie your research as you currently understand it?

- ❏ The Xs and Ys which are the focus of your research.
- ❏ The kinds of thing which these are, for example 'natural kinds' like stones or bacteria, or 'discursive constructions' with no existence beyond language itself, or 'social categories' derived from theories about people and how they organise themselves, etc.
- ❏ The kinds of questions which it is possible to ask about these kinds of things with a reasonable expectation of obtaining a meaningful answer.
- ❏ Whether your goal is mainly to provide a description of these things, or to measure or count them – or a combination.

Finally, take another look at your research questions and consider once more whether your research, as planned, will answer them, and what the answers are likely to look like.

DATA COLLECTION

This unit begins with four examples of research into various aspects of language, where the main focus was on either written or spoken data. These are taken from published studies by experienced researchers, and for each one I have extracted accounts of the processes of selecting and collecting data. In each case, consider the decisions the researchers took about the data they would need, and how these can support you as you face equivalent decisions about your own project.

C6.1 Written texts as data: example 1a

Focus of the research
C3 includes an example of a project researching 'discourses of refugees and asylum seekers in Britain', with a list of questions which the researchers were seeking to answer. In a different article about this study, the authors explain how they found the data they would use to investigate these questions.

Description of the data
> The data were collected through an online interface of newspaper and periodicals (LexisNexis) by way of the following search query:
>
> > refugee* OR asylum* OR deport* OR immigr* OR emigr* OR migrant* OR illegal alien* or illegal entry OR leave to remain AND NOT deportivo AND NOT deportment
>
> Data were collected from nineteen UK newspapers, including six daily tabloids (*Sun, Daily Star, People, Daily Mirror, Daily Express, Daily Mail*) and their Sunday editions (*Sunday Express, Mail on Sunday, Sunday Mirror, Sunday Star*), five daily broadsheets (*Business, Guardian, Herald, Independent, Telegraph*), two Sunday broadsheets (*Observer, Independent on Sunday*), and two regional newspapers (*Evening Standard, Liverpool Echo*). Data were obtained for most of the newspapers from January 1996 through October 2005, although in a few cases data were not available until 1999 (*Business*), 2000 (*Sun, Daily Star, Sunday Star*), or 2001 (*Liverpool Echo*). The data were stored in separate files containing articles spanning one calendar month from each newspaper. The resulting corpus comprised 140 million words, consisting of 175,139 articles.
>
> (Gabrielatos and Baker 2008: 9)

One of the authors explains in a different paper (Gabrielatos 2007) how they devised these query terms, and the process may remind you of the discussion in strand 2 about how to identify the most useful search terms for finding library resources for your literature review.

> ⭐ **Activity**
>
> ### Questions to consider
> ❏ If you were interested in a similar issue, but could not hope to replicate such a large, well-resourced study, how would you scale it down?
> ❏ Which elements of the data collection process used in this study would you (a) retain, (b) learn from, and (c) which could you reasonably dispense with?

C6.2 Written texts as data: example 1b

Focus of the research

The focus was a particular application of the 'appraisal' framework for analysing discourse. This is 'an approach to exploring, describing and explaining the way language is used to evaluate, to adopt stances, to construct textual personas and to manage interpersonal positionings and relationships' (White 2005). Macken-Horarik (2003) was interested in how this approach to textual analysis could illuminate narrative address and reader positioning in narrative fiction.

> ⭐ **Activity**
>
> ### Questions to consider
> ❏ If you were interested in a similar issue, what kind of data would you collect for analysis?
> ❏ How much data would you need?
> ❏ How would you select from all the possible narratives you might include?

Description of the data

Macken-Horarik chose a short story used in an examination as a text for secondary school students to respond to and comment on; to succeed in the exam, they need to 'discern and articulate' the 'emotional and ethical message' contained in the narrative.

> The texts in focus in this article were first published by the New South Wales Board of Secondary Education in the late 1980s (Board of Secondary Education 1987). Although both the narrative and the two responses are now more than ten years old, they are typical of examination narratives and also of responses to these by students over the ensuing years. They have generated continuing discussion among educational linguists in Australia about contemporary specialized requirements of school English.
>
> (Macken-Horarik 2003: 288)

Further questions to consider

Some of the justifications for the author's choices are rather implicit: can you identify what they may be? What conclusions do you draw about appropriate kinds and amounts of data from the brief description of this project?

Written texts as data: further questions to consider

These two studies take very different approaches to research using written texts as data. How good is the fit in each case between the focus, the questions and the way data has been selected?

C6.3 Spoken interaction as data: example 2a

Focus of the research

Dailey-O'Cain (2000) was interested in 'the sociolinguistic distribution of and attitudes toward focuser *like* and quotative *like*' (where *like* is used 'as a highlighting device', on the one hand, and, on the other, 'to cite reported speech or thought', p. 60). She collected two kinds of data, including using questionnaires to explore people's attitudes towards this usage, and casual conversations to identify how various speakers actually do use these two kinds of *like*.

Description of the data

Here is what the author says about the empirical part of the study:

> In order to study the actual sociolinguistic distribution of this phenomenon, informal conversational data was taken from 30 speakers in a sample stratified by age and gender. This data was collected in the spring of 1995, and consists of sociolinguistic interviews in which each informant conversed informally for approximately half an hour with one other person (the author, in each case). All speakers, as well as the conversation partner, were from a middle-class to upper-middle-class socioeconomic background, and had grown up in southeastern Michigan. The informants were chosen to form a quota sample equally distributed among three age groups (ages 14–29, 30–49, and 50–69) and both genders. 671 occurrences of *like* taken from this data were analyzed with reference to the age and the gender of the speaker. 576 of these occurrences were examples of focuser *like*, and 95 were examples of quotative *like*.
>
> (Dailey-O'Cain 2000: 64)

Activity

> ### Questions to consider
> ❏ Although you are unlikely to be able to collect as much data as this, what principles would you apply to the selection and collection of a smaller amount of data?
> ❏ How would your decisions relate to different emphases in researching the phenomenon?
> ❏ In A6, I advise against being a participant in recordings you intend to analyse, but this researcher was an interlocutor in all this data: is this a problem in this study, do you think, or are the disadvantages mitigated in any way, by her greater experience as a researcher, for example?

C6.4 Spoken interaction as data: example 2b

Focus of the research

Two researchers with an interest in formulaic language wanted to test their prediction that routine physical procedures such as paying for goods at the supermarket check-out are likely to be accompanied by 'routine speech tasks', which will be performed 'primarily using speech formulae' (Kuiper and Flindall 2000: 188). Their interest, they explain, was in 'the formulaic inventory and discourse structure used by checkout operators [and] . . . the ritual aspects of the interactions' (p. 189) – and not in 'socio-linguistic variables'.

Description of the data

This study was undertaken in 1991 at two supermarkets from two different super-market chains, in two different suburbs of Christchurch, New Zealand over a period of about a month. One was in a lower socio-economic suburb, the other in a higher socio-economic suburb. About two hundred interactions were collected as follows.* Nine checkout operators were recorded, two male and seven female. [. . .] Customers were informed of the project by a large notice at the beginning of the checkout aisle and informed that the other aisles were not fitted with recording equipment. After the recording sessions, the taped interactions were transcribed onto cards and thence onto computer. Given the aims of the study there was no attempt to control for social variables such as the age, socio-economic status or gender of the customers.

(Kuiper and Flindall 2000: 188–9)

*The checkout operator was fitted with a lapel microphone and the customers were recorded using a semi-directional microphone, the two channels being fed into a Sony TCD 5M stereophonic cassette recorder. (p. 204n)

 Activity

Questions to consider
It is possible that, at least in the UK, the ethical constraints operating today would make even a partial replication of a study such as this quite difficult, but you may have access to a workplace where these challenges could be overcome, perhaps on your university campus.

❏ If so, how many interactions would you aim for and why?
❏ Which details identified in this description would you attend to and which would you modify? Why?

Spoken interaction as data: further questions to consider

These two studies take very different approaches to research using speech as data. How good is the fit in each case between the focus, the questions and the way data has been collected?

Now refer back to the diagram in Figure A4.1.1. Whereabouts on the notional continuum suggested there would you place the kinds of data used in each of these four examples?

The next section of this unit presents some examples of studies where the researcher takes a more direct role in the generation of data. Again, consider as you read each one what you can learn about the process of making decisions about data (type, amount, means of collection), and how far the approaches and principles represented by each example may be applicable to your own project.

C6.5 Elicited data: example 3: diaries and journals

Asking participants to keep a log, journal or diary is a method of collecting data found particularly in educational research, where the informants are learners, teachers or both. As noted in A6, it is also used by parents to record children's early vocalisations and utterances, and by bilingual informants, to record various features associated with the use of different varieties. One example of a diary of this kind, where the objective was to investigate patterns of language use, is reported in Lawson and Sachdev (2004). This is how they summarise their data collection procedure, which yielded 364 diary entries altogether:

> 21 Sylheti-Bengali (16 female, 5 male; ages 12–15) students who had opted to study Bengali as a subject at school, kept a diary of their language use in different contexts over a period of 4 days (pilot work had suggested that 4 days was the optimal period of time for obtaining maximum cooperation among our sample). To obtain information about the widest range of settings possible, the period covered days at the weekend and during the week. Participants recorded categorical information on where they were during the conversation (setting), the topic, information about their interlocutor (age, gender, relationship), and the language(s) used. They were asked to do this by completing a table at various points throughout the day (including mealtimes) to encompass the widest range of interactions in a structured manner. All participants completed their diaries in English.
>
> (Lawson and Sachdev 2004: 52)

Activity

Questions to consider

These authors claim that '[t]he fact that the diary is completed relatively soon after the interaction has taken place, and that it refers to concrete instances of language use, should allow interactions to be recorded with a high level of accuracy and detail' (p. 52).

❏ Do you agree?
❏ Which kinds of linguistic interaction are suitable for this method, and which may not be?

C6.6 Elicited data: example 4: focus group interviews

Focus of the research

The focus here was how people talk about a particular issue – in this case, environmental sustainability. The aim was 'to explore the sorts of meanings within which participants interpreted these issues, and how participants related these issues to their daily lives and concerns' (Myers 1998: 88).

Description of the data

The data comprises transcripts from seven focus groups, and Myers explains the ways in which the procedures were:

[...] typical of many, though not all, focus-group studies in several respects:

(a) The number of participants: Eight in a group, while other studies may have from about five to about twelve.

(b) The selection of participants: Selection was conducted by a professional recruiter on criteria of age, gender, urban or rural residence, newspaper readership, and socio-economic class – variables relevant to the theoretical categories of the study.

(c) The homogeneity of the groups in terms of the theoretical categories of the study: Four in the northern UK, four in the south, with two groups of mothers aged 20–30, two groups of men 35–45, two groups of rural middle-class men and women 55–65, and two groups of urban professionals 25–35. Most handbooks suggest that homogeneity within groups encourages discussion.

(d) The structure given by the topic guide: A section of introductions, in which participants said where they lived and what environmental issues concerned them; a central section of discussions of given statements about sustainability and environmental actions; and a brief closing section of responses to leaflets.

(e) The length: Two hours, which many handbooks say is the limit for such a group; other groups may be as short as an hour.

(f) The role of the moderator: There were three moderators in the course of the eight groups, all trained in a style of intervention that emphasizes constant minimal response with occasional probing and no evaluation.

(g) The audiotaping and transcription of the discussions: Orthographic transcriptions by a typist were checked and further annotated by another listener. Some studies use videotape, while others may rely on the moderator or an observer to take notes.

(Myers 1998: 88)

Myers goes on to explain how 'short statements printed in large letters on cards' were used as a stimulus to the discussion:

> For instance, the first statement on the first card was drawn from a leaflet put out by the UK government's Energy Efficiency Office, and was included with other statements focusing on the general idea of environmental limits: 'Every time we use gas, electricity, coal, or central heating in our homes, we are damaging our other home, the earth.' Participants were first asked to attribute these statements to someone or some organization that might say them, and then to agree or disagree.
>
> (Myers 1998: 88–9)

Again, you can find more extensive details in Myers' paper about exactly how the moderator encouraged participation, sought to allay anxieties and minimise any sense that the interaction was a test of any sort, and to communicate the acceptability of disagreement among the participants.

Activity

Questions to consider

You are unlikely to be able to employ a professional recruiter to select participants for a focus group, but could you use a small-scale version of this approach to collect data of your own? For example, suppose you were interested, like the student in B6, in discourse about the armed forces. He used army recruitment literature as his data, but he could have used a focus group to collect data on how a group of young people, say, interpret accounts from different sources about the armed forces and their activities, and how these participants relate these to their own lives.

❏   What stimulus texts might he use?
❏   What other topics might be explored using this approach?
❏   Which aspects of the focus group technique described here are essential and which could be modified, do you think?

C6.7 Elicited data: example 5: experimental data

Focus of the research

This study explored 'whether color representations are routinely activated when color words are processed' (Richter and Zwaan 2009: 383). It involved two experiments, using 30 psychology undergraduates (where the second replicated the first but with one detail altered). Experiment 1 is described as follows:

> [. . .] participants first saw a colored square, then performed a lexical decision task on a color word (or a filler word of another type), and finally judged for a second colored square whether or not it was identical in color to the first one. The color words either matched or mismatched the colors.
>
> (Richter and Zwaan 2009: 384)

Description of the data

In an experiment such as this, the data consists of the outcome of a series of 'trials', where the researchers record participants' reactions to the stimulus. Having gathered the whole set of responses, they analyse the data to see whether reading the word which names a colour leads people to think of that colour even as they see an image of a different one.

> Participants performed lexical decisions on the verbal and non-word stimuli and a color-discrimination task on the visual stimuli. In each trial, a colored square (the reference stimulus) was presented in the middle of a light-grey screen for 1500 ms. Following a blank screen (500 ms) and a fixation cross (250 ms), a color word, a non-color word or a non-word was shown in black letters (Arial, 20 pt) in a white rectangle in the middle of the screen until participants provided a lexical decision via key presses. Subsequently, a second colored square (the test stimulus) appeared whose color was identical to that of the reference stimulus or differed from it gradually. Participants' task was to indicate via key presses whether or not the color of the test stimulus was identical to that of the reference stimulus. After a blank screen (2500 ms) and a fixation cross (250 ms), the next trial started. Thirty-six trials were experimental trials that included a color word as the target stimulus of the lexical decision task. In half of these trials, the color word matched the verbal label of the colors of test and reference stimulus, in the other half, it named the complementary color (e.g. yellow if test and reference stimuli were blue).
>
> (Richter and Zwaan 2009: 385)

Activity

Questions to consider
- ❏ Is an experimental method the best way to collect data which is appropriate for a study such as this?
- ❏ Are there other ways you could obtain equivalent data and, if so, what would they be?
- ❏ What other kinds of study would make use of similar methods of data collection?

C6.8 Research about data collection methods

The final set of examples in this unit is of data collection methods on which the researchers reflect explicitly, as they evaluate the pros and cons of various approaches. As noted in A6, there are countless manuals on how to design effective interviews and questionnaires, and details of several of these are included in the list of further reading at the end of the book. This section of this unit takes a slightly different approach. In the first example, Low (1999) uses his applied linguistic expertise to investigate how people process the discourse demands of one kind of questionnaire.

Example 6 – questionnaires and think-aloud (TA) protocols

I invite you in A1 to construct a Likert scale to help you decide on your own interests and preferences as a potential researcher, and many questionnaires in applied and sociolinguistics include such ranking scales as a means of collecting data, particularly about people's attitudes and priorities to some detail involved in learning or using language. Low (1999) reports on a study he did to try to understand more fully 'what respondents do' when confronted with such questions, in light of the fact that 'respondents often fail to respond in the desired way' (p. 504). Citing previous studies, he points out that '"reacting to statements" and "selecting ratings" are social, discourse-related activities', and that respondents are likely to interpret the task as such, which may produce results not anticipated or desired by the researcher. Low had nine students complete a questionnaire he had designed and asked them to 'think aloud' as they did so. He recorded what they said, as well as interviewing them immediately after they had answered the questions. (As Low himself acknowledges, his study operates at several levels, using language to research language about language!) Issues he explored include how they interpret intensifiers such as *very* in the rank scales; whether respondents read accurately (do they notice words such as *far* in the statement 'academic work is far harder than I expected'?); how they cope with incongruity: Low deliberately mixed types of response ('agree/disagree' and 'approve/disapprove'), causing respondents to puzzle over what they were actually being asked; how they felt about, and responded to, implicit biases in the wording of the statements. Low concludes: 'In the light of the repeated reinterpretations, substitutions, and transfers found in the TA data, we should I think be cautious about just how far the designer's perspective does ultimately guide and constrain respondents in Likert-type questionnaires' (p. 527).

Example 7 – discourse completion tasks (DCTs)

As discussed in A6, the practical difficulties of collecting unforeseeable linguistic events such as apologies have led researchers to devise ways of simulating the interactions in which they occur. Doubts about the validity of the data produced this way have led to some studies aimed at comparing it with alternatives. Billmyer and Varghese observe that 'no written instrument gathering data in a controlled setting which affords respondents the benefit of time to plan can ever approximate the complexity, ambiguity, and ever-present unpredictability of live face-to-face interactions' (2000: 545), which supports the findings of Beebe and Cummings (1995), who collected simulated refusals in writing and in phone calls, and found more words and more repetitions and elaborations in the spoken medium. One of the conclusions of Billmyer and Varghese (2000) was that, if research does demand DCTs, then the scenarios presented to participants should include more contextual information than is typically the case.

Schauer and Adolphs (2006) approached the issue by comparing elicited discourse completion tasks with a corpus of spontaneous speech. They asked 16 speakers to complete eight scenarios adapted from those used in a previous study, all concerned with expressions of gratitude. The data for comparison was drawn from a large existing corpus and was, by definition, much less controlled, so that the types of expressions of gratitude from this source could not be manipulated to cover such a wide range of situations. About these two kinds of data they observe:

[...] the original purpose of the DCT has traditionally been to create a controlled setting and to gather cross-linguistic data for analysis. The corpus as a resource stands in stark contrast to the DCT as the individual interactions in a corpus do not occur in a controlled environment. The aim of most corpus linguists is to describe patterns of general language use rather than to analyse individual utterances in a highly controlled context. And while the DCT may go a long way in providing data that is controlled for speaker relationship, language proficiency or nationality of the subjects it can never provide the same variety of discourse contexts as the corpus.

(Schauer and Adolphs 2006: 131)

They go on to reflect on the advantages and disadvantages of each kind of data in their summary of the findings from this comparison:

[...] the discourse completion task contained a great variety of interactional formulaic sequence categories that can be linked to a controlled contextual environment, while the corpus data provided detailed insights into additional situational thanking contexts and the use of expressions of gratitude over several conversational turns.

(Schauer and Adolphs 2006: 131–2)

An implication of this study for you as a potential collector of data about speech acts such as these is that, as I stress throughout the book, it is important to clarify not only what your Xs and Ys are (in this case, 'expressions of gratitude', though they might be 'apologies' or 'compliments'), but also what you want to know about them – that is, what kind of question are you asking (see strand 3)?

While this should be something you continue to think about, it shouldn't constrain you so much that you feel unable to begin until you are completely confident about it. However, be aware of the possibility that the practicalities of data collection may lead to you having to modify your original plans. If this does happen, don't forget to look again at your research questions, as modifications to the data available may entail modifications to these too.

C6.9 Housekeeping

As ever, you are advised at the data collection stage of your project to keep records of your work, just as you do with your reading for the literature review, and of progress in general in your research diary or notebook. The final authentic example in this unit is of the record made by a student of the data she collected; this was included as an appendix in her submitted dissertation.

Example

Table C6.9.1 is an extract from a table listing some of the data which Caroline collected for her project on apology strategies. She listened out for instances of people apologising to each other in her presence, and made a note of who said what to whom and in what circumstances. She noted the sex and age of each participant in the interaction, using approximations of age-groups for anyone she did not know, and indicating these with question marks. Columns have been given to each participant (P1, P2, etc.), and each is identified as male or female (M/F), with a unique number, assigned simply on the basis of the order in which the incidents occurred. At the analysis stage, Caroline was able to locate the detailed information by the reference number, and to group her data according to the criteria she devised for analysis. This initial log is a useful summary of the data collected, before analysis proper began. Seven of the 30 examples she collected are shown here.

Table C6.9.1 Extract from a summary of a data set in a student project

Ref. no	Context	P1	P2	P3	Relationship
1	At home	F1 (20)	M1 (22)		Acquaintances
2	Informal meeting at uni (1)	F2 (21)	F3 (22)	F4 (21)	Course mates
3	Informal meeting at uni (2)	F5 (40?)	8 other students, all F (20–5)		Course mates
4	At home	F6 (21)	M2 (21)		Partners/intimates
5	In the library	F7 (20?)	F8 (20?)		Strangers
6	At M3's home	M3 (55)	M4 (40?)		Friends
7	In public car park	M5 (50?)	M6 (30)		Strangers

C7   DATA ANALYSIS AND INTERPRETATION

> I . . . encourage analysts to reflect on their conceptual lens and to formulate their theoretical assumptions prior to analysis, even though subsequent analysis might modify the nature of these assumptions. In doing so, researchers . . . make their assumptions clear, conceptual constructs explicit, and analyses replicable.
>
> (Pavlenko 2007: 175)

As with all other stages of research, the analysis of data involves various theoretical assumptions – about what constitutes 'data' and what kind of data is appropriate to shed light on the questions you are trying to answer; about the relationship between things you can perceive directly and record (such as people's utterances) and things you can't (such as what they think and believe); and about the extent to which the data to which you have access (usually an infinitesimally small proportion of all that could have been collected) represents the more general phenomenon in which you are interested. A7 and D7 both include some discussion of the challenges posed by converting speech to a transcription. This particular aspect of processing and analysing data can be seen as a telling illustration of the way in which all aspects of data analysis involve dealing with issues such as those listed above. This unit begins, therefore, with an exploration of the links between research questions, data and analysis as demonstrated in the transcription of spoken language. We then look at ways in which researchers identify patterns and themes in linguistic data of various kinds (building on themes presented in B7), and finally we return briefly to the analysis and interpretation of numbers and statistics, as these relate in particular to people and the language they produce.

C7.1 Transcription as a stage in data analysis

> ### Transcription and data analysis 1
> Even if your own (likely) data will not involve the transcription of speech, I advise doing these activities anyway, as they illustrate some general issues about analysing data.
>   Make a list of all the possible features of both speech and the context of its production which a transcript *might* potentially include.

★ **Activity**

Commentary
In an article which he calls 'Transcribing infinity', Cook (1990) discusses the problem of specifying, and communicating to readers, the 'context' of the talk which may be of interest to researchers. He reviews some of the many elements which could potentially be included in a transcription. These include, he says:

1   the text itself, by which I mean the linguistic forms realised by graphitic or phonetic substance . . .
2   the physical characteristics of the text – graphetic and phonetic;
3   paralinguistic features (defined here as movements and postures of face and body); [elsewhere in the article, Cook discusses prosodic features as well]
4   the physical situation: the properties and relations of objects and bodies;
5   the co-text: text judged to belong to the same discourse, which preceded or is believed to have preceded, follows or is expected to follow, that under analysis;
6   the intertext: texts which the participants associate with the text under consideration;
7   thought: the intentions and interpretations, knowledge and beliefs, beliefs about beliefs and knowledge about knowledge (and so on, and on!) of the participants, as well as their interpersonal attitudes, affiliations and feelings;
8   the observer: the inevitable selection and interpretation by the analyst.

(Cook 1990: 2–3)

How does your list compare with Cook's? At the time he was writing, the 'multimodal' approach to the analysis of discourse was relatively new. With the rapid development of technology, there are now even more possibilities both for communicating in virtual ways, and for analysts to investigate how we do so. Did you include visual and computer-mediated communication in your list of potential features in transcripts?

Having explored the challenges associated with his list of potential dimensions of transcription, Cook (1990: 15) concludes that '[t]he full transcription of discourse context is . . . a theoretical as well as a practical impossibility'. Like most of the commentators on this aspect of data processing and analysis (see Reading D7.1), he argues for transcribers to select what to include with reference to principled decisions, alongside an acceptance of practical constraints, and you are invited in the next activity to consider both.

Activity

Transcription and data analysis 2

Figure C7.1 contains eight examples of data from research studies which have each investigated some aspect of spoken language, and whose analysts have transcribed this speech in order to answer various research questions. I have not reproduced the transcription conventions here, partly for reasons of space, although the studies usually do include them – and you should do so in any equivalent work of your own. Even without them, you should be able to make a good guess about the kinds of things the authors have chosen to indicate. From the limited evidence available to you, consider the following questions for each example, discussing them with fellow students if possible:

❑ Which features of speech and context have been transcribed and which omitted?
❑ If symbols other than the basic alphabet and punctuation marks are used, can you work out what they may be intended to represent?
❑ What do you think the analyst's main concern was in the study? Can you infer which aspects of spoken language they are interested in?
❑ From the kind and degree of detail included in the transcript, what kinds of research question can and cannot be answered?

Participants: Alysha, Katrina and Irene

1
Al: what I'm saying (.) cos the- people *do* come late (.) **you know** |I should| come
Ka: |mmm|

....

2
Al: late Irene innit (.)   I should innit (.)
Ka:
Irene: it's up to you (.)   it's up to you

Figure C7.1.1 Transcribed data from Irwin (2006: 517)

1	Mary:	[So]
2	Fred:	[We're al]ways the nerds.
3		We like it.
4	Mary:	You@'re the nerds?
5	Fred:	We're <creaky> {glad} to be the ner:ds,
6		a@nd the squa:res and,
7	Mary:	Is that what
8	Fred:	[we don't–]
9	Mary:	[you say] you are?
10	Fred:	<[i?]> Well,
11		we don't exactly s:–
12		We don't always say it,=
13		=I say it. n@
14	Mary:	@@[@!]
15	Fred:	[But-]
16	Mary:	@ You're [[prou:d.]]
17	Fred:	[[you]] know,
18	Mary:	[@@]
19	Fred:	[we don't–]
20		We just don't (0.5) drink,
21		we d [on't (.) <rapid> {d]o
22	Mary:	[Mm]
23	Fred:	any drugs,}

Figure C7.1.2 Transcribed data from Bucholtz (2007: 787)

| *Jones:* | Big day for you Prime Minister. What will you be seeking to do in this address to the nation? |
| *Prime Minister:* | I will lay out again the reasons why it is directly in Australia's national interest to see that Iraq is disarmed without delay and loses the chemical and biological weapons Iraq clearly has. [. . .] And I'll be making it very plain that the ultimate nightmare of the new world we now live in is that weapons of mass destruction can get into the hands of international terrorists and that *the more rogue states like Iraq are allowed to keep them the more will try to do the same and that is why the world must take steps to disarm Iraq.* That in essence is what I'll be saying. (Transcript of interview on Radio 2GB, 13 March 2003) |

Figure C7.1.3 Transcribed data from Young (2008: 632)

30.45	0.16	G:	do you have a can i can you do you do you have a field station marked on
35.45	−0.08	F:	uh-huh
35.53	−0.32	G:	the left-hand side
36.34	−0.17	F:	do i go down that far
37.18	−0.27	G:	go no go down halfway between the the
41.94	*1.20*	F:	the diamond
42.27	−0.30	G:	the diamond

Figure C7.1.4 Transcribed data from Forsyth et al. (2008: 232)

04:56:56
T: so (2.0) do I feel I or that they're really friends?::

Figure C7.1.5 Transcribed data from Harley and Fitzpatrick (2009: 684)

[001]	DA:	You knew that you were going to be asked questions only twelve
[002]		hours ago. It was only twelve hours isn't that right?
[003]		(1.1)
[004]	AM:	Yes.
[005]		(7.3)
[006]	AM:	((*slight head tilt forward and back at 7.0*))
[007]	AM:	((*lip smack/alveolar click and head movement forward toward microphone with thinking face display at 7.3*))
[008]	AM:	I would like to complete my answer on uh:: the question (.)
[009]		about (.) saying that Senat[or Kennedy was watching.
		[((gaze moves to DA))
[010]		(0.9)
[011]	AM:	((*raised and sustained eyebrow flash with mouth open-close co-occurring with three micro vertical head nods*))
[012]		(3.3)

Figure C7.1.6 Transcribed data from Matoesian (2008: 199)

INF 15 '[tell her] about that celery'
INF 12 'Oh yes'
INF 15 'It was your Mum and Dad [wɒnt]it that overheard it where was it up Great Bridge [Tipton EA]?'
INF 12 'No it was me when I went to er up Dudley on the market(.)and erm this woman said [avjoʊsɪn] that [sɛlərɛɪ]? It's like a [tɹeɪ]' (*laughs*)

Figure C7.1.7 Transcribed data from Asprey (2007)

Mother: おいしい　なあ
           oishii   naa
           delicious + particle
                 [It's delicious]

Figure C7.1.8 Transcribed data from Kurimoto (2009)

Commentary

Most transcripts are set out like play-scripts, with speakers' identities in a column on the left and what they said on the right. Among the examples here, the most basic approach of this type is C7.1.3, where the researcher's interest is in the discourse strategies of the interviewee, which accounts for the highlighting, by means of italics, of particular sections of his turn in the extract. Not only does this illustrate the analytical approach to transcription, but it also demonstrates one of the themes Young identified within her data: the politician's use of repetition and 'staying on message'. Unlike several of the other examples, Young does not try to indicate interruptions, as these are not her concern, whereas Forsyth et al. (2008: 225) report on their attempt to make analysts' recognition of these more objective by developing 'a novel orthographic transcription layout based on word timings'. C7.1.4 therefore includes figures representing the precise 'timestamp' from the recording in the first column, and 'inter-speaker intervals' in the second. The participants were doing a map-related task, with one giving the other instructions, but the study is primarily methodological, exploiting technology to identify 'how the speech stream is divided into segments and assigned to the participating interlocutors' (p. 226).

C7.1.1 departs from the play-script format, as the author explains: 'I have used the stave format of transcription suggested by Edelsky 1981 and developed by Coates 1986, 1988, and 1996. This aims to show conversation as a collaborative rather than a "one at a time" venture' (Irwin 2006: 505). The research was concerned with the function of 'I know' and 'you know' among adolescents in London, and the analysis identified patterns in the use of these expressions. The other example which uses a multi-line format is C7.1.8, but in this case the extract contains an utterance of only one speaker.

The transcription is given in Japanese script, then in an approximate phonetic version, using English orthography, which is translated word-for-word on the third line, before a more idiomatic English equivalent is supplied in the final version. The researcher's interest is in how Japanese and English mothers, respectively, regulate the behaviour of their very young children. As the grammar of the two varieties is quite different, she needed to demonstrate some aspects of the linguistic potential available in Japanese but not in English.

Phonetic symbols are used in C7.1.7 – but not throughout. This researcher's interest is in the dialect of the West Midlands, so her interviews were designed to elicit local pronunciation, and when the target sounds were produced, she was careful to transcribe these phonetically. C7.1.2 displays perhaps the most detailed use of symbols, and is in fact a re-transcription by the author of data she originally published several years previously. She did this, she says, because on returning to the transcript she was, 'astonished and horrified to realize that in the interests of focusing on content, my transcript had systematically erased every interactional nuance of the data' (Bucholz 2007: 787). Her study was about girls who self-identify as 'nerds', and the passage from which this example is taken provides, she says, 'an encapsulating statement of what it means to be a nerd'.

Various attempts have been made to include visual information in transcriptions, and examples of this can be seen in C7.1.5 and C7.1.6 – the former using screen-grabs alongside transcriptions of utterances recorded on YouTube, and the latter using descriptions of 'multimodal communicative practices (e.g. gaze, facial expression, body alignment, and realignment)' in an analysis of evidence given by a crucial witness in a rape trial, who, the author maintains, 'implements numerous discursive and extralinguistic resources for manipulating, negotiating, and resisting' the speech exchange system which in court is conventionally seen as particularly asymmetrical.

You may well have found many other aspects of these snippets to comment on, and the more you engage with the process of transcribing spoken language, the more you will no doubt recognise that, as Bucholtz (2007: 802) claims, 'variability in transcription practice has analytic, social, and political meanings that we would do well as researchers to examine more closely'.

C7.2 Identifying patterns in data

The choice of presentation of transcribed data is tightly linked, as I have suggested, to the process of identifying which aspects to focus on. The lists of transcription conventions which usually accompany studies such as those in the previous activity are, effectively, keys to a code, and even data which does not involve transcription may make use of codes. Transcribers aim to represent things of a similar kind in a similar way, so that in C7.1.2, for example, the '@' symbol has been used consistently to represent laughter, 'each token mark[ing] one pulse' (Bucholz 2007: 804).

Analysts working with linguistic data of all kinds may use codes to mark up their data, whether the specific features of interest are phonemes, phrases (like 'you know') used as identity markers, discourse strategies or themes emerging from personal narratives or focus group interviews. Where the production of material to use as data is more tightly controlled, the researcher has already 'coded' the material to some extent, by deciding, for example, to elicit instances of specific behaviour, or choices from a predetermined set of options, so that some sorting and classifying underpins the data collection phase. When data of a less structured kind is collected (at the other end of the notional continuum depicted in Figure A4.1.1), then the process of classifying and coding is likely to be more concentrated in the analysis phase.

There are several approaches to coding 'free-form' data, but the most basic step is to identify areas of potential similarity across different parts of the data. These similarities could be at any level, from phoneme through words and phrases to larger themes, and the necessary tools for analysis will vary accordingly.

Activity

Coding data

This activity invites you to consider three summaries of research studies involving the coding of data. I have simplified and abbreviated them, giving you basic information about each one. In each case, consider – and discuss with other students, if practical – the following questions:

- ❏ If you had to analyse this data, are there any Xs and Ys that you would know in advance you wanted to identify? If so, what would they be?
- ❏ To which levels of language would you pay attention and, potentially, attach codes (sounds/words/clauses/themes, etc.)?
- ❏ What categories might emerge for classifying the particular kind of data collected for the study?
- ❏ What difficulties in coding the data might be anticipated?

Example C7.2.1 (adapted from Song et al. 2009)

Focus of the research
Young children often omit the inflectional –s morpheme for third person singular verbs, which may be explained by their immature grasp of syntax. Could an additional reason be 'the phonological complexity of the verb stem to which [this morpheme] is attached' (Song et al. 2009: 623)?

Data
As well as some elicited imitations from 2-year-olds, the researchers used 'longitudinal data from the spontaneous speech of 6 English-speaking children between ages 1;3 and 3;6 (years;months)'.

Example C.7.2.2 (adapted from Al-Ali 2006)

Focus of the research

(1) When Jordanian Arabic-English bilingual undergraduates write cover letters of application in L2 English, what genre components do they employ to
articulate their communicative purpose?

(2) What pragmatic politeness strategies, positive or negative, do Jordanian
undergraduate students of English utilise to achieve the communicative functions in the component moves of a job application genre?

(3) Are the Arabic-English bilingual undergraduates able to produce a job application letter in English that contains the essential genre-specific meaning
components and the appropriate politeness strategies?

(Al-Ali 2006: 124)

Data

The researcher collected a corpus of 90 job application letters written by 90 Jordanian
Arabic-English bilinguals. '[S]tudents were given a simulated, but tailor-made, job
advertisement describing a fictional situation in which each student was asked to
write a letter of application in response to the ad . . . as if s/he were actually applying
for the job' (p. 125).

Example C.7.2.3 (adapted from Marshall and Goldbart 2007)

Focus of the research

This study was about how families where there is a child with 'complex communication needs' make use of 'Augmentative and Alternative Communication' (Marshall
and Goldbart 2007). This includes facial expression, signing and gesture, 'eye pointing' (looking hard at the object or person you want), picture charts and technological
aids, such as those used for electronic speech output. The aim of the project:

> was to explore the lived experience of parents of children in Britain who used AAC
> [Augmentative and Alternative Communication], with particular emphasis on
> the ways in which children's need for and use of AAC impacts on family life and
> communication.

(Marshall and Goldbart 2007: 78)

Data

The data consisted of transcripts of 11 individual interviews with parents, conducted
in participants' homes using a semi-structured approach that 'permitted the participants to raise issues that were felt by them to be relevant to the overall topic, whilst
allowing the particular topics of interest to the researchers to be addressed through
follow-up questions' (p. 83).

> [T]he only elements of the interview that were kept consistent were obtaining
> some limited biographical data (which also served to relax participants) and an

opening request to 'tell me about a typical day with [child's name]'. Participants were encouraged to raise and discuss any and all issues that they considered to be relevant to the overall topic.

(Marshall and Goldbart 2007: 82)

Commentary

In C.7.2.1, Song et al. began by identifying every example of third person –*s* and selecting those whose stem ends with no consonant or with one or two (in other words, their Xs were at the very detailed end of language production and analysis). They discarded examples of several types which could have confused the issue (such as those where the sound following the target was also –*s*, for example). They report that, '[t]he resulting data set included 323 verb tokens (11 verb **types**) in simple C contexts and 284 verb tokens (40 verb types) in complex CC contexts' (p. 628). They looked next at where in the utterance each example occurred, and recorded the results as percentages. '[I]items were then coded either as –*s produced* or –*s missing*, depending on whether the third person singular morpheme –*s* was present or not' (p. 628), and the authors explain how they handled – consistently – cases which did not clearly fall into either category; for example, if the child did articulate the –*s* but omitted the final consonant of the stem. The calculations then done on the resulting figures revealed that, '[o]verall, the 6 children produced third person singular –*s* more often in simple C contexts as compared with complex CC contexts (75% vs. 54%)' (p. 628). As you may have anticipated, a calculation of statistical significance was then done, allowing the researchers to conclude that their hypothesis was supported: if the stem of the verb ends in a complex consonant coda, these young children are less likely to produce the inflectional third person singular –*s*, so there may be a phonological, as well as syntactic, developmental explanation.

Al-Ali (2006) drew on previous studies to identify, as frameworks to use for his analysis of job application letters, move structure analysis and politeness theory (C.7.2.2). He began by identifying the typical components of texts in this genre, and then 'coded the component moves in each of the letters and assigned a function to each text segment', using as clues 'content, text divisions [and] explicit linguistic clues' (p. 126). This process is inevitably rather subjective, and one way to mitigate that criticism is to involve someone else in categorising the same data (see B3.3 on inter-rater reliability). Al-Ali's use of this process is described as follows:

To validate my coding of the move components contained in each letter, 30 letters, selected randomly from the corpus, were then coded by two other trained linguist assistants for the component moves identified earlier. The coders worked independently and coded all moves in each of the 30 letters of application. On a check of intercoder reliability, there was an 86% agreement rate in identifying the constituent moves of the 30 letters coded by the researcher, and the other two raters. For items on which there was disagreement, the coders together with the researcher reviewed the coding guidelines and recoded the data until they came to a consensus.

(Al-Ali 2006: 126)

Al-Ali also identified and coded instances of both negative and positive politeness strategies in his data, and he includes examples of the sub-categories to which he assigned each one – such as 'showing interest' in the job and 'offering a contribution or benefit'.

The strategy of checking interpretations among several analysts was also used by Marshall and Goldbart (C.7.2.3). They made use of one of the software packages developed to support interpretive research, and these are a resource you may want to investigate at some stage if you do larger projects of this kind. Without these, however, it is still possible to adopt the same kind of procedure, which entailed, in this example as with the previous example, marking 'meaningful segments of the transcripts . . . according to the issues(s) they addressed' (p. 83). From this stage – and this is easier with a computer – recurring themes were grouped together, before developing, at the third stage, 'the thematic networks', each of which was illustrated with quotes from the data: 'The structure consisted of Basic Themes which were grouped into more abstract Organizing Themes. In turn, the Organizing Themes were grouped together to reflect super-ordinate Global Themes, each of which reflected a major issue in the transcripts' (p. 83).

The team of researchers then presented their provisional analysis to a workshop of people with an interest in this subject, and 'invited the audience to consider alternative explanations of the data' (p. 84). This is not so practical for lone undergraduate researchers, but it may be possible to involve others in the analysis of your data in some way – and if not, it illustrates the advantages of presenting your data when you submit your project for analysis.

Two of these examples involved both qualitative and quantitative interpretations of data: once patterns have been identified, the data is explained further by establishing which things occur more frequently than others and, in one case, statistical procedures were used to establish a correlation (complex consonant contexts being strongly associated with the omission of inflecting –s).

One final word of warning, though, about applying statistical operations based on assumptions about random distributions to authentic linguistic data: neither people nor language tend to be distributed randomly. The usual illustration in basic statistics of outcomes attributable to chance is of repeated tosses of a coin or throwing of a dice. However, as Kilgarriff (2005: 263) points out, 'Language users never choose words randomly, and language is essentially non-random'. Some branches of language research, and corpus linguistics in particular, as well as other social science disciplines, are actively engaged in exploring ways of identifying appropriate quantitative operations for the complex inter-relationships that characterise people and the language they use. If you find any of this intriguing, then I hope you will consider extending your studies and perhaps becoming involved in these developments. Unfortunately, I do not have the space here to elaborate on this controversial but exciting dimension of researching English Language.

WRITING UP YOUR PROJECT

> To use Hyland's (2001: 560) metaphor, while the text is a shared journey of exploration for both reader and writer, it is always the writer who is leading the expedition.
>
> (Harwood 2005: 348)

In A8 I suggest various sources of information which can support you in knowing what kind of text you are aiming to produce. One of these is the journal articles which report research findings in your area of interest. As with many of the dimensions of researching English Language that are discussed in this book, applied linguists have considered the language of academic writing as a research topic in its own right. I am adding to that reflexivity in this unit, by using some studies *about* writing as examples *of* writing which is itself in the genre you are learning to contribute to. I have tried to demonstrate how you can read such texts 'with an eye to their genre rather than their content' (A8) but, because of their themes, the content should be of interest too.

C8.1 Making use of abstracts

The abstract of an academic article should indicate succinctly all the main components of the study. The first example given here is from Harwood (2005), whose research question is related to one explored in B8 about pronoun use in academic writing. His study assumes that academics will use the first person pronouns, but his interest is in the variation across disciplines, and in what the word *we* can mean. The second example, even more reflexively, uses as data the abstracts of research articles in the discipline of linguistics. To make it easier to address my questions, I have presented the abstracts side-by-side (Table C8.1.1), and have introduced line breaks which are not there in the original. I have placed these after sentences in Abstract 1, and have divided the text of Abstract 2 into units of roughly similar length.

 Activity

Read both abstracts, and then consider the following questions in relation to each one:

- ❏ What kind of information is included?
- ❏ In what order is the information presented?
- ❏ As you read around your subject, you will need to consider whether to read articles in full, and abstracts should give you enough information to make that decision. Does this one tell you enough to help with that?
- ❏ Is anything omitted from the abstract which you would expect to see there?
- ❏ What similarities are there in these two abstracts?
- ❏ What differences are there?
- ❏ Based on the abstracts, can you draft a list of headings likely to be used in each article?

Table C8.1.1 A comparison of two abstracts from published research articles

Abstract 1 Harwood (2005: 343)	*Abstract 2 Lorés (2004: 280)*
This paper is a qualitative and quantitative corpus-based study of how academic writers use the personal pronouns *I* and inclusive and exclusive *we*.	This paper reports an analysis of research article (RA) abstracts from linguistics journals from two related angles: rhetorical organisation and thematic structure.
Using a multidisciplinary corpus comprising of journal research articles (RAs) from the fields of Business and Management, Computing Science, Economics, and Physics, I present data extracts which reveal how *I* and *we* can help writers create a sense of newsworthiness and novelty about their work, showing how they are plugging disciplinary knowledge gaps.	Based on a small-scale study it reveals two major types of rhetorical organisation, here called the IMRD type and the CARS type.
Inclusive pronouns can act as positive politeness devices by describing and/or critiquing common disciplinary practices, and elaborating arguments on behalf of the community.	
They can also organise the text for the reader, and highlight the current problems and subject areas which preoccupy the field.	
The quantitative analysis reveals that while all instances of *we* in the Business and Management articles and all but one of the instances of *we* in the Economics articles are inclusive, only a third of the instances in the Computing articles and under 10 per cent of the instances in the Physics articles are inclusive.	When thematic analysis, in terms of thematic progression and method of thematic development, is applied to the two types of structure, distinct patterns of thematic distribution and choice are revealed, showing that the study of thematisation can shed light on the complex profile of the RA abstract and contribute towards the understanding and explicit description of these texts.
The study ends with a brief discussion of what a few English for Academic Purposes (EAP) textbooks tell students about inclusive and exclusive pronouns, and offers some suggestions for EAP classroom activities.	Moreover, the approach taken in this study shows potential for further research and pedagogic applications.

Commentary

To some extent, your answers to my questions will indicate as much about you as they do about the texts: if meanings are co-constructed by readers and writers, in varied contexts of reading, then factors such as your previous knowledge of, and interest in, the subject of the studies will influence your interpretations. More objectively, we can note that both abstracts include a succinct summary of the whole article, including the findings; this is a key difference between the 'abstract' and the 'introduction' in reports of research studies. Abstract 1 is longer than Abstract 2, which may reflect the constraints of the different journals in which each one appeared. Abstract 1 includes more detail about the data and the analysis, whereas Abstract 2 introduces some labels for the analytical categories used which are not fully explained at this stage. Both abstracts mention in their final sections that the article concludes in a more speculative vein ('suggestions' (1), 'potential' (2)) and with reference to applications of the research ('classroom' (1), 'pedagogic' (2)).

C8.2 Relating abstracts to whole texts

In most word-processing packages there are facilities to view writing in draft in different ways, and the online view of articles can also be manipulated. This is because it is recognised that both readers and writers need to 'zoom' in and out of the texts they are engaging with, sometimes attending to the minutiae of individual punctuation marks, and sometimes needing to get a sense of the whole picture. One program often used to read downloaded articles from online sources, Adobe Reader, has been used here to illustrate the outline of the article from which Abstract 2 is taken. It appears here as a kind of tree, with major themes forming the first tier of 'branches', while some of these have their own branches in turn (Figure C8.2.1).

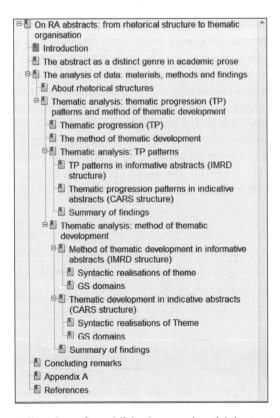

Figure C8.2.1 An outline view of a published research article's structure

You may find it useful as you write your own dissertation to keep updating versions of both an abstract and an outline as integral parts of the writing process. Move between writing the text itself and making adjustments to these two kinds of summary, especially when you're feeling a bit lost and 'unable to see the wood for the trees'. Even if you are not required to submit an abstract, and the outline is something no one else sees, both of these can be a great help in maintaining your sense of control over the writing process.

C8.3 Components of the text

In A8, I include an example of the kind of advice students are typically given about what to include in an undergraduate dissertation. As noted there, such advice is usually tempered with the recognition that different kinds of research project will be written up in different ways. Nevertheless, there are some predictable patterns to the ways in which projects and dissertations are deemed successful. Students who achieve lower grades are likely to be criticised for: not demonstrating that they are familiar with the literature about their topic and how it can be researched; devising research questions which are too general, vague or practically unanswerable; failing to explain how they did their analysis; losing track of the investigation and presenting results which seem unconnected to what they claim to be researching; submitting work which is hard to read because of confusing syntax and/or lots of typographical errors. Conversely, the highest marks go to work which has obviously engaged the writer over a period of time, and which clearly and effectively answers one or more well-devised questions, related to previous research, using defensible methods.

In the final section of this unit, I include some examples from students' work illustrating some specific choices they made about the contents and organisation of their final texts (Table C8.3.1). The extracts are limited to short pieces which are relatively accessible to readers who are not familiar with the full texts, and so I have usually used introductory sections; alternative selections would have illustrated different features, of course. My comments distinguish between the content and the style of the writing, each of which needs careful and repeated attention as you work towards your final draft.

Activity

> Read through the extracts and comments on style in Table C8.3.1, and consider how far you agree with my observations. What else would you comment on in respect of each extract?

Table C8.3.1 Annotated extracts from some students' dissertations *(on pp. 153–4)*

Topic	Section	Extract	Comments on content	Comments on style
The effects of a particular kind of teaching on children's spelling	Introduction	Spelling is a contentious issue both in and out of education. Many adults struggle with it at one time or another and the problem for learners is even greater. Despite causing almost universal confusion, it does carry a great deal of prestige. This study aims to look at two different teaching methods (practising and learning rules) associated with spelling in the primary classroom in an attempt to demonstrate their successes and failures.	This opening section makes immediately clear to the reader what the study is about, while at the same time implying that this area of research is important. The fourth sentence encapsulates very neatly what kind of research was done.	I would prefer 'In this study I investigated' to 'This study aims to look at', since the latter suggests that the aims may not have been met; the same is true of 'in an attempt to'. It's difficult to strike a balance between claiming too much and seeming unsure of yourself. Try reading different versions of parts of your writing aloud, including to other people – or get them to read your text aloud to you.
Gender differences in young people's use of text messaging	Literature review (introduction)	This section covers aspects of the literature concerning computer-mediated communication (CMC) as it has the asynchronous qualities of text messaging and the same 'face'-saving features that are gained from non face-to-face interaction. It also looks at the literature concerning language and identity in terms of gender and, more broadly, identities created through the mobile phone itself. The review of the literature then goes on to examine the youth culture of SMS, uncovering the mobile phone's place in everyday life and its portrayal in the mass media. The final area reviews literature concerning gender differences in spoken discourse and the stereotypes associated with gender.	The writer conveys a sense of control over the different kinds of previous research relevant to her own study. It is clear that she has identified and classified several areas of literature, and she justifies their inclusion in her review.	I find the first sentence a little difficult to process, and would suggest 'fronting' the justification for inclusion, which begins 'as it has'. Sometimes, in the process of redrafting, you realise that you are making too many points in one sentence. My suggestion would be: 'Text messaging has several features in common with computer-mediated communication (CMC). These include its asynchronous nature, and its potential, like other non-face-to-face interactions, to mitigate face threats. This review therefore presents relevant findings from the literature on CMC'. I think that 'The final area reviews . . .' may be a redraft involving 'area' and 'review', as it's not the 'area' that's presenting the 'review'!
Children's SLA at a school	Method (introduction)	The interviews were designed to gather information about the school's approach to SLA. The staff questionnaire then intended to gauge how teaching staff put this approach into practice and their evaluation of the methods. Gathering parental opinions of the school's methods with EAL [English as an Additional Language] students was done with the parent questionnaire.	This is another very clear indication for the reader of the different research instruments used in the project. More detail is subsequently provided about each one, and the actual questionnaires and interview schedules are included as appendices.	I have a minor quibble with 'The staff questionnaire intended to gauge . . .', because it is people who have intentions, while texts, such as questionnaires, do not. I would suggest, therefore, 'The staff questionnaire was intended to gauge . . .'. (The passive voice here, of course, leaves the reader to infer that it was the writer who held this 'intention', see B8.)

Topic	Section	Extract	Comments on content	Comments on style
The discourse of charity appeal texts	Analytical method	The analysis was concerned with the way in which the distinctive clausal features in this discourse presented a picture of the social situation's reality, and revealed a mixing of genres, through which the reader is informed and persuaded to donate to the charity. The results of the functional analysis were tabulated into a tally chart, illustrating the number of counts of each process in the main and the subordinate clauses separately.	Here, the writer summarises her approach to the analysis of the texts which constitute her data. She used a Hallidayan, functional approach to clause analysis, which generated some quantitative results, as she explains. She later describes how raw frequencies were converted to percentages, to facilitate comparisons.	The first sentence is quite long, and I would suggest breaking it down. Three important ideas are referred to here, and each one warrants attention and therefore, potentially, a separate sentence: (1) clause-level analysis; (2) genres; (3) the functions of informing and persuading. I would also reduce the phrase 'the social situation's reality' to 'the social situation'.
Lexical erosion in a regional dialect	Results	Tables 1 and 2 immediately indicate a strong discrepancy in knowledge and use of dialect terms between the age ranges. Of the 15 dialect terms included in questions 4 to 7, seven were known and understood by all the participants aged 60 or over. In stark contrast, just three terms were understood by every member of the other two age groups, an immediate indication of lexical erosion in the dialect.	While the actual detailed results are available in an appendix, this summary of some key findings highlights the most salient figures. The text goes on to explain which terms were universally familiar, and which were differentially understood by speakers of different ages.	There is a slight sense in this account of the writer's evaluation of her findings: note the use of 'immediate(ly)' (twice), 'strong' and 'stark', and I would counsel a little more detachment at this stage. I would also delay the claim about 'indication of lexical erosion' until a later point in the text, when more evidence has been presented.
Differences between second language learning in two contexts	Conclusion	In this study, the German subjects showed higher levels of both instrumental and integrative motivation and more positive attitudes towards the L2 community. Although the German subjects performed on the psycholinguistic tests in ways that could indicate that their L2 is more independent of their L1 than the English subjects, these differences were not statistically significant.	Several key points are condensed into this concise summary, demonstrating the writer's ability to stand back from the detailed evidence and analysis presented in earlier sections and identify the main things which she found out. These points should (and did) mirror quite precisely the questions she identified at the beginning of the dissertation. She also demonstrates her awareness of the technical meaning of 'significant'.	The points are clearly expressed, and the introductory 'in this study' reminds the reader that the claims are about these particular people and not to be generalised too widely. As I read this passage, I would expect 'than the English subjects' to complete the two comparatives 'higher' and 'more positive', but the meaning is clear in context. I would also break the final sentence into two, removing 'although' and beginning a new sentence with 'However . . .'.

LOOKING BACK, LOOKING AHEAD

> If [Applied Linguistics] is to fulfil its aspirations, if it is to be listened to, and if it is to intervene successfully in the many urgent language related problems of the modern world, then it must . . . have a voice of its own. [This voice] will be . . . an emergent, autonomous, dynamic, exciting and influential voice – one which can speak authoritatively, to and about the abstract formulations and findings of linguistics, and the experience of language use which dominates all of our lives.
>
> (Cook 2003: 78–9)

In writing this book, I have been obliged to conform to a number of conventions and constraints – as you must do when writing your dissertation. This book is, among other things, a commodity: the time and labour of the author and the many other people who contribute to its publication is one economic cost, as are the physical materials of which it is made, and as are the storage, distribution and display in the shops and websites where it is sold. Because of these costs, there is a strict limit imposed on how much material I could include (although new technologies allow for the exchange of virtual material via the internet at less expense). Your dissertation is similarly constrained by the realities of your time and that of your assessors, as well as by a word limit, linked to notions of fairness and equity among the cohort of students whose work will be assessed alongside yours. My publishers have the resources of copy-editors and proof-readers, as well as others with expertise in the presentation of writing for publication, whereas you must attend to all these aspects yourself. Like you, however, I am obliged to abide by extensive sets of conventions in my choice of vocabulary, grammatical constructions and punctuation, as well as the house style of my publishers and this series of books.

In all these ways, both students and academics are constrained by the norms of the community which has established, and continues to regulate, the practice of conducting and writing about research in English Language. These are some of the realities of structured social relations. Another example of such relations is that, at the time of writing, new graduates in the UK are facing much stiffer competition for jobs than they were just a few years ago, in the wake of a global financial crisis. This context – like the contexts mentioned above, in which books are written, produced and marketed – is not of any individual's making, but it affects people's life chances. Likewise, the numbers of places available for postgraduate study, and the subjects prioritised for funding, will be affected by changing policies and priorities over which any one of us has only very little influence. Some work in our favour – they are 'enablements' – while others are 'constraints', limiting what we can hope to achieve. And some people's aspirations are more enabled than others. The following statistics, all taken from a report published by UNESCO in 2008 (EFA 2008), illustrate the disparities between people able to take advantage of education and people who cannot. 'In 2006, some 75 million children, 55% girls, were not in school' (p. 4). 'An estimated 776 million adults – or 16% of the world's adult population – lack basic literacy skills. About two-thirds are women'

(p. 5). 'Global wealth inequalities are mirrored by inequalities in education spending. In 2004, North America and Western Europe alone accounted for 55% of the world's spending on education but only 10% of the population aged 5 to 25' (p. 6).

These economic and political inequalities are real: they cannot be reduced to mere discursive constructions. When people do have access to education, they benefit from its enablements, and if we are at all engaged in research, we have the opportunity to make a small contribution to the production and dissemination of knowledge. I want to finish this book with some brief reflections on what I see as the responsibilities that that opportunity brings.

The study of practically everything in the social world involves language. Various scholars in our discipline have investigated the features of political discourse, for example, and the way it shapes people's perceptions of their experiences – including the economy, migration and settlement, what it means to be a 'good' parent, and so on. Such scholarship cannot be 'pure', nor untainted by: the contexts within which it is produced; the traditions and conventions of scholarly writing; and the fact that it is reported, and to a large extent conducted, through the very medium it investigates – language. Nevertheless, all of us, at whatever level of engagement – whether at a government briefing, an academic conference, or in a debate with friends – have a responsibility to strive to make a contribution to the production and dissemination of knowledge which is defensible when measured against the standards of serious academic endeavour. I have tried in this book to describe and exemplify these expectations. They include expectations about:

- the obligation to familiarise yourself with existing knowledge about your topic, while reading critically as well as extensively,
- being clear about what you hope to find out, recognising that your questions may develop as you do the study,
- identifying the properties of your Xs and Ys, including the recognition that both people and language have characteristics that distinguish them from other kinds of things in the world,
- designing a study whose methods are practical and theoretically appropriate both for your questions and for the Xs and Ys you are investigating; and recognising that 'methodology' entails understanding these choices and what lies behind them,
- knowing how to look for patterns in your data, and how to provide a warrant for the claims you make about it, and
- reporting your findings about your project honestly; making use of the writing conventions associated with the discipline while making your own contribution.

The philosopher Karl Popper suggested that knowledge exists in a space he called 'world 3' – 'the world of products of the human mind' (Popper 1994: 24). Education is largely about coming to know world 3, and doing research is partly about making a contribution to that world, albeit necessarily a tiny one. We are all privileged to have the opportunity to take what we do from our educational opportunities; as researchers, we have the opportunity to give something back. Yet, as Popper recognises, 'we can get more out of world 3 than we ourselves can ever put into it. There is a give and take between ourselves and world 3 in which we take more than we ever give' (Popper 1994: 31).

Section D

EXTENSION

READINGS IN RESEARCHING ENGLISH LANGUAGE

D1 **THE ORIGINS OF SOME RESEARCH PROJECTS IN ENGLISH LANGUAGE**

The readings in this section each give us insights into the processes by which research develops from initial ideas into substantial projects. I have chosen the extracts because they can help to make the link between the novice researcher setting out to design their first extended independent study and the 'big names' – established scholars whose books and articles you may have come across, but whose personal biographies probably haven't caused you much concern. You and they are linked in what seems to be a one-way connection: they have carried out significant research and written about it, while you occupy the position of relatively passive consumer, reading what they have published. However, it is quite likely that at least some of the readers of the present book will go on in due course to be researchers, producing the writing that the next generation of students will read. This will be a small minority, of course. Most readers of this book will probably go into entirely different careers, and may never write for publication. As I note throughout strand 1, however, you will take with you the knowledge you have gained about the topics you have researched, and the skills you have gained in identifying relevant material to read, devising appropriate methods for research, analysing evidence and documenting the whole process.

In addition to this, though, you are linked with these eminent scholars in other ways too. Like you, they had to learn the conventions and expectations of doing academic work. Like you, they may have felt constrained at times by these conventions, and wanted to push the boundaries, or at least question why academic traditions have come to take the forms they have. And like you, they did not produce their work in a vacuum. There is no absolute difference between the revered professor preparing to submit his or her hundredth article to a prestigious journal and you scratching your head about where to begin with the draft of chapter 1 of your dissertation. In some ways – though with many differences, of course – you are both members of a 'community of practice' which involves making use of personal experience and interest in particular ways, following approaches to doing so that make a distinction between the knowledge producer – the researcher – and the knowledge produced – the research. As the philosopher, Karl Popper, conceptualised this, the products of human thought and observation occupy a virtual world – the world of ideas – from which we can all learn, and to which we can all, potentially, contribute (see C9).

As the following extracts show, each of these contributors to the world of knowledge about the English language has had a unique biography, and all have been motivated to find out more about particular things. As you read them, see whether you can make connections between the thinking you have done so far about your own research project and the trajectories outlined here of these researchers' interests, motives and contributions to knowledge.

D1.1 John McH. Sinclair and corpus linguistics

→ "real word" texts. (handwritten)

The first extract is by John McH. Sinclair, who was one of the founding fathers of corpus linguistics. Like all such eminent scholars, however, he was once an undergraduate, and required to find research topics, as you have to do. His first degree was in English Language and Literature, at the University of Edinburgh, and he did national service before embarking on a research career. He produced an extensive range of research publications, and there have been special issues of academic journals discussing his work. Sinclair himself contributed the preface to one of these, and he begins by acknowledging the collaborative nature of the research enterprise. He notes that, when based in the English department at the University of Birmingham, '[a]lmost all the work I did there was teamwork . . . I was frequently spokesperson for a whole research group, or I found myself relying on current work of colleagues and senior students, some of whom were surprised to find themselves referred to with academic solemnity'. Although it is unusual, it is not unheard of for the work students produce in their dissertations, at postgraduate and sometimes even undergraduate level, to be recognised as worthy of publication – and everyone has to start somewhere. In what follows, Sinclair reflects on the insights he developed about the nature of language, and how these motivated him to carve out an original and highly significant avenue of research.

John McH. Sinclair (2007) Preface, *International Journal of Corpus Linguistics* 12 (2), pp. 155–7

John McH. Sinclair

[T]here are underlying themes that run through several [of the] papers [in the collection]; I would like to pick out a few of these and comment briefly on them. One is obvious – that I have placed text more and more centrally during my career and paid ever-increasing attention to it. As a young scholar I had assumed without checking that all linguists spent all their time examining text, and I became more and more disillusioned as the scales fell from my eyes. Now I have very little time for any work, including my own backlist, which is not rooted in the actual patterns of occurrence of words in text.

Another increasingly recurrent theme is meaning. Again I had assumed that the whole point of linguistic investigation was to discover the detailed relationship between the textual patterns and the meaning that they created, or showed, or catalysed. I worked for many years under the illusion that all the valuable meanings in sentences were conjured up by the syntax, and it took some years more before I realised that steps towards formalism in language description are steps away from meaning.

Because of remarks like the above, I am sometimes accused of carrying out a one-man crusade against grammar. I hope I am not guilty, because my aim is to free grammar from the burdens that have been placed upon it during the period when it was the only observable kind of meaningful patterning. In those days the only thing that scholars could do with the words was to put them in a long list and despatch them to lexicography; semantics, the study of meaning, was obliged to develop in a completely abstract arena, not in any way accountable to language text.

The papers of mine that are reviewed here show various attempts at coming to grips with corpora. The advent of the corpus has been the most thrilling development in language study during my career, and much of my work has been in celebration of this bountiful resource. A recurrent theme in the papers is the attitude I have to corpus evidence; the corpus has things to tell me, and I try to work out where it is heading. I have been surprised at the confidence of so many scholars, who seem to think that they have something to tell the corpus. While my position always runs the risk of appearing naïve, of reinventing the wheel or stating the obvious, I feel that I am on safer ground.

The fact that the theories available to me did not alert me at all to the strongly recurrent patterns found in a corpus nor explained them when they emerged caused me to view theories with increasing suspicion. I did not assume that they were necessarily all wrong or even just a little wrong, but that they needed some revision, some reorientation to evidence of which their authors could not have been aware when the theories were propounded. It is most unlikely that the best brains in linguistics have been hoodwinked by their intuitions for centuries; more likely that their positions just need some updating. However, I see it as a danger sign that very little if any updating is taking place at a theoretical level. There are encouraging signs from the coal face (where text miners work, no doubt) that the first and strongest messages from corpus research are gradually being rephrased and naturalised within adjacent disciplines, but this has not yet carried through to the more abstract realms.

I hope that despite recurrent themes like the above there has been enough variety in the approaches and the research targets for eclecticism to be a feature of my work and that of my colleagues in Birmingham. The formation of 'schools' of linguistics is a constant danger, and one that I have been at pains to avoid, neither instituting one nor joining any. They relieve members from thinking for themselves, passing the burden up to the guru. Worse, they corral members inside a protective coating, so that uncomfortable ideas can be either ignored, or sanitised before circulation, or percolated through a fine mesh. I am pleased to see that the variety of approaches shown in these papers, the lack of any party line, makes it clear that the 'Birmingham School' is still a phantom. The range of opinion expressed here is a sign of an extremely healthy academic environment.

D1.2 Fischer and sign languages

The following extract was originally published in the context of a *festschrift* for two eminent American scholars. A *festschrift* is an edited collection of articles written by experts in a particular field, partly in order to demonstrate the contribution made to an area of knowledge by the individual(s) whose work is celebrated. The author of this extract, Susan Fischer, uses her chapter in the collection to pay tribute to these two pioneering researchers in the field of sign languages. Another contributor to the *festschrift* (Battison 2000: 5) explains how significant their contribution has been:

> For those who work intimately with sign languages or Deaf culture, it is self-evident that sign languages are autonomous languages with their own linguistic principles. But this has not always been the case: The development of this idea owes much to the seminal contributions of Ursula Bellugi-Klima and Edward Klima, as well as to those they inspired and guided through the years.

Fischer remembers the very beginnings of her academic career, and reflects on why she decided to find out more about the links between the general linguistics with which she was already familiar and the particular issues raised by the signed languages used by deaf people.

Susan D. Fischer (2000) More than just handwaving: the mutual contributions of sign language and linguistics, in K. Emmorey and H. Lane (eds) *The Signs of Language Revisited: an anthology to honor Ursula Bellugi and Edward Klima.* Mahwah, New Jersey: Lawrence Erlbaum Associates

Susan D. Fischer

Preface

The academic year 1965/66 was a momentous one for me. I started protesting against the war in Vietnam, I got my first job as a linguist, I saw Noam Chomsky for the first time, and I was first introduced to the work of Ursula Bellugi. In an otherwise execrable psycholinguistics course, she gave a guest lecture about her work on language acquisition that truly excited and inspired me. *This* was what psycholinguistics should be about! Little did I imagine then as a lowly undergraduate that 5 years later I would have the opportunity to work with her as a fellow pioneer in the field of sign language studies. From the beginning of my 3 years in her laboratory (1970–1974), I was fascinated by such questions as the effects of channel on language structure, the commonalities between signed and spoken languages, and what sign language structure can tell us about language in general. The fact that that interest has persisted for the 25 years since I left serves as a tribute to the lasting influence Bellugi's (and Klima's) ways of thinking have had on me and on the field. I am therefore grateful to Ursula Bellugi for providing me with a chance to get in on the ground floor of an exciting new field of research and to Ed Klima for spurring me on to gain recognition for the field of sign language study as a legitimate area of linguistics.

Introduction, history, and background

It is a universally acknowledged truth that a young person in possession of an intact mind must be in want of a language (with apologies to Jane Austen). If that person happens to be Deaf, the language is likely to be a language conveyed by gesture. Virtually any time Deaf people form a community, even a community of two, some kind of gestural system will develop. If the community has historical continuity, as in the case of a school or a Deaf family, that gestural system will evolve into a language, that is, a sign language. The persistence of sign languages in the world, even in the face of well-meaning but misguided attempts at repression and elimination, stands as a tribute to the robustness of the language faculty and the human need to communicate.

As I have come to know more about sign language, I have gained a great deal of respect for American Sign Language (ASL) in particular, and for sign languages in general. The past 25 years have seen a burgeoning of published research on the structure of an ever-increasing number of sign languages. The study of these languages has much to teach linguists, just as the field of linguistics has much to teach students of sign languages. I am very happy that thanks to our efforts, fewer and fewer people hold the standard – often mutually contradictory –misconceptions about sign languages, such as the notion that sign languages are not languages and are degenerate forms of spoken

**Susan D.
Fischer**

languages, or that they are iconic and primitive. Thanks to those years of research, we know that sign languages are able to express just as much and have grammars just as complicated (and in similar ways, although perhaps not always with similar means) and just as constrained as those of spoken languages.

The study of sign language first fascinated me because although it was (and is) communicated in a different channel, it was unmistakably language and therefore a worthy subject for a linguist to study. I continue to be fascinated with it for what it can tell us about language and the human mind.

D1.3 Carter and creativity

In this third reading in strand 1, Ronald Carter, a researcher who is well established in a number of fields in Applied Linguistics (including the grammar of spoken language, language education policy and many aspects of language learning and teaching), introduces a book that represents another strand of his research by recounting some personal experiences that intrigued him.

**Ronald
Carter**

Ronald Carter (2004) *Language and Creativity: the art of common talk*, London: Routledge, pp. 1–6

Introduction

The genesis of the book
In the Beginning was the Word

Starting points for books can often be accidental. It was several years ago now when the starting point for this book was found, somewhat unpropitiously, one dark and slightly misty autumnal morning as I was making my trolley-pushing way towards the check-in of a local regional airport. My eye was caught by a single line of red and blue letters spread out across a large glass-fronted placard. They were arrayed in a straight line against a plain white background. The letters were the letters of the alphabet. Momentarily intrigued by the sight of the alphabet occurring in this form and in this context, I looked more closely, not at first noticing that one of the letters was missing and that its absence was accentuated by a gap between the letter *p* and the letter *r*, more or less as follows:

abcdefghijklmnop rstuvwxyz

Closer inspection revealed, of course, that the placard was an advertisement for an airline which counted among the proclaimed benefits of travelling business class the fact that there were no 'queues' at its check-in desk and that check-in for passengers with hand luggage only could be undertaken automatically by a machine.

Several minutes later when I was sitting in the departures lounge my thoughts were disturbed by the person next to me, a young Irishman who was holding a child (a little girl about 18 months of age) in his arms and moving her rhythmically back and forth while gazing intently into her eyes and occasionally rubbing his nose against hers. He was softly singing nursery rhymes which I had long forgotten having sung to my own children but which were soon recalled almost verbatim with a surprising immediacy.

> Hickory, dickory dock
> The mouse ran up the clock
> The clock struck one
> The mouse ran down
> Hickory, dickory dock

> Diddle, diddle dumpling my son John
> Went to bed with his trousers on
> One shoe off and one shoe on
> Diddle, diddle dumpling my son John.

Later that same day I found myself in a seminar discussing with a group of teachers some differences between spoken and written English, and during the course of the discussion I put the following short conversational exchange (extracted from a computer-based corpus which I had been compiling) onto a projector in order for us to examine some of the ways in which spoken discourses utilise lexical vagueness ('a bob or two', 'things', 'and stuff', 'and things'). Almost involuntarily I becam e distracted by the repetition of the word 'bob/Bob', a feature of this text to which I had not previously paid any particular attention:

[Three students in Bristol are talking about the landlord of a mutual friend]
- A: Yes, he must have a bob or two.
- B: Whatever he does he makes money out of it, just like that.
- C: Bob's your uncle.
- B: He's quite a lot of money erm tied up in property and things. He's got a finger in all kinds of pies and houses and stuff. A couple in Bristol, one in Clevedon I think.

I began to consider why the word 'bob' was repeated, why there appeared to be no straightforward semantic connection between the two 'bobs', what kinds of attitudes and feelings may have been aroused for the speakers by the particular choice of echo and just how conscious or otherwise such a choice might be.

These three seemingly unconnected instances are provoking and I have since then begun increasingly to puzzle over them and to explore the parallels and points of connection between them.

[. . .]

In exploring these questions further I have become more engaged by examples 2 and 3 than by example 1.

[. . .]

In undertaking these explorations I have been fortunate to have access to a corpus of spoken English, the CANCODE corpus (the Cambridge and Nottingham Corpus of Discourse in English), which is one of the largest of its type in the world. [. . .] The

Ronald Carter

main purpose of its compilation has been to provide a research resource from which better understandings of the differences between spoken and written English could be obtained in order to develop better-grounded materials for the teaching of English grammar and vocabulary. Yet, as this work has progressed, one salient and striking feature of the corpus samples appearing daily on my computer screen has been the frequency with which examples similar to that of text 3 are observed.

Issues to consider

❑ What are the experiences in their own biographies that led each of the researchers represented here to focus on the particular topics that became central to their research? How far are these peculiar to the times and circumstances in which they happened to find themselves, and what, if any, are the implications for you, working when and where you do?

❑ From what is written by or about these researchers in the extracts included here, what were the established ways of thinking about language that they wanted (a) to explore further and/or (b) to challenge and invite people to think about differently? What are the links between these and the factors you identified in response to the questions in the previous paragraph?

❑ What are the indications in each of these extracts that research is rarely, if ever, reducible to the work of isolated individuals? What are the implications of this for the enterprise you are engaged in, of submitting a dissertation to be assessed as evidence of your sole achievement?

❑ I said above that it is part of the tradition that you and I have both inherited to try to separate the researcher from the research. Do you agree with this as a goal? If it is desirable, is it possible? What light do these readings shed on this issue?

D2   ## REVIEWING PREVIOUS ENGLISH LANGUAGE LITERATURE FOR RESEARCH

The readings in this section represent various approaches to presenting surveys of existing literature about topics in English Language research. The way this is done is likely to vary in relation to the specific topic, the kind of publication in which the review appears, the overall aims of the article or chapter and, to some extent, the disciplinary background of the authors. That is to say, since 'English Language' research is done by people in the social, human and natural sciences, the expectations of both research methods and literature reviews may vary quite widely. Part of the challenge for you as reader and writer of a literature review is to recognise what is appropriate for your particular purposes. This is connected with the discussions of communities of practice and of criticality in other units, and so the final reading I have chosen is not an example of a literature review, but a discussion of the much wider issues that are raised if we consider what it means to learn different kinds of literacy. The present book is a text that has arisen from a particular kind of pedagogical context, and it privileges particular kinds of learning. I should not have written the book if I did not share many of the values associated with this kind of academic work – but I also believe that it is important to remain critical and open to persuasion about new kinds of evidence and argument.

D2.1 A survey review of Conversation Analysis and its relevance to Applied Linguistics

Reading D2.1 represents one kind of literature review, namely that which appears periodically in certain types of journal or edited volumes of an encyclopaedic kind, where experts in a particular field are commissioned to compile an overview of other publications. This may be intended to give busy readers a digest of recent studies or, as in this case, it can serve to draw out the links between complementary areas of research. Here the authors set out to explain how the quite specific traditions of Conversation Analysis may be of interest to applied linguists. Many researchers identify with both these approaches to research in English Language, but the main audience for this journal, the *Annual Review of Applied Linguistics*, is people who are interested in Applied Linguistics, particularly language teaching, but are perhaps less familiar with Conversation Analysis, abbreviated to 'CA'. Like many of the other examples of literature reviews considered in this strand, they begin by delimiting the field of what they include in their survey. The extracts provided here are those most relevant to the theme of reviewing relevant literature; I have omitted some of the explanatory discussions about CA and Applied Linguistics.

Emanuel Schegloff, Irene Koshik, Sally Jacoby and David Olsher (2002) Conversation analysis and applied linguistics, *Annual Review of Applied Linguistics* 22, pp. 3–31

Schegloff, Koshik, Jacoby and Olsher

1. Conversation analysis and applied linguistics

[W]herever humans engage in talk in interaction, or in interaction in which talk can spontaneously "break out," there will be an orientation by the participants to the practices of talking in interaction. Understanding interaction in such settings can be enhanced by the findings of conversation analysis, and by the research practices underlying those findings. This is to say that "CA" refers to not only a corpus of findings and accounts of talk-in-interaction, but also—perhaps preeminently—to a method of inquiry, one addressed to distinctive data and embodying a distinctive research stance. [. . .]

[The sections that follow begin by sketching areas of conversation analytic work and some of their prime bibliographical resources and then suggest areas of potential intersection with applied linguistics.]

Turn-Taking

The practices of turn-taking organize distribution of opportunities to talk among parties to interaction and constrain the size of turns, by making the possible completion of a turn "transition-relevant." This interactive dimension—in which possible completion can (but need not always) occasion or trigger the start of a next turn by another—has consequences for speakers' construction of turns, and thereby for the form which turns (and their building blocks, "turn-constructional units") take. The main bibliographical resources in this area are Sacks, Schegloff, and Jefferson (1974) on turn-taking and Schegloff (1982, 1996a) on turn organization, but see also Sacks (1992), Jefferson (1973, 1984), Lerner (1991, 1996, in press) and Schegloff (1999a, 2000a, 2001a).

[. . .]

Repair

The practices of repair constitute the major (though not the sole) resource for parties to talk-in-interaction for displaying that they are dealing with trouble or problems in speaking, hearing, or understanding the talk. The main bibliographical resources are Schegloff, Jefferson and Sacks (1977); Schegloff (1979, 1987, 1992c, 1997a, 1997b, 2000b); and Jefferson (1974, 1987).

[. . .]

Word Selection

The final area of CA work which can be taken up here is that of word selection by speakers in the course of talk in interaction. There are two main lines of inquiry in this area. One examines the deployment of words or multiword usages by reference to other words or usages in the immediate environments of the talk—for example, for its "punning" relationship to that talk (Sacks 1973) or its sound relationship to the surrounding talk, which can, it appears, even induce mis-speakings (Jefferson 1996). The other line of work examines the practices for referring within semantic domains, such as person reference, place reference (Schegloff 1972), measurement formulations (Sacks 1989), etc. The main bibliographic resources are Sacks (1972a, 1972b, 1992 passim); Schegloff (1991, 1996b, 1997c, 1999b, 1999c, 2001a); and Sacks and Schegloff (1979).

[. . .]

Talk in Institutional Contexts

From the beginning, CA has included in its research data material from so-called institutional settings, such as a suicide prevention hotline (Sacks 1972a, 1992), group therapy sessions with adolescents (Sacks 1992), or calls to the police (Schegloff 1967, 1968), though the practices analyzed were, for the most part, not distinctively institutional ones. Subsequent work has examined talk in a variety of institutional or functionally specialized settings, such as legal settings (e.g., Atkinson and Drew 1979; Drew 1992; Manzo 1993; Maynard 1984), broadcast media (e.g., Clayman 1992; Clayman and Heritage in press; Greatbatch 1988, 1992; Heritage 1985; Heritage and Greatbatch 1991), business organizations (e.g., Atkinson, Cuff, and Lee 1978; Boden 1994), pedagogical settings (e.g., Koshik in press a, b; Lerner 1995; Mori 2002; Olsher 2001), research work groups (e.g., Jacoby 1998c, Jacoby and Gonzales 1991), medical settings (e.g., Heritage and Maynard in press; Heritage and Stivers 1999; Lutfey and

Maynard 1998; Robinson 1998), emergency dispatch centers (e.g., Whalen and Zimmerman 1987; Whalen, Zimmerman and Whalen 1988; Zimmerman 1984, 1992), airport operations rooms (e.g., Goodwin 1996; Goodwin and Goodwin 1996), and counseling sessions (e.g., Peräkylä 1993, 1995; He 1995, 1998b), among others.

The key point about talk in such "special" contexts is that one cannot properly understand how the parties come to talk as they do and to understand one another as they do without making reference to special features to which they are oriented—whether legal constraints as, for example, in the case of broadcast news interviews (cf. Heritage 1985; or Clayman 1988, 1992, on "neutralism"), or organizational and functional ones, as, for example, in some classroom settings, etc. Institutional talk has often been of special interest to applied linguists because of the bearing of such special contextual features on the special populations with which applied linguists are concerned—as, for example, with second language learners targeted at a special purpose usage, a special purpose which can impinge and have a bearing on how talk in such settings is organized.

[. . .]

Grammar and Interaction

Despite its origins in sociology, CA research has always had a keen interest in the lexical and grammatical details of everyday and institutional talk. From the syntactic typology of turn-constructional units (Sacks, Schegloff, and Jefferson 1974), through discussions of reference terms for persons (Sacks and Schegloff 1979; Schegloff, 1996b), lexical phenomena such as "and"-prefacing (Heritage and Sorjonen,1994), "okay" (Beach 1993, 1995), "uh-huh" (Schegloff 1982), "yeah" and "mm hm" (Jefferson 1984), "oh" (Heritage 1984a), and "actually" (Clift 1999, 2001), reported speech (Golato 2000, in press, a, b; Holt 1996), and the collaborative construction of one turn unit by more than one participant (Lerner 1991, 1996), CA treats grammar and lexical choices as sets of resources which participants deploy, monitor, interpret, and manipulate as they design turns, sort out turn-taking, co-construct utterances and sequences, manage intersubjectivity and (dis)agreement, accomplish actions, and negotiate interpersonal trajectories as real-time talk and interaction unfold (e.g. Ford 1993; Ford, Fox, and Thompson in press, Ford and Wagner 1996; Fox 1987; Goodwin 1979, 1986; Hayashi 1999; He and Tsoneva 1998; Heritage and Roth 1995; Ochs, Schegloff, and Thompson 1996; Schegloff 1972, 1979, 1990; Selting and Couper-Kuhlen in press). Recently, the number of studies has begun to expand and benefit not only from the insights of scholars rooted in CA studies of language use, but also from scholars rooted in linguistic traditions of analysis who have embraced a CA perspective, in some instances under the rubric "interactional linguistics." These scholars discuss not only ways in which 'grammar organizes social interaction', but also ways in which 'social interaction organizes grammar' and how grammar, itself, can be seen as a mode of social interaction (Schegloff, Ochs, and Thompson 1996).

[. . .]

D2.2 A review of literature as preparation for the presentation of a new study: talk about remembering in oral narratives

Reading D2.2 is extracted from a research article in which the author is presenting an analysis of some data of his own, from corpora of oral narratives. Norrick's concern here is how speakers signal both remembering and forgetting when they tell stories to others about episodes in their lives. He uses his data to argue for a particular interpretation of this aspect of oral narratives, and begins by demonstrating that he is familiar with the existing literature about it, pointing out that, while it has been discussed, it has not been a central focus of research before. There are two reviews of this literature, the first (D2.2.1) providing a summary overview, and the second (D2.2.2) exploring the details of these sources, insofar as they are relevant to Norrick's own topic.

Neal Norrick (2005) Interactional remembering in conversational narrative, *Journal of Pragmatics* 37, pp. 1819–44

Neal
Norrick

D2.2.1

Comments by storytellers on searching for names, words and details, reconstructing ages, dates and chronologies, as well as comments on clarity of memory have received little attention, except for casual comments in research on related areas like repair (Schegloff et al. 1977), clarification (Ochs 1984), forgetfulness as an interactional resource (Goodwin 1987), corrective exchanges (Norrick 1991), reference as process and negotiation (Cohen 1985; Clark and Wilkes-Gibbs 1990), and discursive psychology (Edwards and Middleton 1986; Middleton and Edwards 1990). In natural conversational settings, storytellers frequently evoke their own memory or that of other participants. Storytelling goes beyond the recapitulation of past experience, allowing tellers to revisit and re-evaluate past experience. Narration may even put the teller back in touch with specific names or details assumed forgotten. But all this talk about remembering has interactional functions as well as cognitive underpinnings, and these interactional functions assume center stage here.

   Research on tip-of-the-tongue states and related phenomena gives us a way to think about how speakers deal with difficulty in accessing names. James (1890: 251) speaks of 'a gap that is intensively active' in states of consciousness when we try to recall a forgotten name. Gaps in scripts (Schank and Abelson 1977) or cognitive models (Lakoff 1990) can account for tip-of-the-tongue states and related problems of remembering, as well as for the sudden clarity of memory tellers sometimes mention.
[. . .]

D2.2.2 Interactional remembering

Edwards and Middleton (1986), Middleton and Edwards (1990) and Middleton (1997) have demonstrated that remembering is an organized social activity contingent on the direction and purpose of talk in context. From their perspective of discursive psychology, they recognize the social-discursive basis of memory. They stress the importance

Neal
Norrick

of the interactional context and the joint nature of remembering. We interactively construct versions of past events as the basis for shared understanding. The ways we talk about uncertainty and remembering reflect the activity we are engaged in and our interactional goals. We recall events during talk, not just in talk explicitly focused on the past, but also in conversation with other goals. We do not simply remember and forget in a vacuum; we construct forgetfulness and remembering in various ways appropriate to particular discourse contexts. It is precisely the construction of forgetfulness and remembering in conversational storytelling and its interactional significance that lies at the center of interest here.

Goodwin (1987) investigates forgetfulness as a conversational resource. He recognizes that expressions of forgetfulness and remembering have interactional consequences. He examines passages of conversation in which participants display uncertainty not only to mark as problematic a particular name or detail, but also to invite participation. Goodwin stresses the interactional functions of talk about forgetfulness, but I will highlight the functions of talk about memory here. Goodwin focuses on the structures and trajectories of such interludes and their significance for the interaction. By contrast, I investigate passages of a parallel type in oral narrative, extending the purview to include expressions of particular clarity of recall, especially because these recur near expressions of forgetfulness. Cohen (1985) and Clark and Wilkes-Gibbs (1990) demonstrate that reference must be understood as process and negotiation between the speaker and hearer rather than as something the speaker accomplishes alone. Searches for appropriate names and descriptions as well as queries as to correct identification with various expressions of uptake all belong to the interactional establishment of reference. Talk about forgetfulness and remembering in personal narratives illustrates these functions and others. Norrick (2003) investigates displays of forgetfulness and remembering in conversation by comparison with psychological research on remembering and tip-of-the-tongue phenomena and recent work on metacognition. There I argued that the psychological notion of an 'active gap' in a cognitive model accounts for many of the internal cognitive phenomena surrounding forgetfulness and remembering. I showed how recent research in cognitive linguistics allows congruent description of related states like a feeling of knowing and a special clarity of memory. Still, more research is necessary to describe the interactional roles of displaying forgetfulness and memory in various conversational contexts, and the present paper will focus on this goal.

Tip-of-the-tongue phenomena and metacognition

As I argued in Norrick (2003), research on tip-of-the-tongue phenomena and metacognition gives us a way to think about how speakers talk about remembering and forgetfulness in conversation. Thinking on tip-of-the-tongue phenomena begins with James' (1890) comments on the intensively active gap in a state of consciousness, cited above. Early diary studies report interesting attempts to record mental processes in written form. In diary studies, subjects self-report results like the following (Brown and McNeill 1966: 325).

> Unable to recall the name of the street on which a relative lives, one of us thought of Congress and Corinth and Concord and then looked up the address and learned that it was Cornish.

Neal
Norrick

When a tip-of-the-tongue state occurs, according to Burke et al. (1991: 545), 'a lexical node in a semantic system becomes activated, giving access to semantic information about the target word, but at least some phonological information remains inaccessible because insufficient priming is transmitted to enable activation of connected phonological nodes'. In James' (1890: 251) terms, the active gap 'corresponds to the phonological nodes that cannot be activated'. Subjects in the tip-of-the-tongue state often report 'persistent alternates', words related to the target, which come repeatedly and involuntarily to mind and block the target word.

What Burke et al. (1991) call the 'semantic system' is a network of nodes connecting concepts, e.g. the concept 'chastity' with 'is a virtue' and 'take a vow of'; and connecting the concept 'baker' with 'bake bread', 'get up early', 'sell cakes' and 'knead dough'. The scripts of Schank and Abelson (1977) and the cognitive models of Lakoff (1990) represent a more highly structured version of such networks. In addition to the connections between nodes, a cognitive model for 'chastity' would identify prototypes for the virtue like the goddess Diana, and they would distinguish characteristics like 'is a virtue' from linguistic constructions in which the word *chastity* occurs such as *take a vow of chastity*. A cognitive model for 'baker' would identify prototypes for profession like the owner of the bakery at the foot of the hill. What Burke et al. (1991: 548) call 'priming from many semantic nodes' is the sort of richness which leads to a feeling of knowing, as described below. One word may 'prime', or facilitate recognition of, another word. As Burke et al. (1991: 572) write, 'the activation of *nurse* facilitates activation of *doctor* because priming spreads and summates via these many shared connections'.

Burke et al. (1991) also developed an experimental task, in order to generate tip-of-the-tongue states, and to encourage subjects to introspect about names, related words, syllables, and spelling. They used prompts like those in a trivia game presented on a computer, e.g.

What is the old name of Taiwan?
Target: Formosa   Foils: Taipei, Canton, Ceylon

This experiment design involves a special set of cognitive tasks. Subjects are primed to self-reflect on tip-of-the-tongue states, and they have the leisure to introspect. Nothing personal is at stake for them, as it would be in a narrative from their own past experience. Since they are interacting with a computer rather than other human beings, they have no fear of being wrong and no responsibility to keep talking. Moreover, the experiment treats tip-of-the-tongue as a single word phenomenon.
[. . .]

D2.3 Critical reading and language pedagogy

Reading D2.3 comes from the concluding section of a chapter about different ways of thinking about 'literacy'. In this chapter, Hasan reflects on what it means for young children to begin to enter the world of print, 'the onset of literacy', linking this with 'the ability to make sense' as well as 'the ability to read and write' (Hasan 1996: 379, 386). She extends this rather restricted view into 'literacy as language-based semiosis' where literacy is one among many systems of signs, but one that, crucially, uses language as its resource. Readers and writers need 'recognition literacy' (the skills to decode and encode print), but they also need to develop 'discursive ability' (p. 393), in varied contexts of social action – leading to 'action literacy' and, further, to 'reflection literacy' (p. 397, 408). In this extract, Hasan raises questions about how people learn, from infancy onwards, how to read in the ways demanded of them by the education system, and whether that same system can be emancipatory when it is making demands of learners that require them to conform to certain norms. Although you are no longer a school student, you may find it stimulating to consider your experience of reading for your dissertation in the light of Hasan's arguments about how different learners are positioned in relation to the literacy practices required of them.

Ruqaiya Hasan (1996) Literacy, everyday talk and society, in R. Hasan and G. Williams (eds) *Literacy in Society*, London: Addison Wesley Longman, pp. 414–16

Ruqaiya Hasan

Language is not a mirror that just reflects the social inequalities and hierarchies which exist in our society, mocking our claims of egalitarianism. Language is, in fact, actively involved in the creation and maintenance of social inequalities, because human social systems are *unmakeable* without language.

[. . .]

Keeping teachers of literacy uninformed about the close relation between the development of language, everyday talk, learning, and society, plays into the hands of the dominating segments of society, whose ideologies remain the ideologies of education.

[. . .]

[L]anguage-based semiosis under whatever name will occupy a central position in any discussion of education. We can, if we choose, turn language classes into sites for the discussion of wider social issues, for raising pupils' consciousness about any pressing social problems. The choice is not between bringing such issues to the students' attention *or* developing understanding of language as a powerful social semiotic. Both need to be done, and a more relevant question is: what is the best way to do both? Those who argue against focusing on language, on the explication of its internal character, on the power of lexicogrammar to construe reality, or on the efficacy of discursive knowledge speak from a less than adequate understanding of the role of language in the living and shaping of social life. Whatever else literacy pedagogy needs to be, one thing it cannot avoid is to help pupils to 'intellectualise' in the Vygotskian sense of the term the nature of language. Learning about the nature and structure of language is not an expendable educational activity.

I have talked about the three facets of literacy, [recognition literacy, action literacy, reflection literacy] each being presented in a rather idealised form, as if each existed or was able to exist on its own. This is of course not true. What is true is that different educational systems, different institutions attach different degrees of importance to these facets. Each facet has its own focus. Recognition literacy is concerned primarily with language as expression; action literacy focuses on language as expression and content in relation to social processes, while reflection literacy is concerned with the reflexive capacities of language when it functions as meta-discourse, analysing both the nature of expression and of content by relating both to the exchange of meanings by

**Ruqaiya
Hasan**

socially positioned speakers for the living of life in society. Different as these three per-spectives on literacy are, they are none the less logically related to each other. To see this we need to separate analytically what the various facets focus on as the material for teaching and how they actually do it. It is the former that is important for my claim of the interrelatedness of the three facets of literacy developed here. Let me elaborate this point.

I have suggested that the pedagogy of action literacy pre-supposes the sorts of under-standing about language that form the content of recognition literacy. I will ignore once again the comprehension-composition and self-expressive, creative pedagogies on the grounds that from the point of view of understanding language as a social semi-otic system such pedagogies are deplorably inadequate. Consider, however, genre-based literacy: to talk about the structure of a text is to talk about what meanings construe its various elements/stages, and to talk about the meanings is to talk about the lexico-grammar that will construe those meanings, with the implication that an awareness of lexicogrammar as functionally focused on the construal of meanings is important. But lexicogrammar is the most abstract part of language (Hasan 1995a); what impinges on the human senses is the manifestation of these categories in phonic and/or ortho-graphic form. Thus the phonology-orthography correspondence to lexis and grammar is an essential part of the understanding of language. The success of genre-based lit-eracy – and there is no doubt that it is successful at teaching language – resides in the fact that it has appropriated these aspects of recognition literacy, harnessing them to language in use in social contexts. A similar relation can be shown to exist between reflection literacy and genre-based literacy. If, for example, we wish to understand why politicians toss language education around like a football in the field of political gains, if we wish to ask why sociology only pays lip-service to language, if we want to ask why literary scholars sidetrack issues of language when the universe of literary art is anchored to our intelligence purely by the mediation of linguistic meaning, if we wish to understand how critical literacy can be a program for literacy development with-out a viable basis in an understanding of the workings of language, if we wonder how and why women have colluded in the processes of their own oppression, then we will need to be able to read, and read with understanding the many discourses that reveal the principles underlying these positions. We will need to become familiar with how 'they do it' – how they put these perspectives across, what justifications they offer, from whose perspective. It means being sensitive to discursive strategies, and being able to deconstruct the already constructed discourses in one's society. Reflection presupposes understanding; and understanding a point of view is synonymous with understanding discourse. – written or spoken communication
– Write or speak authoritatively about a topic.

[handwritten margin note: Consider this in relation to SEN students (Autism, Speech + Language etc.)]

[handwritten margin note: ✱ Genre Issues]

Issues to consider

❑ How far do the two examples of literature reviews conform to the conventions identified in this thread of the book?

❑ Textbooks typically advise research students against the 'shopping list' approach to presenting their literature review. In other words, the practice of simply sum-marising what various writers have said, in no particular order, is not highly valued. Do the authors of Readings D2.1 and D2.2 manage to avoid this and, if so, how?

❏ Apart from their contrasting topics, in what ways do these two examples differ from each other? How far are these differences attributable to the different functions of these two kinds of review?

❏ Does either of these reviews include examples of linguistic features that might alert your critical antennae, in the sense of the 'reflection literacy' advocated by Hasan? If so, what are these features, and how do you account for them?

❏ From your own experiences of learning literacy, from infancy to the present, how far do you identify with Hasan's account of the issues linking language, literacy, education and ideology?

❏ How does your awareness of these debates help (or perhaps hinder) your efforts to review the research literature for your project?

QUESTIONS IN ENGLISH LANGUAGE RESEARCH

D3

The two readings in this unit offer different perspectives on identifying research questions. The authors of extract D3.1 describe the questions they set out to answer, and how the data collected modified their assumptions about their topic. The rather tidy categories they had hoped to explore did not appear in the interactions they recorded, causing them to refocus their approach to the inquiry. Brumfit, in extract D3.2, reflects on a much wider set of issues about what it is appropriate and important for applied linguists to inquire about. He writes in the context of research into language teaching, but makes some general points about how research questions can and should be evaluated, in his opinion.

D3.1

S. W. Smith, H. P. Noda, S. Andrews and A. H. Jucker (2005) Setting the stage: how speakers prepare listeners for the introduction of referents in dialogues and monologues, *Journal of Pragmatics* 37, pp. 1865–95

Smith, Noda, Andrews and Jucker

In the present paper we want to explore how speakers guide listeners in constructing representations of new characters in narratives, looking at both dialogic and monologic settings.

[. . .]

This study is part of a larger project in which we look at the establishment of reference as a communicative task. We believe that the ability to coordinate what it is we want to talk about is one of the most remarkable of human accomplishments. We are interested in the variety of strategies, both structural and interactive, that speakers use in doing so. We are especially interested in how their strategies convey assumptions about both their general common ground with their audience and also about the current cognitive status of concepts for their audience (Smith and Jucker 1998; Smith et al. 2001; Jucker and Smith 2004).

We will analyze strategies used by speakers in either dialogic or monologic settings to introduce four characters from a silent movie. In all cases, speakers have just watched the same Charlie Chaplin video. In the dialogic setting, the audience is present and shares knowledge of the first half of the movie, while in the monologic setting, participants are asked to describe and discuss the movie for a missing partner. We will be interested in contrasting, for example, how they introduce characters who are already familiar to all audiences (Chaplin) or new to all audiences (an artist).

[. . .]

Our plan was to build on work dealing with basic issues in reference (e.g. Ariel 1996; Chafe 1994, 1996; Gundel 1996) and also on previous work on interaction (Clark 1992, 1994, 1996). We began with a set of assumptions that seemed reasonable at the time. We assumed that the introduction to a character would be discrete and easy to identify and that most of the work in creating the representation of the character would occur in a given noun phrase that constituted the introduction. We thought most referents would be readily classified as given or new, and for the remaining introductions it would be easy to identify the script or conceptual link (Cote 2001) that served as the basis for inferring the referent. We also thought that it would be easier to characterize strategies used in monologues than those used in dialogues; strategies used in monologues would be both more discrete and more uniform. Finally, we expected that interactive devices would function mainly to correct or clarify an inadequate introduction.

Our original plan had been to identify the use of a specific set of strategies based on common ground ('from the boat', 'that we saw'), common presentation devices ('there was', 'he saw'), and structural discourse markers ('and then', 'so'). We would then determine whether they were distributed differently for dialogues and monologues. We had prepared examples of introductions for our coding such as excerpts (1) and (2).

> (1)   *Then he saw* **the young woman from the boat.**
> (2)   *There was* **a man with a large mustache.**

Instead, we found introductions that looked like (3) and (4).

> (3)   B: and then he was turning around,
>   *and it's you know*
>   *there's* **that lady** *remember* **that lady** *that he saw on the ship*?
>   A: uh huh
>   B: *that* **he kind of fell in love with** *or whatever?*
>   A: yeah.
>   B: *so* and he saw **her,**

GLBCC 29, 148–54

(4)   B: (H) *so then* **some other guy** he is kind of like chubby
             <SV fat SV>
             he comes straight down where he's sitting at
       A: <SV mhm SV>
       B: and they're like wondering who he is,
             he's like <Q oh I'm **an artist** Q>,
             I think that's what it said an artist
             (H) [so] they are talking and everything
       A: [mhm]
       B: (H) and then the bill comes and then the artist is like <Q oh I'll pay
             for it Q>.

GLBCC 29, 222–31

Smith, Noda,
Andrews and
Jucker

That is, the introductions appeared to take place over a series of utterances and turns. There was not necessarily a discrete and identifiable introduction as such. Nor was there a clear line between the introduction and other elements that either foreshadowed or elaborated on the first direct mention. At first we were tempted to think that our speakers were somehow incompetent. But soon we realized that these examples were quite typical of everyday conversations. The challenge then was to understand what it is that speakers are doing when they introduce a character in this apparently messy way.

That led us to a reformulation of our original question—how does an introduction occur? Instead of asking which noun phrase serves as the introductory referring expression, we asked what strategies make it possible for the listener to construct the needed representation. Does it make sense to say that this representation results from a given noun phrase, the referring expression? Or might it make more sense to say that it is constructed incrementally, in a multi-stage unit?

We propose then to define reference in general and introductions in particular in terms of a reference episode, with a sequence of potential elements that together are used by the listener to establish a referent. This approach would be consistent with earlier advice that linguists should think in terms of discourse units (cf. Linell 1998; Watanabe 1998) rather than structural units to define referents.

D3.2

Christopher Brumfit (2001) *Individual Freedom in Language Teaching: helping learners to develop a dialect of their own*, Oxford: Oxford University Press, pp. 145–8

Christopher
Brumfit

Approaches to research

Researching may be defined as 'systematizing curiosity'. Its ultimate purpose is to provide better and better explanations of phenomena.

Research is essentially a cumulative process, building on what has gone on before. Unfortunately, the term 'research' has become debased, so that anyone enquiring into the necessary background facts for a television programme will be listed in the credits as a 'researcher'. However, it is worthwhile to list some of the features that should distinguish serious research from simply the search for information.

Christopher
Brumfit

Competent research will involve:

1   Careful formulation of the questions to be investigated, to ensure that they are not phrased in such a way as to confuse major issues with minor ones, or to embrace many different questions within one vague, general topic which is incapable of being investigated systematically

2   Careful exploration of the best means of investigation for the particular question being addressed

3   Consideration of the major previous attempts to explore the same and closely related questions, in order to borrow and adapt appropriate formulations of the questions, and appropriate modes of investigation

4   Explicit accounts of the process of question formulation, the criteria for selection of the research techniques, and the reasons for the questions being felt to be important in the first place

5   Full documentation of the procedures used, the means by which information has been gathered, and the methods of interpretation and analysis which have been adopted

6   Explicit acknowledgement of all previous work which has contributed to the conceptualization, means of collection, and procedures for analysis of the data collected

7   Specific interpretation of the data collected, to assess its usefulness in relation to the initial research questions

8   Evaluation of the extent to which the project has achieved its aims, together with an account of the ways in which the process of research has led to changes in the initial formulation of questions – and any other relevant judgements that the researcher may wish to pass on to interested readers

9   A willingness to publicize the research, so that it can contribute to further development by others to the exploration of the same, or related questions.

By the definition I am proposing, research is characterized by being a public, systematic, and useful activity. It is public, because it needs to be distinguished from simply improving one's own private understanding: it is not another name for personal study. It needs to be public because private work is necessarily inefficient. Public work benefits from having procedures throughout being open to scrutiny by others who will lack the biases of the original researchers (though they will have others of their own), who will bring further understanding to bear on the same problems, and who will be able – above all – to offer public criticism as a result of which methods and formulations can be improved upon in subsequent work. Private research would not benefit from this, and would thus risk being tied to the idiosyncrasies of one set of researchers, being limited to what one person or group of people knew about, and being sympathetic to the interests of those who formulated the proposal, and thus possibly unintentionally biased.

Research must be systematic, because it needs to be explicit about its procedures if it is to be distinguished from mere hunch. What kind of systematicity will be sought depends on the question being investigated, but for every question, the means of exploration will be examined exhaustively to ensure that it is the best that can be devised for

Christopher
Brumfit

the time and resources available, and the formulation and interpretation of the research will be systematically examined as rigorously as possible.

Research must be useful, in a particular sense. It will not necessarily be useful in its immediate results – otherwise we would be committed to producing the results which most fitted with what we most wanted to find out! But the question to be investigated must have some useful point to it; it must be something that we need to know. A recognition of where particular problems are is a necessary control on irresponsible mind games. While irresponsibility, divergent thinking, and imagination will all contribute to the wide range of potentially fruitful ideas that researchers may exploit, funding, time, and expertise are limited. Justifying a particular area for investigation involves necessarily showing how the study will contribute, directly or indirectly, to improving our understanding of language teaching.

But for this understanding to be useful, we do not need to adopt a narrowly utilitarian point of view – all we need to do is to show that we have thought clearly about why we should indulge our curiosity (in a way that is relatively expensive in time and effort) on this topic rather than another. The benefits are the public scrutiny which should improve the effectiveness of what we do by laying us maximally open to advice and criticism. But the right to these benefits needs to be argued by a demonstration that we are not merely being self-indulgent.

Within this framework, there are three main types of research. Often researchers may be dependent on external funding, but individual investigations may fit into these categories also.

[. . .]

What distinguishes these three types of research is not so much the procedures used, as the context in which they operate. Typically, pure research will be performed by professional researchers (who may also work simultaneously as higher education teachers), perhaps in collaboration with practitioners. The formulation of the problem will depend on the work of scholars and researchers, and the work may be funded by research councils, private charitable trusts, or government agencies, and will usually carefully describe its relationship with all previous relevant research.

Action research will be performed by practitioners, on topics formulated by practitioners. If there is external funding, it may well come from sources whose main concern is with activating the teaching profession rather than with a prime interest in whatever results are obtained.

Policy-related research will be performed by professional researchers, sometimes in formally set-up research institutes attached to official organizations. The work may be collaborative with practitioners. The formulation of the research topic will usually be defined by the policy, and the funding agency will usually be the policy-making body. Relationships with previous research may be made explicit, but this is not regarded as essential.

None the less, in spite of these contextual differences, if the research is to be of more than personal value (and hence to justify the term 'research' at all), they will all be the same in following the general procedures I have outlined above.

Issues to consider

❏ The authors of D3.1 are quite frank about the expectations they had in advance of collecting their data. Did these expectations constrain them? Do you think their revised analytic approach was successful?

❏ From the extract presented here, can you formulate some explicit questions which would be likely (a) to have been in the original plans for this study and (b) to be the questions they were actually able to answer?

❏ As a beginning researcher yourself, do you find the narrative of the changed focus of this inquiry reassuring or unsettling?

❏ The author of D3.2 is quite prescriptive in his list of features of good research. Do you agree with all of his criteria? If not, which ones would you take issue with?

❏ Are these criteria relevant to students doing research for accreditation, or only professionals at a later stage in their careers?

❏ What light does each of these readings shed on your attempts to identify and refine questions for your own project?

D4   METHODS IN ENGLISH LANGUAGE RESEARCH

The readings in this section represent just some of the various methods used in researching aspects of English Language. D4.1 discusses the role of experimental approaches in studying the language of very young children, giving examples of a range of techniques that have been used in this area. D4.2, by contrast, is from a book-length account of a large ethnographic study of literacy practices in a single community. In this extract, the authors explain and justify various methodological decisions they took in the context of collecting data in this way. D4.3 is from a survey article introducing various approaches to researching the teaching of English to speakers of other languages (TESOL). Rather like extract D3.2, this reading steps back from the specific issues raised by any one study, to place choices about both the methods and goals of research into a broader social and political context.

D4.1

Karmiloff and Karmiloff-Smith

Kyra Karmiloff and Annette Karmiloff-Smith (2001) Experimental paradigms for studying language acquisition, in *Pathways to Language: from fetus to adolescent*, Cambridge, MA: Harvard University Press, chapter 2

Language production experiments

Spontaneous interactions between children and adults, as well as between children and siblings or peers, are regarded as an ideal source of data in language production studies. But observation of spontaneous speech is increasingly accompanied by semi-structured and/or structured experimentation. Pioneers in child language research, like Daniel Slobin, Lois Bloom, and Susan Ervin-Tripp, recognized that a combination of research methods can significantly enrich the data—and not only research carried out in a strictly experimental setting of the laboratory. Even in the naturalistic setting of the home, a researcher who associates a number of different approaches can more fully assess new language developments. For instance, the use of semistructured, ad hoc experiments can help ascertain whether the appearance of a new linguistic structure produced by the child in one context will generalize to other language contexts. Take the following example. During an observational session, a child who has until now only ever used the singular word "car" suddenly says "cars." Does this represent the application of a newly acquired grammatical rule for forming the plural of nouns? In other words, did she purposely apply the rule "add s" to the singular "car"? Or was the infant simply repeating a new word she has heard for a collection of cars? Does she even realize, at this stage, that there is a relationship between the words "car" and "cars"? Simple on-the-spot experimentation allows the researcher to capitalize on this important moment of language observation. For instance, by presenting the child with pairs of other objects that the child is able to name in the singular (such as perhaps cups or dolls), the researcher can determine whether the novel utterance of the plural "s" generalizes across different linguistic contexts.

Elicited production using nonce words

Different children have different linguistic experiences. For instance, some may know words that others of a similar age do not know. How, then, can the researcher avoid confounding individual experience and linguistic knowledge? One solution has been to use nonce terms, which are invented words that obey the phonotactics of the language (what combinations of sounds are legal in the language being studied). So, for example, "lopet" is a possible English word, whereas "lpote" is not, because English never combines the phonemes "l" and "p" at the beginning of a word. In a sense, then, nonce terms are words that could have existed in the language (say, a noun like "wug" or a verb like "gorp") and to which we would quite spontaneously add an "s" for the plural "wugs" or an "ing" or "ed" for tense marking ("gorping" or "gorped") if we learned them as new words. Such nonce terms can be used in conjunction with the elicited production approach, whereby young subjects are prompted to produce the missing part of a sentence in which a critical grammatical rule is called for.

Jean Berko-Gleason pioneered this approach with the Wug Test in the 1950s. The technique has been used extensively and forms part of developmental psycholinguistic research to this day. Berko-Gleason invented a series of nonce terms, including "wug," and encouraged children to use such terms in different linguistic contexts within carefully planned experiments. The general idea is that when prompted by the linguistic context in which the terms appear, children will transform these when necessary to obey obligatory grammatical markings like plural "s" on "wugs" or past tense "ed" on "wugged." During the Wug Test, the child is shown a picture of, for instance, a bird-like creature and told that it is called "a wug." She is then shown another "wug" and told: "So now there are two of them," and finally asked, "now I have two . . .?" (rising intonation). At this point the child is expected to produce the plural "wugs."

The use of nonce terms enables researchers to find out whether, in new situations, young children are capable of generalizing to new words obligatory grammatical markers relevant to their native tongue. With nonce terms, the child's response cannot be explained simply by past experience, because she had never heard the words "wug" or "wugs" before. In contrast, rote learning could explain the production of various real words containing such plural markers in children's spontaneous everyday language. For instance, if a child has only ever heard the plural of the word "clouds" when she looks up at the sky, she may use this plural "clouds" correctly in her speech, but not actually know the word "cloud" in the singular. In this case, therefore, the correct usage of the word "clouds" cannot be taken as evidence that the child is correctly applying a plural marker. Rather, she may simply be using a familiar lexical item that, to her, refers to a fluffy white mass in the sky. To this young child, therefore, the word "clouds" is not formed by adding an "s" to "cloud" but is a lexical term in its own right. It is through the use of nonce terms that researchers can overcome these confounding factors and discover the true status of the grammatical markers present in the child's output.

From our knowledge of written language we conceptualize the plural rule as simply "add an 's'" to singular words. In spoken language, however, the sounds we actually produce when pluralizing are influenced by the rest of the linguistic context of the word. So the plural of "dog" is pronounced "dogz," whereas "cat" becomes "cats," and "dish" becomes "dishez." The Wug Test allows the researcher to ascertain not only whether children can add the plural marker in general, but also whether they are sensitive to the different allomorphs (varying forms of the same addition) on the endings of the nonce terms to be pluralized. So an experiment might examine whether a child correctly transforms "sich" into "sichez," "fap" into "faps," and "gog" into "gogz."

The nonce word approach can also be adapted to investigate a range of other grammatical structures such as tense marking on verbs. For instance, the experimenter may tell the child:

Every day I gorp. (Pause)
Just like every day, yesterday I . . . (rising intonation)

At this point the child should produce the past tense "gorped." Again, although we think of past tense as the addition of "ed," there are in fact several allomorphs, so the actual pronunciation changes as a function of the sounds that precede the marker. Thus, we pronounce "worked" as "workt," in contrast to the past tense of the verbs "to end" and "to plan," which are pronounced "ended" and "plannd." The Wug Test can be adapted to examine these allomorphs as well as to test both regular and irregular tense markings. Most verbs in English are regular (walked, speeded, planned). But some frequently used verbs like "come," "go," "sing," and "eat" have irregular endings: we say "came," not "comed"; "went," not "goed"; "sang," not "singed"; and "ate," not "eated." Such exceptions to language represent further challenges to children. To test children's knowledge of such variations, we can present them with nonce verbs whose endings differ to make them sound either like regular or irregular verbs. An example would be comparing nonce terms like "ting" and "gick" to see if children transform them to "tang" and "gicked."

Children seem to be particularly receptive to invented words if they "sound right," and they will spontaneously treat them as if they were real words. The experiments are designed to be fun and creative. So the elicited production approach with nonce terms can be both gratifying for the child and informative to the researcher. The data are unique in uncovering how children integrate their growing knowledge of grammar as well as new words (also known as lexical items).

Elicited imitation with spontaneous correction

Elicited imitation is a useful and much used tool for probing language development. This method involves placing the child within an experimental context that elicits repetition of different types of model utterances and examines the child's ability to repeat them. Some of the utterances to be repeated are constructed with correct grammar, whereas others contain mistakes that the child is expected to correct spontaneously. The experiments are presented in the form of a game, to encourage the child's active cooperation. For instance, the child may be shown puppets that "speak" and that make language errors. At the onset of a trial, the child is prompted to "repeat what the puppet says." It is assumed that if the child is sensitive to violations of particular grammatical rules, she will correct them spontaneously in her repetitions. For example, the child might be asked to repeat the incorrect sentence:

(1) I've got two foots.

If she possesses the knowledge that there are certain exceptions to the "add s" rule for plural transformation, she will actually change what she heard and repeat it in the right way as in (2) below:

(2) I've got two feet.

Alternatively, the puppet may make a syntactic error:

(3) This is my blue big tractor.

A child who is sensitive to word order rules should spontaneously imitate this utterance as:

(4) This is my big blue tractor.

The manner in which children correct sentences provides us with vital clues to their levels of language knowledge.

D4.2

Barton and
Hamilton

D. Barton and M. Hamilton (1998) *Local Literacies: reading and writing in one community*, London: Routledge, pp. 57–8; 72–3

> The idea is not so much to prove one's existing hypotheses as to try to reach beyond the old problematics . . . to look at societal phenomena from fresh, unprejudiced, yet well-founded points of view . . . and to call into question the self-evident.
>
> (Alasuutari 1995: 145)

The research goal in this study is to uncover patterns and regularities in the organisation of one aspect of cultural life. Our aim is to be explicit about the methods used in this research, by describing what we did, and by explaining why we did it. The point has already been made . . . that having a social theory of literacy, as something which is contextualised in time and space, implies that certain research methods are appropriate. Methods which take literacy out of its context of use are not appropriate. Instead, methods are needed which enable us to examine in detail the role of literacy in people's contemporary lives and in the histories and traditions of which these are a part. [. . .]

In terms of methodology, this research draws heavily upon ethnographic research traditions, as developed by anthropologists and utilised in several fields including education. Traditionally there are four aspects to this approach (see Goetz and LeCompte 1984: 3). Firstly, ethnography studies real-world settings; we do this by focusing on a particular place at a particular point in time. We deal with people's real lives: we never ask anyone to take a decontextualised test and we never stage a photograph. Secondly, the approach is holistic, aiming at whole phenomena; the phenomenon we are studying is this cultural artefact, literacy. Thirdly, the work is multi-method, drawing on a variety of research techniques; we combine extensive interviewing with detailed observation and with the systematic collection of documents. Fourthly, ethnography is interpretative and it aims to represent the participants' perspectives; we endeavour to do this by highlighting the actual words people use and by discussing our data and our interpretations with them. Contemporary ethnography is not without its intellectual and methodological debates and reflections upon how it is written (as, for example, in Clifford and Marcus 1986; Atkinson 1990), and we intend to contribute to these discussions. In designing our study we also drew upon other named traditions of qualitative research, including case study research and oral history.

Rather than just naming an approach we describe carefully what we did in our study and provide some rationale for each step. One reason for this is that many of the terms used, including basic terms such as ethnography and qualitative research, have different meanings to different researchers. In addition, the way these meanings are turned into a practical research strategy is frequently only vaguely described, often deliberately so: ethnography has a tradition of not being explicit about methodology. We make our methodology explicit, in order to provide some possibility for it to be evaluated by others, but also in order to aid others who wish to do similar work. In doing this we have to address issues such as sampling procedures, the nature of the database, validity, reliability and generalisability. These are terms which are transformed and challenged by qualitative research, but which need to be addressed in some way if research is to be evaluated. [. . .]

An additional reason for being explicit is that we were not taking one specific well-tried methodology off the shelf for this project. Significant methodological decisions were made as the research progressed, allowing the topic of the research to shape the methods, adapting and evolving new strategies over time. We are consciously developing methodology in this research. [. . .]

Barton and Hamilton

What can be learned from an ethnographic study of literacy

This research starts by describing the particular. It is also about connecting the particular to a larger context of patterned practices, how specific things, people and processes are related, how the specific is connected with its social and historical context. This relationship between local activities and global patterns is described differently by different disciplines where people are working to understand the social construction of technologies and how cultural systems operate (as in LaTour 1993; Silverstone et al. 1994; Myers 1996). LaTour refers to a 'thread of practices and instruments, of documents and translations' which 'allow us to pass with continuity from the local to the global' (p. 121). In this research we are engaged in tracing the threads of literacy practices through contemporary social life.

There are many ways of relating a local study, a finding or an explanation to broader entities, including referring to statistical studies, to other literature, concepts and theoretical traditions, and appealing to the relevance of an explanation. It is the task of the researcher to specify in what ways the data relates to broader entities (see Alasuutari 1995). At various points we contextualise [our] findings by juxtaposing other studies which offer different sources of information. These include national survey data and other studies of literacy.

We do not need to prove to our readers the existence of literacy, but we are trying to interpret and explain the data we have collected – to make these examples of everyday literacy intelligible within the framework of cultural practices and social theory which we have adopted, producing classifications, conceptual tools and theoretical explanations which can be used to extend understandings of literacy in other contexts. Such theoretical explanations are essential to empirical study of any kind, and without them, data, whether quantitative or qualitative, cannot be interpreted. Ultimately, this study will be evaluated in terms of the ways in which it fits in with the theoretical frameworks we make use of, with other research data on literacy, and, not least, its relevance to our readers' concerns about literacy.

D4.3

Alister Cumming (1994) Alternatives in TESOL research: descriptive, interpretive, and ideological orientations, *TESOL Quarterly* 28 (4), pp. 673–5

Alister Cumming

What orientations to research currently exist in TESOL? What value might each alternative orientation have? What limitations do they possess? TESOL's Research Interest Section invited several noted researchers to address these questions, [and] . . . they collectively convey three important themes on the current state of inquiry in TESOL internationally.

**Alister
Cumming**

First, a multiplicity of orientations to research exists. There is not simply a finite number of these orientations, nor is there a simple dichotomy between qualitative and quantitative approaches. Many more orientations exist than the seven outlined here, including methodologies like narrative, historical, or survey inquiry; various techniques to plan or evaluate language programs or policies; and ways of validating specific linguistic theories or psychological models. Similarly, many of these orientations are complementary, overlapping in their methodologies and interrelated conceptual foundations, acknowledging the need for multiple and divergent perspectives selected according to the purposes that guide specific projects or are appropriate to particular contexts. Moreover, what might be designated as one research orientation actually entails a variety of potentially different analytic units and methods as well as competing interpretive and situational perspectives—each embracing diverse ways of collecting data in addition to analyzing, interpreting, and making recommendations from them.

Second, these orientations illustrate different purposes of inquiry. That is, each orientation aims to establish somewhat different kinds of knowledge and to make somewhat different contributions to educational practices. Some orientations aim to establish scientific knowledge about systems of human behavior: describing, for example, linguistic systems acquired by learners of a new language, the formal conventions through which language can be structured as texts, common patterns of strategic behavior in language learning or communication, or systems of discourse interaction typical of language classrooms. Other approaches aim to produce local knowledge relevant to understanding and improving particular language programs, policies, or educational circumstances. Research in this area may focus on whether distinct patterns of classroom interaction yield learning results appropriate to a certain curriculum, consider how the cultural life of a school interacts with its local societal circumstances, or assess how language policies are being implemented in specific educational jurisdictions. A third research orientation may aim to transform the social relations of participants in language education, using the potential in research processes to achieve political results (not just scholarly information or institutionally determined goals), such as change in individual and intergroup relations, people's critical awareness of their historical and societal positions, and the redistribution of cultural power and privilege.

These research orientations focus to different degrees on descriptive, interpretive, and ideological purposes. That is, these orientations distinguish purposes of (a) describing and analyzing the verbal behavior of individual language learners in reference to theories of learning, language, or society; (b) documenting and interpreting the cultural practices and experiences of learning a language in a specific institutional setting; and (c) advocating and fostering ideological change within particular contexts and broader domains. On the one hand, these alternative purposes present us with a kind of "paradigm war" between competing views of how educational research should be conducted (Gage 1989, p. 4). But on the other hand, these positions interact, as does the knowledge they produce for language education (Johnson 1992) and for educational inquiry generally (Jaeger 1988). Indeed, these purposes are often interdependent, each aiming to conceptualize and enhance different but mutually related aspects of our knowledge about language education. For example, definitions of text genres, accounts of classroom interaction, or ethnographic techniques may inform critical analyses

Alister Cumming

of pedagogy, and in turn critical or participatory approaches to research may shape approaches to text analyses or learners' strategic options for action within their communities. Similarly, theories of language acquisition may inform classroom observation schemes or emit interpretations of language socialization, just as verbal reports may be used to gather data for participatory action research or ethnographies.

Implicit in the multiplicity and differing purposes of these orientations is a third theme, that of choice and values. To do or use research in TESOL implies making decisions about the purposes research will serve, the value it may contribute, and the foundations of knowledge or action appealed to: specific academic disciplines and theories of learning, language, or society; practices and actions in particular educational programs; or openly political agendas. Conversely, to ignore or fail to engage in such inquiry may imply neglecting such choices and the value of their contributions, an implication that invites us all to examine and understand each of these alternative orientations to research carefully and responsibly.

Issues to consider

❏ In other units in this strand, I have drawn a distinction between 'methods' and 'methodology'. To what extent does each of these readings draw a similar distinction?

❏ 'Experiments' are often defined quite tightly, and I have suggested that they are more appropriate methods for researching specific aspects of language production and reception. To what extent would you say that the methods described in D4.1 are actually experiments? Could they be classified in any other way?

❏ How convincing do you find the very explicit rationale given by the authors of D4.2 for their use of ethnographic methods? Could they have collected equivalent data in any other way?

❏ Compare extract D4.3 with D3.2: what are the differences and similarities in the two discussions of factors which Applied Linguistic researchers should consider? How far do these issues of applications of research findings, and of social responsibility, relate to other areas of English Language research, including that of your own study? In what kind of research area, if any, are they not relevant?

PROBLEMS IN ENGLISH LANGUAGE RESEARCH

Research reports have traditionally focused mainly on the substantive findings of the studies conducted, and some research traditions, as noted elsewhere in this book, set considerable store by the foregrounding of the knowledge generated, frowning on any discussion of the people involved in its generation. Sometimes, however, researchers do allow themselves to be represented in their own reports of their work, even to the extent of describing things that have not gone according to plan, and the readings in this unit represent some examples. In different ways, they illustrate the potential messiness of the research process, and the fact that, since language is an aspect of human behaviour, collection of data for linguistic research, particularly authentic, interactional data, entails negotiating relationships with other people, who have their own interests and priorities, which may well not coincide with those of the researcher. Between them, these examples depict the influences on the research process of a wide range of such interests.

D5.1

The author of this reading, Jennifer Coates, is a widely-read writer on issues of language and gender. Like some of the authors included in D1, she introduces one of her books, *Women Talk*, with an account of 'how it all began', revealing that, 'In 1983 my marriage had broken up and I was looking for a full-time university post in linguistics' (Coates 1996: 2). She goes on to write about the importance of her friendships with women in getting her through this difficult period, and the insights into feminism acquired while writing an earlier book on *Women, Men and Language*. This very personal perspective serves as an introduction to her account of collecting data from this same group of women friends.

Jennifer Coates (1996) *Women Talk*, Oxford: Blackwell, pp. 3, 4, 5, 6

I became increasingly uncomfortable about the ethics of writing a book which claimed to be (briefly at least) the last word on Language and Gender (or Language and Sex, as the field was quaintly known at that time) when I myself had done no original sociolinguistic work in the field. I decided that I would start a research project focusing on all-female talk, as I was unhappy at the extent to which Language and Gender research denoted research involving mixed-sex talk. Beyond this, I was vague about details. My main thought was that I must start collecting data, and that things would fall into place. It's probably a terrible confession to admit to, having had no clear research goals. Though it may be foolish of me to lay myself open to criticism in this way, I do so because I can't believe I'm the only researcher who's started a project in this way, and by speaking out I hope to draw attention to the question – how do we go about 'doing research'? I also want to challenge the notion that there is necessarily one right way of doing things.
[. . .]
   At this point, the germs of a research project and my support network of friends on Merseyside came together. Over several years (since 1975 to be exact), some of us had established a pattern of meeting once a fortnight at each other's houses. We would meet in the evenings, around 8.30 or 9.00 (when with any luck we had got our children to bed) and sit round and drink wine and talk.
[. . .]
   The initial group consisted of five women, all with young children, two with newly-born babies. . . . In the autumn of 1983 – incredible as it may seem in these days of Ethics Committees – I took the decision to start recording these meetings

Jennifer
Coates

surreptitiously (I will return to this issue). Initially, I intended to record each meeting, moving from one house to another as the fortnights rolled by. My first attempt was a disaster: we were meeting at Helen's house, so I took her into my confidence and rigged up some unsophisticated machine behind the sofa. The resulting tape was unusable for various reasons. First, not surprisingly, the recording quality was appalling, and, although I already knew that I was more interested in conversational features such as questions and repetition than in the minutiae of phonetic variation, these recordings were not good enough. This meant that I had to use better recording equipment. Secondly, the stress of managing the tape-recorder meant that I was distracted all evening: I began to realize that my awareness of the recording procedures was a methodological problem that had to be addressed; I needed to find a way of reducing my awareness to a minimum.

I decided that a solution to both problems lay in restricting recording to meetings held at my house. This had several advantages. First, I felt much more comfortable about recording my friends on my territory. Secondly, I could use the in-house hi-fi equipment which was in the living room where we always sat, coupled to my son's microphones. My elder son, Simon, was in a rock group and therefore had some reasonably sophisticated microphones: he reorganized the hi-fi system to become a recording system, with two microphones judiciously placed one on each side of the fireplace. Thirdly, I negotiated with Simon that, on the pretext of scrounging a glass of wine, he would come into the room during the evening and turn on the recording equipment. These new arrangements worked well: the recordings were of reasonable quality (apart from unexpected interference from the two-way radio of our neighbour's minicab firm) and, to my surprise, I was often so immersed in conversation that I barely noticed Simon's brief interruption of proceedings, and forgot for most of the time that recording was in progress. The only snag to these new arrangements was that meetings in my house only occurred at quite long intervals – after all, there were six or seven of us, and we met once a fortnight, with breaks for major holidays such as christmas and in the summer. So there were often three months or more between recordings. At the time this didn't worry me, but in the event I was offered a lecturing post in London, starting in September 1984. This meant that I had to move away from Birkenhead, away from my Oxton friends, with only four recordings completed.

Coming clean

At this point I chose to tell the group that I had been recording them for nearly a year. I was staggered by their reaction: they were furious. In retrospect, I'm amazed by my own naivety. Recording people talking without their consent is a gross violation of their rights. These people were my friends; they had come to my house in a spirit of trust. But I would ask readers to bear in mind that at that time, surreptitious recording still seemed methodologically acceptable. I had worked since 1968 as a research assistant for the pioneering Survey of English Usage, at University College London (initially full-time, then part-time after I moved away from London). The Survey was a pioneer in that it included spoken as well as written language in its corpus. Many spoken conversations collected for this corpus were recorded surreptitiously; that is, those recorded did not know they were being recorded (with the exception of the speaker connected with the Survey who was responsible for the recording). Working for the Survey was

Jennifer Coates

a formative experience: I admired the work done there and realize now that I adopted Survey practice uncritically as a model for my own work. Major sociolinguistic work that I knew about – the research of William Labov in the United States and of Peter Trudgill in Britain, for example – deployed the sociolinguistic interview as a tool for gathering data. While this method avoided surreptitious recording, it resulted in talk that was constrained by the asymmetry of the interview situation (the interviewer and the interviewee are not equals) and which was often relatively formal. It was not a method that could be used to collect the spontaneous talk of friends.

The long, and sometimes painful, discussions I had with my friends after my revelation that they had been recorded have informed all research I have carried out subsequently. I have never recorded anyone surreptitiously again. I have had to think carefully about research methods, and am grateful to my friends for challenging me. Fortunately, they gave me permission to use the tapes, and are now pleased that we have a concrete record of our friendship.

[. . .]

Over the two summer vacations following my departure from Birkenhead I started to transcribe the tapes I'd made. Anyone who has done any transcription of spoken language will know that it is an extremely difficult and time-consuming task. When you are working on recordings of conversations involving five or six speakers (as I was), you need to allow at least 30 minutes to transcribe one minute of conversation. But listening over and over again to my recordings, attending to every detail of what was going on in these conversations, proved to be an invaluable experience: it helped me to clarify my research goals. As I became aware of the richness of my data, I also became convinced that single-sex talk among women and girls was what I wanted to work on, more specifically, the talk of female friends in single-sex groups. I started to look for other existing groups of friends who would be willing to record themselves. [. . .] The corpus which I ended up with was arrived at by a hodgepodge of means. I use the word *hodge-podge* deliberately, to draw attention to the fact that this was not a carefully planned exercise, and to underline the serendipitous nature of the resulting corpus.

D5.2

Papaioannou, Santos and Howard

Vasiliki Papaioannou, Nora Basurto Santos and Amanda Howard (2008) University of Warwick, UK, Data collection: real stories from the field, *IATEFL 2007: Aberdeen Conference Selections*, ed. Briony Beaven, IATEFL

In their workshop, three doctoral researchers from the University of Warwick shared some personal experiences of data collection in TESOL environments in the UK, the Middle East, and Mexico. Amanda Howard interacted with the audience and explained that data collection in educational research often appears in the literature to be a relatively straightforward matter. It simply requires planning where, when and how to carry out all the activities associated with collecting data in education settings, and the rest of the process will follow in logical steps. However, educational data collection is often a process full of frustrations, cancelled appointments and tense diplomatic negotiation. First-hand detailed accounts of how access was obtained for fieldwork are scarce in the literature of qualitative research in educational contexts (Delamont 2002) and particularly in TESOL contexts (Richards 2003).

Van Maanen summarises some of the feelings about fieldwork which Amanda shared with the audience:

> Fieldworkers, it seems, learn to move among strangers while holding themselves in readiness for episodes of embarrassment, affection, misfortune, partial or vague revelation, deceit, confusion, isolation, warmth, adventure, fear, concealment, pleasure, surprise, insult, and always possible deportation. (1988: 2)

Vasiliki Papaioannou highlighted that the problems arising while doing fieldwork can cause subsequent damage to relationships and to the quality of the research itself, and it is important to share experiences as this could help novice researchers reflect and identify possible ways to deal with such problems in the future. In her research in a UK-based multicultural school, obtaining a potentially relevant document suggested by a German teacher threatened her relationship with the Head and ruined that with the teacher involved. Negotiating access to this document was problematic, as the Head thought it was very 'shallow' while the teacher was extremely fond of it. When she was asked about the document Vasiliki gave her personal opinion, saying that it was helpful to EFL teachers up to a point, but she pointed out that it was also an annexe to a report, and a non-signed document which used hypothetical instead of real data.

The teacher thought that Vasiliki agreed with the Head and was rejecting a valuable document. He avoided communication in the staffroom, asking daily for the interview transcripts. Although he had seemed to be a difficult respondent it was hard to anticipate the end result.

Once the transcripts were sent to the teacher, he withdrew all data relating to him, saying that his English was 'bad' and the interviews made him seem 'stupid'. All efforts made to save this data were in vain. As a result Vasiliki decided not to send any more transcripts to teachers but only the final quotations which would be used in her thesis, giving respondents the final say about them.

Nora Basurto Santos stated that new researchers may think that negotiating research entry and access is a simple matter because this important aspect of fieldwork has been either played down, taken for granted or ignored completely. Unfortunately, this is particularly true of the few ethnographic studies carried out in secondary or preparatory schools in Mexico.

Although the terms 'entry' and 'access' are often used interchangeably, a very useful consideration to bear in mind is that 'entry' does not mean 'access', or at least not access in an ethical way where respondents are the ones to decide whether to participate or not.

The stories that Nora shared in the workshop demonstrated how entry and access are two distinct issues. The first, *Mexican Wrestling: Technician or Rude?* showed how she had to grapple with dilemmas of power when access to willing participants was ended by a gatekeeper. The second, *Bringing out the Dr Jekyll in Me*, illustrated how she had to adjust her behaviour to fit in with the demands of the setting.

However, not everything that the three researchers had to say about fieldwork was negative, quite the contrary. They all concurred that:

D6

Papaioannou,
Santos and
Howard

The challenge and growing reward of fieldwork is to come to know yourself honestly enough to discover with equal honesty the ways of others, and the process of recording is the balance by means of which this relationship can be weighted (Richards 2003: 135).

Issues to consider

❏ What, if anything, is gained by researchers' exposure of their problems and fallibilities through publications such as these? Are these authors brave or foolish to publish such accounts?

❏ Do you think the experiences described here are likely to be unique, somewhat unusual or fairly common? Why?

❏ To what extent can pitfalls such as those encountered by these researchers be avoided by more careful preparation and planning?

❏ Are the issues such as those raised in these readings peculiar to particular research approaches, or are they always relevant in some form to research in English Language?

D6   **COLLECTING ENGLISH LANGUAGE DATA**

The material that constitutes the data in research projects, as discussed in other units, may be of many different kinds. I have selected examples of three contrasting studies, from different research traditions, to illustrate how experienced researchers reflect on the process of data collection: the first uses questionnaires to investigate the strategies adopted by learners of English in their writing, the second uses corpus methods to explore how written texts represent speech and thought, and the third is an example of linguistic ethnography, focusing in this case on the ways in which children negotiate their identities and relationships through informal talk at school.

It is usual for published research reports to explain what kind of data was collected, with some indication of how this was done, and the first and third readings are taken from book-length texts where the authors have the space to devote to an account of their approach to data collection. In more succinct journal articles, as the authors of the first reading in this unit observe, there are some aspects of data collection which are rarely discussed in much detail. In the abstract of their article, Petrić and Czárl (2003: 187) note that, '[v]alidation of data collection instruments is an extremely important step in research', yet, they claim, 'it is often only briefly reported in research studies'. They therefore choose to explore this aspect of data collection in some depth. The extracts included below illustrate just some of the considerations that Petrić and Czárl found to be important in planning this particular piece of research about writing from the perspective of learners of an additional language.

D6.1

B. Petrić and B. Czárl (2003) Validating a writing strategy questionnaire, *System* 31, pp. 187–215

Petrić and
Czárl

[W]e created a questionnaire in order to obtain a research instrument which makes it possible to survey the self-reported writing strategies of a large number of non-native advanced speakers of English who write in English for academic purposes. Such an instrument would enable researchers to compare findings in different contexts. At the same time, it could also have pedagogical applications in two ways: as a needs analysis or diagnostic tool for teachers and an awareness-raising tool for learners. The instrument was validated using a qualitative and a quantitative method with two groups of participants from the target population.

[. . .]

Instead of investigating what L2 writers do when writing, our approach to this area was to turn our attention to their self-reported strategies in order to find out what strategies they find useful and manageable when writing assignments for content courses (i.e. when writing is used in authentic situations rather than for writing classes only). Such findings may provide insights into issues that have relevance for the L2 writer and thus may complement findings from direct observations of the writing process. This approach is also in line with O'Malley and Chamot's (1990) conclusion that the individuals' perceptions and interpretations of their own experiences can provide explanations for behaviour.

Construction and form of the questionnaire

In this study writing strategies are defined as actions or behaviours consciously carried out by writers in order to make their writing more efficient (based on Cohen's definition of learner strategies, 1998, pp. 10–11). This implies that the study focuses on students' perceptions of the writing strategies they use, which may not be the same as the actual strategies applied. The ideas for writing items came from the researchers' personal experience as non-native writers in English and writing teachers, from informal interviews with students, and from the literature on writing as well as questionnaires on similar issues (e.g. Oxford's, 1990, *Strategy Inventory for Language Learning* (SILL)). The construct was operationalised as a list of written statements, each of which presents an assertion about the use of a writing strategy. This format was taken from Oxford's SILL, as was the five-point Likert scale with options ranging from *never or almost never true of me* to *always or almost always true of me*. The items were sequenced following the structure of the writing process, i.e. pre-writing, writing, and revising stages, so as to provide a clear frame of reference to the respondents. The questionnaire was compiled in English, and not the respondents' native languages, as this was the only language that all potential respondents and the researchers themselves share. The questionnaire was then checked for content validity . . . with both experts and members of the target population, after which it was substantially revised. In addition, the researchers themselves (being members of the target population) did a test–retest of the last draft of the questionnaire. The final form of the questionnaire [included as an appendix] consists of 44 items, of which 38 are strategy items and 6 are background questions. It starts with six questions about the respondents' general background. The main part, dealing with strategies, is divided into three subsections: *planning strategies* (8 items), *while-writing strategies* (14 items), and *revising strategies* (16 items). This division was introduced for the sake of clarity; however, it is not assumed that these processes are completely separate stages. In fact, a number of items point to the overlap of the stages and the nonlinear nature of the writing process (e.g. item 2.5 *I go back to my out-line and make changes in it.*). In addition, care has been taken to include items which would indicate that the respondent does not use any planning or revising strategies (e.g. item 3.3: *When I have written my paper, I hand it in without reading it.*).

Establishing the reliability and validity of the instrument

Although validation of data collection instruments is a necessary step in research, emphasised in research manuals (e.g. MacNealy 1999; Seliger and Shohamy 1989; Hatch and Lazaraton 1991; Gall et al. 1999), there is little detailed and practical guidance on how validation should be conducted. As Converse and Presser (1986: 52) point out when discussing the issue of pre-testing questionnaires, '[t]here are no general principles of good pre-testing, no systematisation of practice, no consensus about expectation; and we rarely leave records for each other'. Other authors (Reid 1990; Alderson and Banerjee 1996; Block 1998) similarly note, and our own experience confirms, that few studies report validation data, which makes it difficult to obtain information about commonly accepted practices and standards in the field. The decisions made in the validation process in this study were therefore based partly on the literature, especially concerning the choice of methods and general principles, and largely on our own sense of plausibility regarding analysis and decisions in dealing with practical constraints. Based on recommendation by Alderson and Banerjee (1996) to combine more than one method of validation, it was decided to pre-test the questionnaire using a qualitative and a quantitative method, and with different groups of members of the target population, i.e. advanced non-native speakers of English, in academic environments where writing in English plays an important role.

[. . .]

The test–retest method was chosen as the main reliability check method, as it enabled us to establish the reliability of the questionnaire for stability over time and as it is a relatively feasible method to apply in a regular school environment. Two considerations are important to bear in mind when using this method: first, that the variables measured could be subject to significant change over time, and second, that a repeated administering of the same questionnaire may result in the sensitisation of the participants to the issue researched. Both concerns are related to the time between the test and retest, which implies that the decision about the appropriate length of time is crucial; however, little information is available on this issue.

[. . .]

Decisions on the choice of validation methods were based on Alderson and Banerjee (1996), who overview the literature on validation of data collection instruments in classroom research, and Converse and Presser (1986), who offer practical guidance on validating questionnaires in particular. In this study, the most relevant types of validity are considered to be content, construct and response validity, whereas predictive and concurrent validity are not discussed since they are beyond the scope of this study.

Establishing content validity was an important step during the construction of the questionnaire. The draft was given to four experts, who are all researchers as well as teachers of academic writing in English, to obtain expert opinions on the relevance of items to the purpose of the questionnaire, possible wording and interpretation problems, and the instructions. At the same time, the research instrument was also piloted with three members of the target population, who were asked to participate in an informal think-aloud session. Wording and conceptual problems were discussed, and additional ideas were invited in order to ensure that all strategies relevant to the target population are covered. As a result of the content validity check, some major changes were implemented, of which the most important ones were eliminating irrelevant items, collapsing related statements, and addressing a number of wording problems.
[. . .]

The factors discussed above are capable of having a significant effect on the way participants respond to the questionnaire and thus also on the reliability and validity of the data obtained. Some of the factors can be controlled by reconsidering wording, devising parallel items, or by gathering information about the research context beforehand and piloting with members of the target population. However, problems related to the idiosyncratic ways in which respondents understand certain words or items, and various issues related to recent experiences, attitudes, reasons, and circumstances behind actual strategy use cannot be solved completely by rewriting and validating items. This is an important limitation of questionnaires that needs to be taken into consideration. As Sakui and Gaies (1999) state, "unless we limit ourselves to questionnaire items which explicitly target a very specific situation [. . .], we may have to accept the inherent limitations of questionnaire items—no matter how carefully developed, field-tested, and revised they may be" (p. 481).

D6.2

In this chapter on their book about how speech, writing and thought are presented in a corpus of English writing, Semino and Short explain the process of constructing their corpus. They had to make decisions about what to include in it, and to decide on explicit criteria for making those decisions. Much of the chapter is concerned with presenting these details, so that readers are aware of the data on which they base their analyses.

E. Semino and M. Short (2004) Methodology: the construction and annotation of the corpus, in *Corpus Stylistics*, London: Routledge, chapter 2

In this chapter we describe our corpus and the system we developed for annotating it. We focus particularly on the many and varied methodological decisions that we had to make in the course of our project, and begin to consider the thorny issue of the status and reliability of the quantitative findings that will be presented in subsequent chapters.

The corpus

Our corpus contains 120 text samples of approximately 2,000 words each, amounting to a total of 258,348 words of (late) twentieth-century written British English. It is divided into three sections, which comprise 40 text samples each and represent three main genres:

- Prose fiction (87,709 words)
- Newspaper news reports (83,603 words)
- Biography and autobiography (87,036 words) (henceforth we will refer to this section as (auto) biography')

[Semino and Short go on to give details of the sub-sections of these genres, explaining why they decided not to include some kinds of texts which might be thought to meet their criteria (such as 'oral or multimodal narratives', p. 20 and '"soft news" items', p. 21). They then provide further details of the way in which they selected texts in the categories they had decided on for inclusion in the corpus.]

Choosing our source texts

When it came to selecting the source texts from which to extract our text samples, we began by considering any suitable material that was already available in electronic form. As far as prose fiction is concerned, approximately half the texts were derived from a combination of the *Oxford Text Archive* (OTA) and the *British National Corpus* (BNC). The rest were selected from novels that had been published relatively recently at the time when our corpus construction phase took place. In order to operationalize the distinction between popular and serious fiction, we relied on a set of explicit criteria:

1   The internal classifications of our electronic resources (in particular the OTA and the BNC for our popular and serious fiction texts).
2   The opinions of nine members of Lancaster University's Stylistics Research Group. These individuals were presented with a list of writers whose works were available in the OTA (which mainly archives serious fiction), and asked to decide, for each one, whether they regarded the author as a writer of 'serious' fiction or not. Texts by authors which six or more of the nine informants judged as writers of serious literature were selected.
3   The strategies used in publishing and marketing books, and in allocating them to different sections in libraries and bookshops.
4   The inclusion in shortlists for prestigious literary prizes (e.g. the Booker Prize) or, indeed, the winning of such prizes.

Criteria (1) and (2) applied to texts which we derived from existing electronic resources, while criteria (3) and (4) applied to texts which we chose from the wide array of recently published fiction.
[. . .]

[Having next provided extensive further information about text selection, Semino and Short introduce the issue of annotating their data.]

The annotation system

The corpus annotation for other types of linguistic phenomena is usually conducted automatically (see Biber et al. 1998; Garside et al. 1987; McEnery and Wilson 1996). However, it was not possible to tag our corpus automatically, because, at this early stage of the development of the system of classification, it was necessary for human analysts to test and refine the categories and to develop guidelines for annotation.

[...]

[Several more pages are devoted to an explanation of the system used to mark up the texts in the corpus, with examples so that the reader can see how this worked in practice and understand instances used later in the book, where the analyses are presented. In the final section of this chapter, Semino and Short reflect on the whole process of collecting and beginning to process the data that they use in this particular research project.]

Concluding remarks

The corpus we have developed was constructed with a very specific set of research purposes in mind, and is much smaller than the multi-million word corpora generally available for lexical and grammatical research. The main reason for this was that our corpus annotation could not be achieved by automatic means. Even programs to tag DS were not as reliable as the annotations currently achieved by grammatical taggers, and the need to take contextual and pragmatic factors into account for the annotation of other speech, writing and thought presentation categories (and especially the free indirect categories) meant that manual tagging was the only possibility.

Humans make mistakes, of course, and so although we have striven to make the annotations in our corpus as reliable as possible (the tagging of each text in the corpus was checked and discussed by at least two people in addition to the original tagger), there are bound to be errors and alternative analyses. Once contextual and pragmatic interpretative factors are involved, other analysts may well be able to propose alternative descriptions. We are very aware that further alternative analyses are possible, and that to some degree the quantification we report in later chapters might not be absolutely accurate. Similarly, we are aware that our corpus could usefully comprise more text types and more samples within each text-type. As a consequence of this, we put little weight on statistical differences that are not large. However, in spite of the inevitable shortcomings of our work, we feel that our annotated corpus is innovative and revealing in many ways, both theoretically and in relation to the text-types we have examined.

Having described the corpus and the annotation system we developed in some detail, it may be helpful for us to make some general remarks about our understanding of the relation between theorizing and corpus annotation. It is clear that the use of any annotation system must assume an initial theorization of the area of analysis to be undertaken, but the process of manual annotation itself leads to insights and changes in what is annotated, and how such annotations are arrived at. Then, in turn, the re-examination of the corpus data in the light of the completed annotation (which allows analysts to examine much more systematically the range of variation within and among categories) can lead to further changes in theorization (in this case, SW & TP theory). There are bound, therefore, to be changes to annotations and understanding as one goes along, and it should not be assumed automatically that the annotation system is an exact replication of the theory and system of description arrived at after the corpus has been analysed with the help of the annotations. Some examples from our own experience will help to illustrate these general remarks.

We introduced some categories and sub-categories during the process of annotation, in order to be able to collect instances of particular phenomena we had begun to notice, so that we could use WordSmith to help us examine them later. The new categories and sub-categories we will describe in chapter 3 were introduced as the process of annotation took place, and therefore required the subsequent re-tagging of texts already tagged. Our use of the annotation system (and the theorization behind it) itself has led us to consider more carefully how SW & TP should be described, and in the final chapter of this book we will discuss a particular area where, if we were in the happy position of being able to start the process of annotation now, we would probably make different tagging decisions. Moreover, some annotations may be specifically introduced to test sub-parts of the overall theory. The fact that we made a tagging distinction between DS and FDS from the beginning was not because we believed that this category distinction was real, but rather because we were already suspicious of that distinction and wanted to examine it more closely.

D6.3

Janet
Maybin

Janet Maybin (2005) Setting the scene, in *Children's Voices: talk, knowledge and identity*, London: Palgrave Macmillan, chapter 1

In the extracts reproduced here, Maybin provides an evocative account of what it feels like to collect ethnographic data. Although in this opening chapter, as elsewhere in her book, she explains the theoretical and methodological rationales for her decisions, the extracts below concentrate mainly on the unfolding experience of collecting this kind of authentic data. I have chosen to bring forward from its place in the original chapter a brief summary statement of Maybin's approach to research.

D6.3.1 The researcher in the data

The starting point for my research on children's talk was Martin Hammersley's (1990) definition of ethnography as social research gathering empirical data from real world natural contexts using a range of unstructured methods, particularly observation and informal conversation. The focus is usually a small-scale setting or group and data analysis involves the interpretation of the insider meanings and functions of human actions. In my own case, I immersed myself as far as I could in the children's worlds through my observations and contact with them in school.

[The first, indented, paragraph of extract 6.3.2 is an actual example of the data included in ethnographic studies, where the researcher makes detailed records of her experiences 'in the field'.]

D6.3.2

Janet
Maybin

> Going into the school I am struck immediately by the amount of talk. Teacher–pupil dialogues in classrooms, the continual low murmur of talk of children carrying on with work. Children talking as they mix paints for art-work in the landing outside the classroom, children joking in the changing rooms before PE. Children chatting at lunchtime while eating their sandwiches . . . a group of older, 11 year-old boys and girls bantering and teasing.
>
> (Fieldnotes, 26.09.90)

In this chapter, I give some flavour of the experience of researching children's talk across the school day: what it actually felt like observing and recording children and trying, as far as I could, to enter into their world. This was an extraordinarily vivid experience, which influenced my later work on the data and shaped my own development as a particular kind of researcher.

[. . .]

What I was most interested in, was not children's individual linguistic or psychological competencies, but their involvement in the messy, contingent, collaborative process of language use in everyday life, and how this might be contributing to their construction of knowledge and identity. Within this process, language has multiple meanings and is often ambiguous; its referential, interactional and emotive functions are closely intertwined. It is also always on the move: elliptical, processual and recursive.

I wanted to find out how children use ordinary complex everyday talk to learn about their world and gain a sense of themselves, and how this language is involved in their socialisation into particular cultural practices and their development into particular kinds of people. I needed to find some way of describing the intensely interactive and fragmentary talk I was recording in school, my research lying somewhere at the junction of anthropology, social psychology and sociolinguistics. Searching for a more dynamic language of description grounded within everyday social activity involved me in a struggle between a more formalist framework from linguistics, with its powerfully precise procedures and terminology for describing patterns within communication, and the commitment within ethnography to particularity and participation, holistic accounts of social practice and openness to reinterpretations over time (Rampton et al., 2004).

[. . .]

I start with a vignette from the first day at my main research site school. I am sitting next to my tape recorder taking notes at the side of the class, a mixed Year 6 and Year 7 group of around 30 10- to 12-year-olds. The upstairs classroom is light and airy, with colourful displays of children's work on the walls. The tables are arranged in clusters, each designated for work in mathematics, science or English. Around me the children are working in small groups, apparently cheerfully, on the worksheets which organise their activity throughout most of the day. As I watch, the teacher moves around the class helping individuals amid a general low buzz of talk which is punctuated every now and then as she raises her voice to instruct or harangue an individual, or speak to the whole class. Some children are restless, getting up frequently to look for pencils and

**Janet
Maybin**

rulers and starting arguments over where they want to sit, while others get on with their work, talking now and then with children seated near them.

On that first day I had an overwhelming sense of the ordinariness of what I was seeing, an impression of 'business as usual' in the schooling of working-class children. Having decided to set aside the lens of curriculum goals and educational competencies, I initially had no alternative way of reading what I was seeing, or of understanding its significance for the children themselves. In my pilot study in a nearby school, I had attached a radio microphone to a 10-year-old girl, Julie, for three days and collected a considerable amount of data about her informal interactions with other children, picaresque anecdotes and rapid switches of style between different contexts. I now wondered if this had been beginner's luck and whether I would manage to collect any interesting data at all from this class where I was going to spend the next three weeks. My main reaction to being in the classroom that first day was an acute awareness of my inability to read beyond the surface of what I was seeing, a lack of meaning for my own presence, and a strong feeling of paralysing boredom.

My misgivings about being able to collect the data I wanted were to radically change over the next three weeks. In order to record the children's talk I used a radio microphone, switched around different children in two friendship groups (three girls and three boys) whom the teacher had suggested were 'ordinary', fairly talkative children. I also collected copies of all the texts they were using and producing. In addition, I used two small tape recorders to record as much as possible of the other talk going on in the classroom, which also usefully deflected attention from the 'wired-up' child. I began to spend my time helping the children who weren't being recorded with their work, creating a role for myself within the classroom community and starting to build relationships with individual children. Break-times were spent checking equipment and notes and playing back tapes and chatting with children who wanted to hear recordings of themselves. Gradually I began to establish a regular set of working practices which carried me through the school day and gave me a sense of my own place and purpose in the classroom. As I spent more time among the children and started listening to the recordings, I began, slowly, to tune into their experience and perspectives.

This tuning in involved dislodging my initial perceptual framework, which had been organised around the official school timetable and curriculum. I began to realise that there was an alternative framework of time and space within the school which was equally, if not more, significant for the children themselves. The contexts where children expressed their own viewpoints and experience most vividly were not within the teacher-managed classroom activities, but in the gaps between the official curriculum spaces. During the minutes before the teacher entered the classroom after break-time, in a classroom corner away from the teacher's gaze, when the children lined up for lunch or chatted in the school coach on the way to the swimming pool, they pursued their own agendas and explorations through talk among themselves. I noticed that recurring themes and personal topics from conversations in these alternative spaces within the school day were fleetingly referred to in talk around a classroom activity, and off-the-cuff remarks in class which I had barely registered before acquired a new significance. My perceptions of the interstices between official spaces opened up and expanded, creating a new lens through which I read what was happening in the classroom.

I now saw Darren moving confidently around the classroom with his sharp haircut,

Kim's hostile glance at the teacher and Kevin and Kieran working quietly together in a corner, in the light of my knowledge about their preoccupations and viewpoints expressed in unofficial talk elsewhere. This lens was strengthened, further laminated, as it were (as when layers of glass are melded together to make a stronger pane) when I returned to Lakeside, my main school site, the next term after the observation and taping to interview the children in friendship pairs about the themes and topics which were cropping up in the continuous recordings. Sitting with a friend and myself in the relative discomfort of a corner of the school store room (the only available private space), children talked at length about different aspects of their out-of-school lives, questions over which they were puzzling and their feelings about particular events and relationships. In addition to providing further recorded data about the ways that children used language to express and reflect on experience, these interviews gave me another point of reference from which to interpret the other data I had collected.

My experience of fieldwork was not only crucial for collecting the recordings and observations, but also for establishing an ethnographically informed lens through which to read and interpret my data. In contrast to research which views children's language through what I have called the educational gaze, my shift into the children's view-points was accomplished, as I have explained, by focussing first on their meaning-making in unofficial spaces and then looking back, in the light of this, at their talk around class-room activities, shifting out again to the experience of the interviews and finally applying the laminated lens from these accumulated experiences in my subsequent work on the data.

Issues to consider

❏   The issues raised by the authors of these readings include:
- The balance between justifying and being proud of the method used, and ac-knowledging potential criticisms.
- How the original research that they report fits into a network of previous studies, both reinforcing aspects of what's gone before and adding something new to it.
- How the researchers draw on various resources to support the development of their own data collection methods. These include: existing literature and precedents; authentic first-hand experience beyond the research domain; the judgements of peers not directly involved in the particular study, but with attested expertise earned from other experiences. What are the implications for novice researchers choosing methods of data collection?
- The balance of practical and theoretical considerations in collecting data (practical: what's easily available in electronic form already; what's possible to do in the researchers' working conditions; theoretical: concepts such as 'validity', 'authenticity').
- The iterative dimension: as repeatedly noted in this book, the execution of a research project is rarely completely linear. Instead, it often involves revis-iting decisions taken at earlier phases, so that, for example, the process of annotating data brings new theoretical issues to light. How is this manifest in these readings?

❏   What would you say are the Xs and Ys explored in the studies? (Why) are these
    methods suitable for investigating them?
❏   Each of these studies was on a bigger scale than yours is likely to be: how can
    you still take useful principles from them, and make them applicable to a smaller
    project?

D7   **ANALYSING ENGLISH LANGUAGE DATA**

As suggested in other units, the analysis of data is not a completely separate stage in
the research process. Underlying any decision about what is to count as data and how
it is to be collected are theories about what kind of analysis is possible and desirable.
This is illustrated quite sharply by the challenges raised in the analysis of spoken language, where the first stage of analysis is the conversion of the data from an oral to a
written medium.

In Reading D7.1, the authors engage in a debate that began many years earlier,
about how the very act of transcribing a recording of speech is in itself an analytical
process. They are responding to a previous short article in the same journal but, as
they quote or summarise the parts they are concerned with, you do not need to have
read the first piece to follow their argument.

D7.1

Coates and
Thornborrow

Jennifer Coates and Joanna Thornborrow (1999) Myths, lies and audiotapes: some
thoughts on data transcripts, *Discourse and Society* 10 (4), pp. 594–7

A response to Kitzinger (*Discourse and Society* Forum, 1998, 9 (1) 'Inaccuracies in
quoting from data transcripts: or inaccuracy in quotations from data transcripts').

Celia Kitzinger, in *Discourse and Society* Forum 9 (1), exposes some of the errors and
inconsistencies to be found in quotations from data transcripts. We share her concern
at the sloppiness which leads writers to misquote others' transcripts, and we endorse
her view that researchers should take care to reproduce others' transcripts exactly as
printed, particularly given the problems that typesetters have with conversational data.
However, we would like to challenge some of the assumptions that underlie her piece.
Kitzinger's argument, that if analysts are making claims which rest on the 'fine detail' of
their transcript, then they should make sure that fine detail is reproduced in the same
way every time it is quoted, raises questions about what a transcript *is*, and what it *does*.

Firstly, there is the problem that transcripts are often treated as if they *are* the data.
At the very least, some researchers make claims that suggest they are treating the
spoken data and the written data as virtually isomorphic. Schenkein, for example, in

his 'Explanation of Transcript Notation' (1978: xi–xvi), uses the phrase 'a reader's transcript', which he defines as 'one that will look to the eye how it sounds to the ear'. This implies that this particular type of transcript has the capacity to communicate to the reader more or less the exact sound quality of the original data tape. This is clearly impossible, given the limitations of written language as a representation of spoken language. Secondly, Schenkein's definition assumes that 'how it sounds to the ear' is unproblematically the same for all hearers. The ear is a subjective instrument at best, and one transcriber's hearing of a given chunk of talk will inevitably differ from another's. We need to bear in mind that transcripts are an analytic convenience to make data accessible to readers.

In the presentation of transcription notations, although some conventions are made explicit by the analyst, many other analytic decisions may be left implicit. Conversation analysis is an interesting case, because it is an approach in which the transcription process has always been explicitly foregrounded, yet the reasons for using certain conventions and foregrounding certain features are not always adequately explained or justified. For example, in the following extract, the word 'just' is foregrounded, while the rest of the utterance is represented using conventional orthography:

MAE: I ju::ss can't come. (Schenkein 1978: xii)

It is not clear to us how the colons after <u::> tell us how we should 'hear' this particular vowel, since in this transcription notation colons are said to indicate an extension of the preceding sound or syllable. Nor is it clear why the final sound is written as double s. If the double s is meant to indicate an extension of the sound, why was this not represented by <s:>? But presumably Schenkein has chosen to spell the word 'just' as <ju:ss> to indicate elision of the final alveolar stop before the following consonant. Yet later in the same utterance, he has used conventional orthography for the word 'can't', even though here again it seems likely that the final alveolar stop would probably have been affected by the phonetic environment of the following consonant (although we would of course need to listen to the tape to be sure of this).

Moreover, representing orthographically how the sound is 'heard' by a transcriber does not guarantee how it will be 'read' by another researcher. The vowel sounds in 'just', 'can't' and 'come' in the example above could have a range of pronunciations depending on the reader's particular variety of English; not only will an American reader differ from a British one, but a northern British reader will differ from a southern one.

The problem is that any deviation from conventional spelling systems suggests that the words so altered are marked in some way, while suggesting that all the other words are pronounced as standard, yet this may not be the case as the quoted example demonstrates. Each analyst makes decisions about what is relevant for her or his particular purposes, and no transcript can possibly capture everything that is going on in a chunk of talk. In our view, unless phonetic or prosodic quality is central to the researcher's analytic focus, or significantly marked in some way, little is to be gained by deviating from the standard orthography.

Our second point is that we want to challenge the assumption that there is such a thing as the perfect transcript, the 'true' version of a recording (audio or video) of

**Coates and
Thornborrow**

spoken interaction. A transcript of the speech recorded on audio- or videotape is always a partial affair. Different researchers focus on different aspects of language: a phonetician will make a fine-grained phonetic transcript; a linguist interested in collaborative talk will use a stave to capture the interaction of different voices: a narrative analyst may transcribe stories in 'idea units' (Chafe 1980). As Kitzinger notes in her introductory paragraph, the decision about how to transcribe is always a theoretical one. In other words, the same chunk of data can be transcribed in many different ways: each method of transcription will represent the data in a particular way and will illuminate certain features of talk but will almost certainly obscure others.

This is not a tragedy but a necessity. As Ochs rightly pointed out many years ago, 'transcription is a selective process reflecting theoretical goals and definitions' (Ochs 1979: 44). Where linguists and discourse analysts have failed is in not always making explicit the fact that theoretical decisions preceding transcription have dictated which method is used: good analysts will justify their choice of method and show why it is the appropriate one, but it will never be the only one. The fact that we as data analysts have failed to be frank about this aspect of our work arises from the pervasiveness of the liberal humanist tradition in academia and the notion that we, the researchers, are objective researchers after truth rather than reflective participants in the analytic process.

Finally, despite the important fact that transcription is always theoretically driven and therefore biased to a particular standpoint, there is another reason why data transcripts may vary. This is that any analyst who is honest will admit that every time he or she listens to a tape he or she will hear new things. A transcript can only ever be the best version at that moment; a month later it may well have changed. One of the co-authors (JC) has published transcripts of conversation over the years which have changed with each revision, so for example the extracts appearing in Coates (1996) differ from those which appeared in Coates (1989). So when Kitzinger accuses Schegloff of 'misquoting himself' when he uses three different representations of the words 'to say': <tihsay> (1992) becomes <tih ssay> in a 1996 transcript and <tih say> in 1997, it could be that these changes are a result of new 'hearings' of the tape (even though, in line with our first point, it is not necessarily clear to us how the three representations might be hearably different).

Kitzinger's diatribe rightly confronts such inconsistencies, but wrongly describes them as 'errors'. What we as researchers and transcribers have failed to do is to make explicit the fact that we are continually revising our transcripts and that we offer any particular transcript as the best we can do at that moment, not as a finished product. Transcription is a never-ending process.

In conclusion, it seems that we often fail to make our theoretical alignment explicit. It is vital that we do so, as well as acknowledge the partial nature of all data transcripts. Even more importantly, we must not lose sight of the fact that it is the original audio- (or video-) tapes which constitute our research data: transcription of these tapes can never be more than a research tool designed to illuminate some – but not all – aspects of the data.

References

Chafe, Wallace (1980) 'The Deployment of Consciousness in the Production of Narrative', in Wallace Chafe (ed.) *The Pear Stories: Cognitive, Cultural and Linguistic Aspects of Narrative Production*, pp. 9–50, Norwood, NJ: Ablex.

Coates, Jennifer (1989) 'Gossip Revisited: Language in all Female Groups', in J. Coates and
    D. Cameron (eds) *Women in Their Speech Communities*, pp. 94–121, London: Longman.

Coates, Jennifer (1996) *Women Talk: Conversation between Women Friends*, Oxford: Blackwell.

Ochs, Elinor (1979) 'Transcription as Theory', in E. Ochs and B. Schieffelin (eds) *Developmental
    Pragmatics*, pp. 43–72, New York: Academic Press.

Schenkein, J. (ed.) (1978) *Studies in the Organization of Conversational Interaction*, New York: Aca-
    demic Press.

**Coates and
Thornborrow**

D7.2

Reading D7.2 illustrates one kind of study where the approach to data analysis is
implicit in the study design. As they explain in the abstract of this report, which is
reproduced first, these researchers were investigating a prediction about a relationship between an X and a Y. In this case, they were exploring whether young children's
exposure to both English and Spanish would inhibit the development of the full range
of sounds needed to use English. Their research design was broadly in an experimental tradition, and both the nature of the data to be analysed, and the approaches
to analysis, were presumably fairly firmly fixed before data collection began.

C. E. Gildersleeve-Neumann, E. S. Kester, B. L. Davis and E. D. Peña (2008)
English speech sound development in preschool-aged children from bilingual English–Spanish
environments, *Language, Speech, and Hearing Services in Schools* 39, pp. 314–28

**Gildersleeve-
Neumann,
Kester, Davis
and Peña**

Abstract
Purpose: English speech acquisition by typically developing 3- to 4-year-old children
with monolingual English was compared to English speech acquisition by typically
developing 3- to 4-year-old children with bilingual English–Spanish backgrounds. We
predicted that exposure to Spanish would not affect the English phonetic inventory but
would increase error frequency and type in bilingual children.

Method: Single-word speech samples were collected from 33 children. Phonetically
transcribed samples for the 3 groups (monolingual English children, English–Spanish
bilingual children who were predominantly exposed to English, and English–Spanish
bilingual children with relatively equal exposure to English and Spanish) were compared
at 2 time points and for change over time for phonetic inventory, phoneme accuracy,
and error pattern frequencies.

Results: Children demonstrated similar phonetic inventories. Some bilingual children produced Spanish phonemes in their English and produced few consonant cluster
sequences. Bilingual children with relatively equal exposure to English and Spanish
averaged more errors than did bilingual children who were predominantly exposed to
English. Both bilingual groups showed higher error rates than English-only children
overall, particularly for syllable-level error patterns. All language groups decreased in
some error patterns, although the ones that decreased were not always the same across

language groups. Some group differences of error patterns and accuracy were significant. Vowel error rates did not differ by language group.

Conclusion: Exposure to English and Spanish may result in a higher English error rate in typically developing bilinguals, including the application of Spanish phonological properties to English. Slightly higher error rates are likely typical for bilingual preschool-aged children. Change over time at these time points for all 3 groups was similar, suggesting that all will reach an adult-like system in English with exposure and practice.

[. . .]

Data collection

A certified SLP and six graduate student clinicians in speech language pathology administered the picture naming task to the children at the fall and spring time points (T1 and T2). The examiners were bilingual English–Spanish speakers who spent time with the children twice a week for the school year in classroom activities as part of a longitudinal study on dynamic assessment and mediated learning.

Children's productions of 65 words in the picture naming task were analyzed. [An appendix shows the stimulus list.] Words were chosen for consonant frequency of occurrence, appropriateness of the word in the regional dialect, ease of presentation in picture format, and to ensure representation of all English vowel phonemes in stressed syllables. At least three words for each vowel were included, targeting the English vowels /i ɪ eɪ ɛ æ ʌ u ʊ oʊ ɑ/. Words of varying length and phonotactic complexity were included in the word list.

Examiners tested the children in a quiet location. Children were encouraged to produce words spontaneously. If the children did not produce a word spontaneously, a delayed imitation procedure was used. All utterances were audio-recorded using a Marantz PMD-201 portable analog tape recorder and a Sony Lavaliere microphone.

Data analyses

The primary author transcribed the data from the audiotapes and entered the information into the Logical International Phonetics Program (LIPP; Oller and Delgado 2000). The second author retranscribed 20% of the data. The mean intertranscriber agreement was 94% for the transcribed data. Independent and relational analyses for each child and by language group were conducted using LIPP. Dialectal features of the adults in the community were not considered errors in the children's productions. For example, both [dɑg] and [dɔg] were accepted for the word *dog* because the /ɔ/ is a phoneme in the English dialect that is spoken by many central Texans.

Independent analyses

Independent analyses explored consonant and vowel inventories, regardless of accuracy. Specific syllable shapes (such as CCVC) were not counted because there were limited opportunities for each in a sample of 65 words; instead, initial, medial, and final consonant singleton and sequence productions were counted. Descriptive analyses included consonant place and manner, vowel height and front/back dimensions, consonant cluster, and syllable and word shape characteristics as they were present in the single-word naming task that was employed. Because the speech samples were single-word responses to pictures rather than spontaneous speech samples, a consonant, vowel, consonant cluster sequence, or word shape type, was counted as being in a child's inventory at each time point if it was produced at least twice. Group comparisons were for both time points and change over time.

Relational analyses

Children's productions were compared to English and Spanish normative data with the intent of examining cross-linguistic effects. Relational analyses included analyses of accuracy by calculating the percentage of consonants correct (PCC; Shriberg, Austin, Lewis, McSweeney, and Wilson 1997) and the percentage of vowels correct (PVC; Shriberg 1993), and analyses of frequency by calculating the percentage of occurrence of 28 phonological error patterns (see [Appendix]). These error patterns were selected based on their occurrence in English and Spanish speech acquisition. Statistical comparisons were made first of PCC and PVC with follow-up analyses for significant findings. There were ten potential follow-up error patterns identified based on their greater than 5% occurrence in the sample of all phonological error patterns analyzed. Five of these error patterns were consonant substitution patterns (final devoicing, gliding, glottal substitution, stopping, and vocalization), two were vowel substitution patterns (vowel front/back changes, vowel tense/lax changes), and three of the patterns affected the syllable structure (final consonant deletion, cluster deletion, and cluster reduction). Statistical comparisons of phoneme accuracy and the frequency of error patterns were completed using the Statistical Package for the Social Sciences (SPSS, v. 14.0). Between-(group) and within-subjects comparisons (time and measure) were conducted using repeated measures analysis of variance (ANOVA). A multivariate solution is reported when Mauchly's test indicated that analysis did not meet assumptions of sphericity. A significance level of $p < .05$ was adopted; trends of $.05 < p < .10$ are also reported as significant due to the exploratory nature of the comparisons. Post-hoc Bonferroni test comparisons were used to follow up on significant interactions. Effect size was calculated using partial eta squared (hp 2), interpreting the effect as follows: .00–.09 = negligible, .10–.29 = small, .30–.49 = moderate, and .50 and greater = large (Rosenthal and Rosnow 1984).

D7.3

The third reading in this unit is rather different from the others in this strand of the book, in that it is the very first piece of published work by a relatively inexperienced researcher: the project on which Macksoud is reflecting is her own Masters level dissertation. I have chosen it partly because so few qualitative published studies explain in this level of detail the procedures their authors adopted in analysing the data, and also because it is a useful model for beginning researchers who seek to apply the advice found in methods books about qualitative methods to their own data.

The extract focuses on yet another topic of language research, this time in the field of language teaching. This researcher used a qualitative approach in her investigation of 'teachers' feelings of preparedness to teach English for specific academic purposes (ESAP)'. Macksoud (2009) explains that she:

> collected data over a three-month period from six university ESAP teachers as well as from six teachers of general university EAP. Each ESAP teacher participated in one sixty-minute interview and completed an attitude questionnaire. For the general EAP teachers, data were collected using an e-mail questionnaire with a similar set of questions to the interviews and an attitude questionnaire. In addition, after each interview and electronic contact, reflective notes were recorded in a researcher journal. These notes were used to cross-examine the data collected using the other techniques as recommended by Nunan (1992).

After a detailed account of the design of her data collection instruments, and the approach she took to transcribing the interviews, Macksoud explains how she dealt with the interpretation of the material she had collected.

Ruby Macksoud (2009) Using interview data in case studies, in S. Hunston and D. Oakey (eds) *Introducing Applied Linguistics: key concepts and skills*, London: Routledge

**Ruby
Macksoud**

Interpreting the data

When the transcribing was complete, I used a coding strategy to identify themes in the interview transcripts that were directly related to the three research questions. I designed the coding strategy based on suggestions in the literature on qualitative data analysis (Lincoln and Guba 1985; Miles and Huberman 1994) and used the original research questions to create a general framework for the analysis. Within this framework, I used an interpretive approach to identify relevant themes in the interview data. Each unit of analysis, or "segment of text . . . [which] contains one idea, episode, or piece of information" (Tesch 1990: 116), related to the research questions was placed into one or more categories that reflected emerging themes. In total, I identified and categorized one hundred and five units of analysis in the interview transcripts for the first research question and sixty-two units of analysis in the interview transcripts for the second research question. (I did not use the interview transcripts to answer the third research question.)

After I completed the initial coding, I performed the constant comparative method as described by Miles and Huberman (1994) and Bogdan and Biklen (1998) with my emergent codes. This meant that I reviewed all of my data to cross-examine the codes which had been applied. This process involved comparing units of analysis within and across transcripts to identify any overlap between coding categories that had emerged from the data. The result was a set of relatively parallel, discrete coding categories.

To illustrate, for the first research question, coding of the interview transcripts resulted in the emergence of eight different categories that represented sources of influence on these participants' feelings of preparedness to teach ESAP (see Table 1). Further, I divided some of these categories into narrower sub-categories in order to generate more detailed findings. For example, when participants said they drew on their teacher training when teaching ESAP, some participants referred to English language teaching (ELT) teacher training, and others referred to non-ELT teacher training.

Table 1 Sources teachers drew on when teaching ESAP

Category	Sub-category
Education	Language-instruction
	Non-language-instruction
Teacher training	ELT
	Non-ELT
Teaching experience	EAP
	ELT
	Non-ELT
Professional training/experience	Non-ELT training
	Non-ELT experience
Current EAP work environment	–
Intuition	–
Personal characteristics	–
Knowledge of broader current context	–

One example of this process of coding units of analysis involves the category *education* (see Table 1). I identified relevant units of analysis in the transcripts by looking for references the participants made to their educational backgrounds as influences on what they did in the ESAP classroom. Some of the teachers' educational backgrounds were in language-related areas like literature, linguistics, and foreign languages; other teachers' educational backgrounds were in non-language-related areas like natural sciences, business, and engineering. In order to take into account the range of educational backgrounds among the teachers, I divided this category into two sub-categories: *language-instruction-related education* and *non-language-instruction-related education*.

The following excerpt from an interview transcript is one of the units of analysis I coded as *education*. This teacher credited his language-instruction-related education with giving him the ability to analyze different texts confidently in his ESAP course:

> Well, one of the things I would say that I draw on consistently is the fact that my *education* was really about close reading . . . I mean, when I was an undergraduate, those texts were romantic literature and Chaucer and those kinds of things. Now they are engineering texts . . . the ability to read closely, the ability to understand the

material from the context, all that kind of stuff you get really at an undergraduate level in an *English language education*, which makes you very in touch with the text. (italics added)

(Teacher E)

The following excerpt is another example from a different teacher. This teacher drew on his non-language-instruction-related education to help him deal with subject-specific content in his ESAP course:

Yes, well, I thought I can understand how things work because I have got *the economics background*. (italics added)

(Teacher B)

To illustrate this coding process further, another category was *current EAP work environment* (see Table 1). I identified relevant units of analysis in the transcripts by looking for elements of the participant's current work environment, such as other colleagues or resource materials, that s/he reported drawing on when teaching ESAP. These elements would have been set up by the institution or the individual teacher. The following excerpt from an interview transcript is an example of one of the units of analysis I coded in this category. This teacher explained specifically how she drew on her colleagues to deal with materials development in her ESAP teaching:

[. . .] You realize though that when you *share materials with other people*, you think, ah yes, and you immediately identify with it and you think that is a really good thing because *it fits the model or framework that you have about pedagogy*. (italics added)

(Teacher F)

When I had completed the coding, I addressed the issue of reliability by asking another individual (who had experience with qualitative data analysis) to re-code 10% of the data using the list of categories and sub-categories that I had generated. I compared the codes that individual assigned to the data with the codes I had assigned to the same data to see how closely we agreed. This resulted in an inter-rater reliability value of 91%. Then, I re-coded 10 per cent of the data myself, and examined how closely my coding decisions overlapped with my original coding decisions with that data. This resulted in an intra-rater reliability value of 98 per cent.

Issues to consider

❏ These three readings, clearly, deal with different approaches to the analysis of data. Nevertheless, can you identify aspects of their discussions which share similar assumptions?

❏ As well as superficial differences (in the topics being researched, for example), are there more profound differences in the three approaches represented by these readings?

❏ As it happens, all of these readings are concerned with spoken language, though in different ways. To what extent can the issues raised in D7.1 be applied to the other two readings?

❏ D7.2 includes some detailed statistical information. How accessible do you find this? How important would you say it is to understand the terms and concepts used here (e.g. 'repeated measures analysis of variance (ANOVA)'; 'Post-hoc Bonferroni test comparisons'; 'a significance level of $p < .05$')? Could the data in this study have been analysed without using these statistical procedures?

❏ The author of D7.3 produced a coding scheme based on her data. How else might she have approached the analysis? How appropriate would it have been to use procedures like those in the previous extract?

WRITING ABOUT ENGLISH LANGUAGE RESEARCH

The readings in this unit report on research into writing in higher education. Although they deal with assignments in general, rather than research projects or dissertations, and although they feature data from several disciplines, and not just English Language, the issues raised will be familiar to anyone who has experienced uncertainty about just what is expected and required when written work is submitted for assessment in a university context. The authors all have expertise in the study both of language and of learning at an advanced level, so their insights are particularly relevant to students writing up their research in the field of English Language studies.

D8.1

The first reading in this unit presents some findings from a study carried out in two universities in the south of England about the expectations of tutors and experiences of students as writers of academic texts. The research approach was ethnographic, and 'included conducting in-depth, semi-structured interviews with staff and students, participant observation of group sessions and attention to samples of students' writing, written feedback on students' work and handouts on "essay" writing. A major part of the research has included a linguistically-based analysis of this textual material' (Lea and Street 1998: 160).

Extract D8.1.1 explains what the authors set out to investigate and how they collected their data.

Mary Lea and Brian Street

Mary Lea and Brian Street (1998) Student writing in higher education: an academic literacies approach, *Studies in Higher Education* 23 (2), pp. 157–72

D8.1.1 (p. 161)

The unstructured, in-depth interviews examined how students understand the different literacy practices which they experience in their studies and in what ways academic staff understand the literacy requirements of their own subject area and make these explicit to their students. We gave participants the opportunity to reflect upon the writing practices of the university, at different levels and in different courses, subject areas and disciplines, and to consider not only the influences that were being brought to bear upon them from within the university but also those from other writing contexts. We asked staff to outline, as they saw them, the writing requirements of their own disciplines and subject areas and to describe the kinds and quantities of writing that were involved for their students. We also asked them to talk about their perceptions of problems with student writing and the ways in which these were addressed at both an individual and departmental level. Students explained the problems that they experienced with writing at the university and their perceptions of the writing requirements of different courses and subject areas. We also collected copious amounts of documentation from both staff and students: handouts on essay writing; examples of students' written work; course handbooks; assignment guidelines.

[Lea and Street go on to report on the perceptions of the staff about student writing, finding that 'The interviews with staff suggest that academic staff have their own fairly well-defined views regarding what constitutes the elements of a good piece of student writing in the areas in which they teach. These tend to refer to form in a more generic sense, including attention to syntax, punctuation and layout, and to such apparently evident components of rational essay writing as "structure", "argument" and "clarity"' (p. 162).

The next extended extract from this article reports on how the students saw the issues.]

D.8.1.2 (pp. 163–70)

Writing requirements: student interpretations

The research interviews with students revealed a number of different interpretations and understandings of what students thought that they were meant to be doing in their writing. Students described taking 'ways of knowing' (Baker et al. 1995) and of writing from one course into another only to find that their attempt to do this was unsuccessful and met with negative feedback. They were consciously aware of switching between diverse writing requirements and knew that their task was to unpack what kind of writing any particular assignment might require. This was at a more complex level than genre, such as the 'essay' or 'report', but lay more deeply at the level of writing particular knowledge in a specific academic setting. Students knew that variations of form existed, but admitted that their real writing difficulties lay in trying to gauge the deeper levels of variation in knowledge and how to set about writing them. It was much more than using the correct terminology or just learning to do 'academic writing' – as what we term the academic socialisation model would suggest – and more about adapting previous knowledge of writing practices, academic and other, to varied university settings:

Mary Lea and Brian Street

> The thing I'm finding most difficult in my first term here is moving from subject to subject and knowing how you're meant to write in each one. I'm really aware of writing for a particular tutor as well as for a particular subject. Everybody seems to want something different. It's very different to A levels where we used dictated notes for essay writing.

Such common descriptions in interviews with students did not appear to support the notion of generic and transferable writing skills across the university.

Students themselves often internalised the language of feedback. They knew that it was important to present an argument and they knew that structure played an important part, but had difficulties in understanding when they had achieved this successfully in a piece of writing. Students would frequently describe how they had completed a piece of work that they believed was well constructed and appropriate to the subject area, only to discover that they had received a very low grade and fairly negative feedback. They often felt unsure and confused about what they had done wrong. What seemed to be an appropriate piece of writing in one field, or indeed for one individual tutor, was often found to be quite inappropriate for another. Although students frequently had guidelines, either from individual tutors or as departmental documents on essay writing, they found that these often did not help them very much with this level of writing. They felt that such guidelines dealt with matters that they knew from A level or Access courses. The guidelines involved issues broadly defined as structure, such as those concerned with the formal organisation of a piece of writing (introduction, main body, conclusion) or as argument, involving advice on the necessity of developing a position rather than providing 'just' a description or narrative. Students could assimilate this general advice on writing 'techniques' and 'skills' but found it difficult to move from the general to using this advice in a particular text in a particular disciplinary context. In both universities, the majority of the documents offering guidelines of this nature that we analysed took a rather technical approach to writing, concentrating on issues of surface form: grammar, punctuation and spelling. They also dealt fitly with referencing, bibliographies and footnotes, and supplied warnings about plagiarism. They rarely dealt with the issues that students reported they had most difficulty grasping – for example, how to write specific, course-based knowledge for a particular tutor or field of study.

The conflicting advice received from academic teaching staff in different courses added to the confusion. For example, in some areas students were specifically directed to outline what would follow in the main body of a traditional essay, whilst other tutors would comment, 'I do not want to know what you are going to say'. Many different conventions were to be found around the use of the first person pronoun in student writing. Even within the same courses, individual tutors had different opinions about

**Mary Lea and
Brian Street**

when or if it was appropriate to use this. Such conventions were often presented as self-evidently the correct way in which things should be done.

[. . .]

Understandings of plagiarism

A similar area of conflict between different perspectives on the writing process amongst tutors and students concerns the concept of 'plagiarism'. We found reference to 'plagiarism' was identified surprisingly often in the interview comments of both tutors and students, and frequently in the documentation available for students as advice on assignment writing and other course documentation. In both universities there appeared to be an unquestioned assumption that both tutor and student would share the same interpretation and understanding of 'plagiarism'. Our evidence, in common with Ashworth et al. (1997), would suggest that we cannot assume this to be the case. Students often expressed anxieties about plagiarism in terms of their own authority as writers. They were unclear about what actually constituted plagiarism and yet at the same time were concerned about how to acknowledge the authority of academic texts. Their overriding concerns were that the texts they read were authoritative and that they as students had little useful to say. They were confused, not only about the conventions for referencing, but more importantly they found it difficult to understand the implicit relationship between acknowledging the source of the text and acknowledging the authority of the text. Their concerns lay more with the latter and how they as novice students could write anything that they had not read in an authoritative source:

> I don't know anything about the subject other than what I've read in books so how on earth could I write anything which was not someone else's idea?

For this student, as with others, the relationship between plagiarism and correct referencing was not transparent and he was worried that he would plagiarise unknowingly. For academics, the issue of referencing sources seems clear; for students the boundary between their sources and their own account is less certain as they feel, like the student quoted here, that all of their knowledge is implicated in others' texts. Indeed, some tutors did express concern during the interviews about student interpretations of plagiarism that recognised this uncertainty. However, at an institutional level plagiarism was treated as clearly definitive and unquestionable. In one particular instance, a standard feedback sheet for tutors to comment on student essays gave considerable attention to plagiarism in a document that was necessarily constrained for space and where the choice of topic in relation to student writing is therefore highly significant. Even if the emphasis on plagiarism evident here could be construed as a valid aspect of a document offering advice and feedback to students learning to write, the discourse here is that of the law and authority rather than of tutor and student engaged in the learning practices of educational discourse:

> PLAGIARISM is an assessment offence (see section 3.7–3.9 of University Assessment Regulations pp. 26–7 in Student regulations). A student who knowingly allows his/her work to be copied, either verbatim or by paraphrasing, will be guilty of an assessment offence.

In this same university, whilst interviewing tutors, we observed notices warning against plagiarism on the walls of tutors' offices and on the notice boards in corridors. Whatever the formal and legal issues involved, as a social practice this focus upon the term plagiarism itself and the legalistic discourse in which it is embedded affirms the disciplinary and surveillance aspects of the writing process. This discourse reinforces the relations of tutor to student as those of authority, backed by the heavy weight of an institution with boards, regulations and ultimately, legal resources.

Mary Lea and Brian Street

[. . .]

Evidence such as this [including a discussion of feedback on student writing that is not included here] has led us to suggest that we consider the analysis of writing in the university as an 'institutional' issue and not just a matter for particular participants. The institution within which tutors and students write defines the conventions and boundaries of their writing practices, through its procedures and regulations (definitions of plagiarism, requirements of modularity and assessment procedures, etc.), whatever individual tutors and students may believe themselves to be as writers, and whatever autonomy and distinctiveness their disciplines may assert.

D8.2

The second reading also results from work in the recently developed tradition of challenging a 'skills' view of student writing in favour of a more rounded 'social practice' view. *The Politics of Writing* (Clark and Ivanič 1997) is a book-length exploration of many aspects of the writing process and, in particular, how people invest in writing so that their sense of self is closely bound up with the texts they produce. As Lea and Street note above, the process of writing is also a political one, in that issues of power and authority are inescapable, especially when students produce writing for assessment.

The extract reproduced here is preceded in the original by a detailed discussion of some of the ways in which writing has been conceptualised. The authors acknowledge that, whereas advice to students often assumes a very linear path 'through a set of discrete steps or stages' (p. 89), some previous research had begun to take account of the recursivity that actually characterises most writing (except the very ephemeral). They examine the model suggested by two previous researchers (Hayes and Flower 1980; 1983), finding in it much that is useful but nevertheless remaining critical of the concentration, in this model, on the individual mind and the cognitive aspects of writing, which they feel leads to a neglect of the relationship between writer and social context, as well as of the cultural shaping of writing practices. Before they move on to a case study from a different type of writing (an interview with a playwright), Clark and Ivanič present their own version of writing processes and practices.

Romy Clark and Roz Ivanič (1997) *The Politics of Writing*, London: Routledge, pp. 94–9

**Clark and
Ivanič**

Towards an alternative view of writing processes and practices

We deliberately avoid using the term 'model' for this view of what is involved in writing, because it suggests a fixed, predetermined and hence prescriptive route through the process and does not allow for differences in practices. (This was borne out by the reaction of a group of students with whom we used our representation early on, who expected to find or to be shown the 'right route'. In discussion afterwards they said that it was the term 'model' that had misled them.) Our representation attempts to capture the dynamic interplay both between all of the elements of the writing process and between the psycholinguistic and social features, and also to convey the message that there are no prescribed routes through the process.

The list is composed of those elements that we think are crucial to writing, including some things that do not generally get included in discussions of writing. Our list is in no significant order other than a division into (a) long-term components (that is, those that develop over time) and (b) components of each individual act of writing. For example, the 'accumulation of knowledge, opinions and feelings' appears in both sections. It is an ongoing, lifelong developmental experience that is always there as something to draw on in our writing. But we also accumulate new knowledge, opinions and feelings specifically as part of each act of writing.

Long-term components:
1   Accumulating general knowledge, opinions and feelings.
2   Developing the ability to use language.
3   Developing familiarity with types of writing (genres).
4   Developing socio-political identity as a writer.

Components of each act of writing:
5   Accumulating knowledge, opinions and feelings for this particular task.
6   Establishing goals and purposes (global and local).
7   Analysing the assignment.
8   Planning.
9   Drawing on familiarity with types of writing (genres) (i.e. making use of what you know about the conventions of different types of writing and deciding whether to follow them or not).
10   Considering constraints of time and space.
11   Making the neat copy.
12   Drafting.
13   Formulating your own ideas.
14   Revising.
15   Experiencing pain, panic and anguish.
16   Clarifying your commitment to your ideas (i.e. deciding what you wish to say, how strongly you believe it and whether you are prepared to risk saying it).
17   Establishing your socio-political identity as a writer (i.e. deciding how and how

much to show the reader who and what you are through the way you write and what you write about and how you treat your reader).

18 Considering the reader (i.e. both being considerate towards your reader and also bearing him/her constantly in mind while writing).

19 Experiencing pleasure and satisfaction.

20 Deciding how to take responsibility: whether to mask or declare your own position (e.g. whether to use the pronoun 'I' or to passivise).

21 Putting your knowledge of the language to use and developing this knowledge.

Before we proceed to a diagrammatic representation of the actual process of writing, we need to make a number of explanatory comments about the components of writing that we have listed. Firstly, because we have presented them in list form, the dynamic and interdependent nature of the relationship between them does not come across. We will come back to this later in this section. Secondly, some of the components we include involve a degree of conflict and opposition that will vary from writer to writer. For example, 'drawing on familiarity with types of writing' as it stands suggests an unproblematic dipping into a well of accepted norms and conventions. But of course some writers will use their knowledge of these conventions in order deliberately to resist or flout them (cf. Chase 1988). And as Kress (1982: 124) points out:

> Other conventions can be imagined; . . . children constantly invent their own modes of organising and knowing, which do not, however, become recognised as such but rather are categorised as errors.

Thirdly, we think it is crucial to include and emphasise the socio-political dimensions to the writing process . . ., as expressed in particular in the components 'clarifying your commitment to your ideas', 'establishing your socio-political identity' and 'deciding how to take responsibility'. The socio-political context is also central to the components 'establishing goals and purposes', 'drawing on familiarity with writing', 'formulating your own ideas' and 'considering the reader'. Also important are the long-term aspects that cover the way in which a writer develops over time, because different elements will come more or less into focus as the writer learns more about him/herself and what is involved in writing and the different genres they have to deal with. We also think it is wrong to neglect the affective factors involved in writing, and these are represented in particular by the components 'accumulating knowledge, opinions and feelings', 'experiencing pain, panic and anguish' and 'experiencing pleasure and satisfaction' (for a more detailed discussion of these components see Clark and Ivanič 1991). We have also tried to represent more truthfully the seemingly 'chaotic' nature of the writing process.

The representation of the process of writing that follows is the result of discussions with thirty students in Lancaster University's department of Politics and International Relations in 1990. Each of the components of the individual act of writing was written on a piece of card, and the students worked in small groups, each with a 'pack' of cards. The students were asked to discuss the meaning of the cards and any difficulties they thought the components might cause them and to share their experiences of writing as they reflected on each component. Finally, they were asked to arrange the cards in such a way as to represent what they thought the process of writing 'looked like'. Figure 4.3

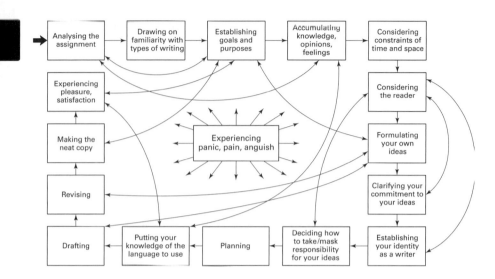

Figure 4.3 An alternative representation of the process of writing as a social practice.
Source: Clark and Ivanič 1991.

is what one of the groups came up with and, not surprisingly, for them 'pain, panic and anguish' was central to the process and 'pleasure and satisfaction' was near the end.

Several points emerged from attempting to incorporate physical, affective and social elements alongside cognitive ones in a representation of the process of writing. Firstly, as Hayes and Flower, we and the students found it impossible to suggest any type of linear progression through the writing process. The use of a word-processor even makes it difficult to see the 'neat copy' as the final stage in the process. Secondly, 'revising' is fundamental to and ongoing throughout the whole process. Writers revise their plans in the light of new thinking or new information; they revise the identity they wish to project to the reader by, for example, changing sexist language to non-sexist; they revise their understanding of the reader's needs in the light of rethinking or after discussing with an intermediate reader. Writers revise mentally and they revise as a physical 'procedure'. So, although it appears on our original list of components it perhaps should not appear separately but be subsumed in the other components. Thirdly, all the components are in some way interrelated; e.g. 'analysing the assignment' draws on 'familiarity with types of writing', 'knowledge' and 'considering the reader', and all these in turn belong in other 'constellations'. In other words, some arrows are missing. Fourthly, different types of writing need a different amount of each component, but probably even the simplest labelling task involves a small amount of each.

Fifthly, neither the list nor the representation shows the often interrupted nature of the writing process: writers often write ourselves into a corner and do not know how to go on; one solution is often to stop and go and do something else! But it is at moments like this, when we are 'stuck' or when we feel we are 'on to' something new, that we most consciously move from one element of the process to another. We may consciously decide that we have to change our overall plan, for example, in order to incorporate new thinking. This in turn can create problems for other parts of our writing and so we stop and maybe go back to goals, etc. This is nicely captured in the following extract from a letter from one of the student writers who had, earlier on in the term, devised Figure 4.3.

> Do you remember our first session that we have drawn the 'elements of an assignment writing'? We had designed a continuous loop/circle of essay/dissertation writing. [. . .] And, this happened to me! At the end of my essay, after reading an article, I completely changed my mind about the construction of my essay! I found out that I missed some very important and interesting arguments!

Finally, even with the directional arrows drawn in and the proviso made under point three above, the printed version of the representation still inevitably looks static.

We have turned the activity we have just described into a pedagogic tool for raising consciousness among learner writers of what is involved in the writing process.

Issues to consider

❑   Lea and Street (D8.1) did their research some time ago. How far does the picture they present of tutors' and students' perceptions and concerns about academic writing reflect your own, more recent experience?

❑   Clark and Ivanič (D8.2) list a number of components of acts of writing. Which of these do you recognise from your experience of writing about your own research, and which are less familiar?

❑   Both these readings challenge the view that learning to succeed in academic writing is largely a matter of mastering a set of skills. If you have experienced any difficulties as a writer yourself, would you place more emphasis on the 'skills' dimension or the 'social practice' dimension of writing?

❑   What is your overall reaction to these two reports of research into students' experience of academic writing? Do you find them reassuring, unsettling, informative – or what?

MOVING ON FROM DOING ENGLISH LANGUAGE RESEARCH

The most obvious way in which you can build on your experience of researching aspects of English Language is by enrolling as a postgraduate student and doing further research for a Masters degree, and moving on from there to a PhD. However, it is only a minority of students who follow this path, especially immediately after graduating with a first degree, when, for many reasons, they may decide that the immediate next step should be to find employment.

D9.1

In this final set of readings, I begin with a study of a young woman whose degree was a vocational one, preparing her to teach English in high schools in the USA. While this account does not draw particularly on her formal research as an undergraduate, it does include reflections on the links between aspects of the knowledge and skills she developed as a student, and the relevance and application of that knowledge in her work.

Smagorinsky, Wright, Augustine, O'Donnell-Allen and Konopak

P. Smagorinsky, L. Wright, S. M. Augustine, C. O'Donnell-Allen and B. Konopak (2007) Student engagement in the teaching and learning of grammar: a case study of an early-career secondary school English teacher, *Journal of Teacher Education* 58 (1), pp. 76–90

> I don't think [a teacher I observed] really looked to see if the kids were interested in what they were doing or not . . . They were bored . . .

This entry is taken from the journal of case study teacher and coauthor Laura Wright, who wrote it in relation to a practicum [teaching placement] prior to student teaching. Her observation voices the dilemma that drives our analysis of her early-career efforts to develop a conception to inform her teaching: how to engage students with the high school English curriculum, particularly the "language" strand most commonly taught as formal grammar.

[. . .]

In the current study we investigate Laura's effort to teach a strand of the English/ language arts curriculum that Weaver (1996) and others have found students consistently experience as drudgery: language, usually interpreted as instruction in English grammar. As Weaver noted, grammar instruction typically comprises the sort of seatwork that Goodlad found pervasive in classrooms: "listening, reading textbooks, completing workbooks and worksheets, and taking quizzes" with "a paucity of activities requiring problem solving, the achievement of group goals, students' planning and executing a project, and the like" (p. 213). These latter, less frequently occurring activities presumably would result in student engagement, a condition that has received considerable attention from observers and practitioners interested in English/language arts instruction.

We study Laura's teaching in relation to the following question: In the four primary settings of her learning to teach—her university course work and practica, her student teaching, her first job, and her second job—how did Laura endeavor to teach grammar and usage as part of her broader goal to teach in ways that were engaging; that is, in ways that her students found enjoyable, interesting, and relevant?

[. . .]

Laura . . . [had taken] a Theory of English Grammar course during her teacher education program; she was a top student at her state's most selective public university; and she did not regard traditional grammar instruction as useful. She did, however, work in a variety of institutional contexts with particular work conditions and imperatives. We look, then, to these settings to help account for her developing a notion of how to teach grammar.

[. . .]

Smagorinsky,
Wright,
Augustine,
O'Donnell-
Allen and
Konopak

We argue that, as conventionally taught, grammar instruction involves little higher order thinking because it works primarily at the level of labeling parts of sentences written by someone else—the nameless and faceless authors of sentences found in grammar books. Although our data do not enable us to make claims about the level of order at which students thought in relation to her instruction, we believe that we can identify a relation between Laura's stated goals concerning students' learning, the teaching methods she practiced, and the degree of engagement that we identified in her students through our observations of her classroom.

[. . .]

Given that each setting appeared to promote, require, or enable a particular approach to grammar instruction, we decided to make Laura's teaching of grammar the focus of our analysis. We were particularly interested in the degree to which she attempted to make grammar instruction enjoyable, relevant, interesting, and engaging—a repeatedly stated value of Laura's and a challenge given the drudgery with which grammar is typically experienced by students and teachers alike.

[. . .]

We trace Laura's approach to teaching grammar through four key settings in her development as a teacher: her university program, her student teaching, her first job, and her second job. Each context provided a different set of mediators to guide her approach to teaching this troublesome topic and helped to shape her conception of grammar as a school subject. We examine her approach to teaching grammar through the filter of her efforts to develop an umbrella conception of engaged learning to guide her teaching as a whole.

[. . .]

Laura attended her southwestern US state's namesake university . . . [where] [t]he Theory of English Grammar course was the teacher candidates' primary orientation to language instruction prior to student teaching and relied on . . . readings [that] strongly critique "traditional" grammar instruction—that is, textbook exercises oriented to labeling parts of speech in clauses and phrases, choosing a correct word to use in a given sentence (e.g. *between* or *among*), correctly identifying whether a collection of words is a phrase or clause, and correctly parsing the language into its component parts without actually using language to generate ideas. The authors emphasize traditional grammar instruction's inability to move students' written or spoken expression toward the textbook version of the English Language presumed to be optimal in language texts and standardized assessments. In contrast, they recommend approaches that teach grammar and usage in the context of student writing, argue for a cultural understanding of language forms and vernaculars rather than insisting on a single "standard" version of English, encourage generative approaches to language study such as sentence combining, view students' own linguistic knowledge and practices (including those believed to be nonstandard) as resources to build on in language study, and in general advocate attention to how speakers and writers use language for communicative purposes in social contexts based on cultural knowledge and practices.

This emphasis often stood in stark contrast to what the teacher candidates observed in schools. During her practicum taken in conjunction with her Theory of English Grammar course, Laura wrote the following journal entry about a teacher she was observing:

**Smagorinsky,
Wright,
Augustine,
O'Donnell-
Allen and
Konopak**

I watch the class while she is teaching and I see nothing but boredom. They hate the class. I hear them say so all the time. At least once every time I have been there I have heard a student say, "I hate this class." I just wonder why my [practicum] teacher cannot see that. Maybe it is harder than the book [Gere et al. 1992] makes it sound to have a classroom that doesn't function on an artifact level [which Gere et al. associate with the formal study of grammar, New Criticism, cultural literacy, focusing on product over process, and an emphasis on the formal aspects of language].

How as a teacher will I be able to stay away from the ruts? I don't want to be stuck somewhere teaching the exact same thing every hour of every day for years and years. I don't want to have to teach what all the other 7th grade teachers are teaching. Is it possible to do that with all the restrictions placed on you by the school board and district and the parents, etc.? My [practicum] teacher this semester told me that she and all the other 7th grade teachers do the exact same lesson every day.

Laura's remarks prior to student teaching suggest much about the approach that she ultimately adopted for her own practice, one in which she sought to avoid boredom and disaffection by engaging students with the curriculum in meaningful ways. As she notes, teaching in engaging ways is harder than most textbooks imply.
[. . .]

We next describe her approach to teaching grammar, one of three primary strands of virtually any secondary school English curriculum along with literature and writing, in her student teaching, her first job, and her second job.
[. . .]

Mary [Laura's mentor] provided what Laura felt was a sensible idea by suggesting that Laura cover grammar by having groups of students teach their classmates particular grammatical concepts. Mary had developed this method by reflecting on the difficulties she'd had teaching grammar and realizing that she herself had only learned grammar when her career required her to teach it. It made sense, then, that having students collaboratively study, discuss, learn, and teach a specific concept would have the same effect on her 10th graders as it had had on her: Students would learn grammar by having to teach it to others.

Field notes and interviews with Laura revealed that students' performance on this activity was uneven. [. . .] The lesson proceeded with mixed results, with students enjoying the activity, and the assessment procedure helping to identify strengths and weaknesses of the presentation; however, some concepts were taught and no doubt learned incorrectly.
[. . .]

[The article goes on to describe how in her first and second teaching positions, Laura had to adapt to different circumstances and requirements regarding the teaching of grammar.]

We have traced Laura's knowledge of how to teach grammar through the idyllic setting of her preservice education course work, the mentoring she received in the mildly constrained environment of her student teaching, the seemingly unfettered curriculum of her first job, and the highly restricted and fragmented curriculum of her second job.

Her grammar instruction did not follow a straight and predictable course; rather, it fit within the contours of the institutions in which she taught. In this sense, we see her development of a conception of how to teach grammar in engaging ways as following what Vygotsky (1987; cf. Smagorinsky, Cook, and Johnson 2003) called a "twisting path." Her instruction was characteristic of much teaching at the nascent stages of a teacher's learning:

[. . .]

Laura's experiences illustrate how this concept development is a function of the settings in which teaching takes place. Rather than moving in a linear fashion from inchoate to integrated, her conception of grammar began with a good theoretical grasp and then was modified as she moved through different institutional settings. As Vygotsky (1987) argued, theoretical knowledge is insufficient for concept develop-ment; formal or academic knowledge must work in concert with practical activity to be refined and further articulated and practiced. The settings of the schools provided different forms of mediation for Laura. [. . .]

She thus used her notion of engagement as a conceptual tool through which she chipped away at the confines of the middle school curriculum in her second job to allow space for herself and her students to grow. We therefore see the importance of empha-sizing concepts in teacher education programs. Such attention involves more than just the explication of theory; it requires a dialectic between theory and practice that con-tributes to a teacher's capacity to adapt either or both to new circumstances. As such, concepts provide teachers with critical tools to shape their decisions and provide them with agency as they move through the multiple settings of learning to teach.

D9.2

Many graduates with degrees in the field of English Language studies, as has been noted, begin their working lives outside of universities. However, it is not at all unu-sual for them to return to academic study after gaining experience in various fields, which will almost certainly include two of the main activities associated with an aca-demic job, namely teaching and administration. The dimensions of research and writ-ing may also be features of a graduate career, and in any case it is not at all unusual for people with quite extensive employment experience to return to study at a later stage. In the next reading, Ben Rampton reflects on the way one particular 'region' of academic endeavour has developed in recent years, describing how different sub-ject disciplines contribute to the enterprise of linguistic ethnography (LE) – a research approach that has been touched on at several points in this book. In the extract repro-duced here, he celebrates the varied contributions of the people and ideas which com-bine to enrich the research discussed.

Ben Rampton (2007) Neo-Hymesian linguistic ethnography in the United Kingdom, *Journal of Sociolinguistics* 11 (5), pp. 584–607

[. . .] as Brumfit noted in 1985, in applied linguistics people often embark on research a little later in life than do students in disciplines like maths, psychology, sociology or indeed formal syntax, phonetics, etc. (1985: 72, 76). Indeed, as 'mature' students in their late 20s and early/mid-30s (or later), the move from work or family commitments into research is often more motivated by interests generated in practical activity than by a fascination with academic theory *per se*. Indeed, in many cases this shift into linguistics and/or ethnography is an attempt to find a way of adequately rendering quite extensive personal experience, and the initial spur involves not just the kind of 'contrastive insight' that Hymes describes (1996: 6), but often quite an intense frustration with the institutional processes in which people have found themselves living (e.g. Rampton 1992: 30–3). After that, once established, it is common for applied linguists to engage in various kinds of consultancy research, where at least initially, the issues to be investigated are identified by people working inside the organizations that are serving as the fieldsite (cf. Roberts and Sarangi 1999). In both cases, the research process involves an overall shift from the inside moving outwards, *trying to get analytic distance* on what's close-at-hand, rather than a move from the outside inwards, *trying to get familiar* with the strange, and this has at least four consequences:

i. First, it meshes well with discourse analysis, which is often centrally involved in stepping back from the easy flow of communicative practice, interrogating its components, underpinnings and effects. For example, in spite of some striking differences (Wetherell 1998; Billig and Schegloff 1999), both Critical Discourse Analysis and Conversation Analysis provide ways of stepping back from the taken-for-granted in order to uncover the ideological (CDA) or interactional (CA) processes that constitute commonsense and everyday practice, and this commitment to de-familiarisation suits researchers whose first ethnographic priority is to achieve greater analytic distance on the activities in which they or their clients/collaborators participate on a routine basis.

ii. Second, a from-inside-outwards trajectory fosters doubt about the classical notion of 'comprehensive ethnography'. On the one hand, it encourages sensitivity to the risks of stereotyping: if you are researching people and institutions in the area where you are based, the kind of people you are studying may well turn up in your classes and/or read-and-reply to what you've written, and this provides quite strong incentives to hedge your claims and clearly specify their limits. At the same time, if you live in a city like Manchester, Birmingham or London, the complexities leap out at you and you can really only aim to produce 'broad, in-depth, and long-term study of a social or cultural group' (Green and Bloome 1997: 183) if you accept dominant ideological constructions uncritically, or are happy to close your eyes to the rest of social science. Instead, particularly if you are sympathetic to discourse analysis, the informants' 'groupness' is itself likely to be treated as a problematic issue, as a category that exists in a much larger ideological field among a range of other claimed, attributed and contested identities, differing in their availability, salience, authority and material consequences for individual lives (Moerman 1974; Gumperz 1982: 26; see Rampton 2005; Harris 2006; Maybin 2006: 5 for UK examples).

iii. In a similar vein – third – if your analytic sensibility is shaped in the inside outwards directionality, you are quite likely to be sensitive to the limitations of the ethnography of communication in exotic/distant locations. If you are a foreigner researching a cultural group that you have little or no direct experience of, starting out with only a rather a rudimentary knowledge of the vernacular, it seems unlikely that you will be able to produce much more than a description of conventional systems, even after a year or two of fieldwork (see Tonkin 1984; Borchgrevinck 2003). It is likely to take you far longer to reach the levels of understanding and familiarity where you can reliably tune into the expressive nuances that generally animate communication, intimating contexts of experience, presupposition and value quite often at a tangent to the articulated propositions (cf. Gumperz 1982; Becker 1995: 299–300). Without that apprehension of the play of dissonant perspectives on convention, the ethnographic description of unknown ways can still be very informative, but if it were a lived tension between experience and dominant forms of representation that drew you to research in the first place, accounts of this kind may also feel reductive, inclining one to sympathise with the view of Varenne and McDermott that '[t]hick brushstrokes of Samoans or Balinese may give some hints as to what Samoans and Balinese must deal with in their daily lives, but they can greatly distort the complexity of Samoans and Balinese as people' (1998: 137; Sapir 2002: 191–2).

iv. Fourth, the inside-outwards directionality probably has implications for one's academic and political demeanour. If you are working in the country where you're a citizen, if you are studying an institution where you have spent a substantial part of your life, and if you are maybe also actually credentialed and paid to draw research into professional practice, then you are also likely to be a lot less vulnerable to the kind of ontological uncertainty about political intervention that anthropologists feel when they are working on distant cultures abroad. Similarly, if you start your working life as an interpreter, a healthworker or a classroom teacher, you often feel empowered as you become more fluent and at ease with academic knowledge. You probably recognise that traditionally, practical relevance has been stigmatised in the academy, but up to a point at least, you made your own peace with that when you first signed up for your professional training. Rather than having marginality to disciplinary knowledge as your principal anxiety, the worry is that you're being seduced into irrelevance to activity in the real world, and this ambivalence about 'merely academic' work makes it easier to follow in pursuit when 'problems lead where they will and ... relevance commonly leads across disciplinary boundaries' (Hymes 1969a: 44; Rampton 2006: 372–7). Indeed, it was this kind of 'habitus' that helped to sustain (and was supported by) the dialogues conducted under the aegis of applied linguistics.

These analytic dispositions have, of course, also found ratification in the broader 'climate of the times', and the post-structuralism associated with Bakhtin, Bourdieu, Giddens, Foucault, etc. has undoubtedly also contributed to their development (e.g. Maybin 2006; Rampton 2006: 12–25). Discourse analysis has moved into a privileged position in the humanities and social sciences (Fairclough 1992: 1; Coupland 1998: 115–16), and this ratifies LE's assertion of linguistic and micro-analytic perspectives within ethnography.

D9.3

The final reading is advice to students who are engaged in postgraduate study, or have already completed a Masters dissertation or PhD thesis. It is an attempt to demystify the process of writing for publication as an academic researcher. If you are currently writing your first dissertation, you may feel that the endeavours with which this piece is concerned are a long way off, but, on the other hand, it can be stimulating to contemplate the kind of niche you may eventually find for yourself and your ideas.

A. Curzan and R. Queen (2006) In the profession: academic publication, *Journal of English Linguistics* 34, pp. 367–72

Academic publication is scholarly bread and butter. Publication is tied to us as individual researchers, representing the result of our deep love for the scholarly enterprise, including conducting original research, reading, and writing. Publication also brings individuals together into a scholarly community by advancing the field—in our case, the field of English linguistics. Without publication, new discoveries, theories, and perspectives remain local and unable to inform subsequent research and understanding. Publication also keeps us accountable to ourselves and each other as scholars and accountable to our data.

As scholars, we may never feel that our research is finished enough or perfectly polished enough for publication: there is always another book or article to read, another set of statistics to run, another set of data to collect and analyze. However, it is critical to the health of the field that we publish our research—our empirical findings as well as our theoretical insights—so that others can respond. That response may be the incorporation of our work as the starting point or theoretical framework for a further study. That response may also be conflicting evidence or a conflicting perspective in support of a different argument. Both responses productively advance the field. In this way, it can be helpful to view publication as an ongoing scholarly conversation, put down on paper and made public. We are all in search of better answers and better understandings, and we use each other's work to move forward in achieving these. This view of publication as scholarly conversation can help us frame our research in the context of previous work in the most productive, critically analytic yet collaborative, forward-looking ways.

In considering the topic of publication in English linguistics, we realize that there is a great deal of variation in the reasons for and goals of publication. We also recognize that standards and expectations for publication differ across institutions, subdisciplines, and departments, and that those differences tend to be more compounded the further we go in our careers. Finally, we appreciate that academic publication, like all human endeavors, cannot always live up to the ideals we imagine, for it is not immune to politics and fashion and is not so privileged as to be above critique. Yet because it is the primary tool of the scholarly trade, it is important that information about it be accessible to those learning the trade. For this reason, we have written this column in a fairly general way with the particular intention of helping graduate students and newly hired assistant professors get an informed sense of the "lay of the land" with respect to publishing in English linguistics. [. . .]

[The authors proceed to discuss the various types of publication where researchers may seek to place their writing, including: books, peer-reviewed journals, edited collections, special issues of journals and book reviews.]

As editors and publishing scholars, we feel privileged to be involved in both sides of the publication process. We would like to take this opportunity to express our heartfelt gratitude not only to our editorial board and supplemental external reviewers but also to manuscript reviewers for all journals and publishers for their invaluable role in the publication of high-quality research. For little to no monetary gain, CV building, or fanfare, reviewers volunteer to provide detailed, constructive reviews of manuscripts that assist editors and authors in ensuring published research furthers the field as much as possible. The upside is that reviewing for academic journals and presses allows scholars to read the newest work in their area, to help colleagues develop that work to its fullest potential, and often to work through their own ideas in responding thoroughly to others' work. It furthers the scholarly conversation of which we are all a part. We encourage all scholars newer to the profession to become involved in both sides of the publication process and to seriously consider requests to review as well as invitations to serve on editorial boards.

Issues to consider

- ❏ In relation to your own research topic, can you envisage how you may, like Laura, bring knowledge you have gained from your study to your likely place of work?
- ❏ If you anticipate a job unrelated to 'the academy', are there nevertheless ways in which you may better understand your place of work because of what you know about language and discourse?
- ❏ If you plan not to do any formal study immediately after graduating from your current programme, could you imagine becoming, at a later stage, one of the mature students to whom Rampton refers?
- ❏ Your experience of doing research is likely to have been, in different ways, both constraining and liberating. What light do these readings shed on the constraints and opportunities of (a) language-related work outside universities and (b) academic work?

GLOSSARY OF TERMS

adjacency pairs   Sequences of two utterances typical in conversational turn-taking, such as greeting/greeting, or offer/acceptance.

collocates   Words are said to be 'collocates' if they repeatedly occur within a few words of each other in running text.

concordance lines   The output from the software specially developed to analyse language stored in a corpus. Concordance lines make visible the patterning around the item under investigation. This item – a word, string of letters or sequence of words – is known as the **node**.

confounding variable   see **variable**

corpus   A large, electronically stored databank of authentic language.

data   In language study, 'data' refers to the material collected for analysis by the researcher. The words in a casual conversation are produced initially by speakers for the purpose of communication, but these words may become data if observed, recorded in some way and analysed. Many other kinds of facts or information may be collected and used as data in language research. (The word 'data' is linguistically interesting in itself. It derives from the plural form of the Latin word *datum*, meaning 'something given'. Some people continue to use the plural form of the verb when 'data' is the subject, but, as the Chambers dictionary notes, 'When referring to collected information, especially in electronic form, *data* is increasingly treated as a singular noun, since a unified concept is often intended'. I have followed this usage in the book – but you may come across assessors of your work who prefer you to treat 'data' as a plural – so be aware of the controversy!)

dependent variable   see **variable**

empirical research   Involves observations using the physical senses (or instruments which extend the senses).

experiential (meta)function of language   In the kind of language description associated with M. A. K. Halliday, the *experiential* metafunction of language is how it is used to construe a model of experience. It contrasts with: the *interpersonal* metafunction, which is how language is used to enact social relationships; the *textual* metafunction, which is concerned with how language is used to create relevance to context; and the *logical* metafunction, by which language is used in the construction of logical relations.

extraneous variable   see **variable**

hypothesis   In the strictest interpretation, a hypothesis is derived from extensive existing evidence which points to a theory about how things of a similar kind will behave in a similar way under the same conditions. For example, a burning substance will be extinguished when deprived of oxygen. To test the hypothesis that 'oxygen must be present for fire to burn', a scientist does not simply keep demon-strating that things burn when there *is* oxygen present, but tries to make them burn *without* oxygen. This is because in such cases a single counter-example can show the theory to be false. Weaker interpretations of hypothesis do not always demand this attempt at falsification, but they are still associated with attempts to develop generalisable theories. This is why, outside of strictly control-led, replicable experiments, references to a hypothesis in research plans may be inappropriate.

independent variable   see **variable**

interpersonal (meta)function of language   see **experiential metafunction of language**

inter-rater reliability   see **reliability**

intra-rater reliability   see **reliability**

introspection   Literally, 'looking inside'. In language research, a means of investigat-ing a linguistic phenomenon by directing language users' attention to particular aspects of language

Likert scale   Named after Rensis Likert, who devised a format for questionnaires and surveys with a continuum of response categories, typically ranging from 'strongly agree', through 'agree' and 'disagree' to 'strongly disagree', etc.

logical (meta)function of language   see **experiential metafunction of language**

method   Research methods are the means by which the researcher tries to gain knowledge of what is being researched. In our field, these include activities and procedures such as interviews, experiments, the generation of concordance lines, and so on. 'Method' contrasts with 'methodology', which is the study of method, the theoretical principles underlying decisions about which methods to use and why.

methodological/methodology   see **method**

node words   see **concordance lines**

objectivity   Contrasts with the *subjectivity* of personal opinion and with claims to knowledge that are influenced by vested interests and/or are unsupported by evi-dence. Philosophers have long recognised, however, the impossibility of human beings' attempts to stand 'outside' the world they are part of and to know it and what is in it as 'objects', unaffected by the language in which they are described. More modest forms of objectivity seek to identify which among competing claims are more coherent and defensible.

random   A sample of the things being researched is a selected sub-set of all the things which are of a similar kind. The sample is *random* if every potential member of the whole population of these things has an equal chance of being selected for the sample. Neither language nor people are usually distributed randomly!

reference corpus   A language corpus which is used as a standard of comparison with another, usually smaller, one. This specialist corpus is compiled by one or more criteria related to a particular kind of language use.

reliability   A research process is *reliable* if the method used produces consistent results across repetitions of the same procedure. When the same analyst applies a consistent procedure in coding examples, this should ensure *intra (within)-rater* *reliability*. When different analysts are consistent in their coding of examples, this is *inter (across)-rater reliability*.

replication   The repetition of a research procedure in order to test its validity. The concept rests upon the belief that the things researched have consistent properties and predictable behaviour, so it is more relevant for some kinds of study than others.

representative(ness)   An item that is typical of a category or group. Selecting items to represent the category as a whole involves knowing what the characteristics of the category are.

research hypothesis   see **hypothesis**

sample   A limited quantity of something, selected to be similar to, and to represent all instances of, things of its type. If the things in question are distributed in a particular pattern, then the sample should be similarly distributed.

significance   Statistical significance is a measure of how likely it is that something has occurred by chance. Be careful about referring to the results of your research as 'significant' unless you have carried out appropriate calculations.

standard deviation   A statistical measurement that reveals how spread apart individual items are around the average or mean of all the items.

tagging systems   In corpus linguistics, items in the corpus may be *tagged* in various ways, such as by adding a label ('tag') to indicate the word-class, or part-of-speech, of each word.

textual (meta)function of language   see **experiential metafunction of language**

tokens   When counting the number of words in a text (or any other given stretch of language), you may include every *token* of every word used. You need to do this when calculating the length of an essay which has a specified word limit, for example. Alternatively, you could count how many *different* words occur in the text – and, possibly, how often each of them occurs. In this case, you would be calculating the 'number of words' by *type* rather than token.

triangulation   In navigation and surveying, several vantage points can be used so as to make accurate calculations about distance and direction. This is extended as a metaphor for the practice in research of using a variety of methods to investigate the topic of interest.

types   see **tokens**

validity   A research process is deemed to be *valid* if it measures what it sets out to measure. This seems a simple idea, but it hides a number of assumptions (about the nature of what exists, as well as about how to measure it).

variable   Something which takes on different values that can be measured or counted. In the context of a research study, particularly an experiment, the researcher may attempt to control one component and keep it constant: this is then described as the 'independent variable'. In response to the procedure, another component (also strictly defined) may change: this is described as the 'dependent variable'. Components of the procedure which may influence it in ways beyond the researcher's control are called 'extraneous' or 'confounding' variables. Many things in the social world are not of this kind, and acquire their characteristics *in relation to* and *in response to* other things, rather than having the intrinsic, measurable properties assumed in research based on the concept of variables.

FURTHER READING

General

There is an enormous number of books about doing research, and quite a few for postgraduate students doing research in applied linguistics (e.g. Dörnyei 2007, Duff 2007, Hatch and Lazaraton 1991, McDonough and McDonough 1997). However, far fewer are both fairly introductory and specifically about researching a range of English Language topics. Two which are of this kind are Wray and Bloomer (2006) and Sebba (2000). The latter spans support for projects at upper secondary and under-graduate level, while McDonald (1992) is aimed at a similar readership.

Particular perspectives/approaches to researching language

Cameron (2001) includes a section on how to do research in spoken discourse. John-stone (2000) covers qualitative methods in sociolinguistics, and Scholfield (1994) gives advice on quantitative approaches.

Language research topics

Some of the titles mentioned above include ideas about how to identify a topic, and many departments offer online advice to students about ways of beginning a research project. These web pages often list previous projects as a way to stimulate ideas. One such site, at the University of Lancaster, provides a detailed account of work done by students on a Literacy Studies course, with links to more than 20 specific studies: www.literacy.lancs.ac.uk/resources/studentprojects.htm.

Literature review

Like the majority of the books published on research methods, Hart (1998) is aimed primarily at postgraduate students. Nevertheless, the style is accessible and the con-tent and approach likely to be of use to beginning researchers. Fink (2005) is aimed not only at research students, but also other researchers (including marketers and policy-makers) and, consulted selectively, may be useful for novice researchers in English Language studies. Two books which are likely to be particularly relevant to students of English Language who are interested in educational topics are Wallace (2005) and Wallace and Poulson (2004). The former includes discussion of theories and approaches in Critical Discourse Analysis and Critical Language Awareness, with examples and case studies from language classrooms, while the latter supports post-graduate education researchers in the process of becoming critical readers and writers, with an exposition of theory as well as checklists and examples.

Research questions

I know of no titles concerned exclusively with research questions as such, but many of the general titles listed here include a section or chapter on framing questions for research.

Research methods

As mentioned above, Johnstone (2000) deals with qualitative research methods, while Rasinger (2008) is an introductory textbook for students of linguistics embarking on research with a quantitative orientation. It presents the basics of statistics and the core concepts underlying conventional quantitative approaches to research, with an emphasis on linguistic and applied linguistic topics, although it tends to take certain methodological assumptions for granted. Many of the titles listed within other sections of this further reading give detailed advice on research methods.

Details

Some publications which explore the ethical and related aspects of social research, including on linguistic topics, are Burton (2000) and Cameron et al. (1992).

Data collection, interpretation and analysis

Again, many general titles on language research methods and approaches include advice about both collecting and analysing data in accordance with the perspective adopted. In relation to specific methods of data collection, Briggs (1986) interrogates the very idea of the interview, as, from a different perspective, does Kvale (1996), while Rubin and Rubin (2005) introduce beginning researchers to many aspects of interviewing as a method. Foddy (1994) deals with the challenge of constructing questions for both interviews and questionnaires. Bloomer (2009) is a good introduction to questionnaire design.

Silverman (2001) covers a range of aspects of language as research data, while there is a very extensive literature on all aspects of discourse analysis. Many of the following titles deal with the processes both of collecting and analysing linguistic data for research: Fairclough (2003); Gee (1999); Schiffrin (1994); Schiffrin et al. (2003); Wetherell et al. (2001); Wodak and Krzyzanowski (2008).

If you are thinking of using corpus linguistic methods, some titles which you may find useful include Adolphs (2009); Baker (2006); Kennedy (1998); McEnery et al. (2006); Stubbs (1996; 2001); Wynne (2004).

Writing up your project

One of many useful sources of reference for the 'nuts and bolts' aspects of writing in an academically acceptable way – 'correctly', 'confidently' and 'with style', as the book's three main sections are labelled – is Peck and Coyle (2005). It covers the details at the editorial level, but also deals with issues such as paragraphing and the overall structure of academic texts. Two chapters by Oakey (2009a and 2009b) focus on composing and editing academic writing, and Becker (1986) will strike a chord with people who find academic writing challenging. The reading and writing processes expected of postgraduate students are linked in Wallace and Wray (2006). Sharples (1999), although mainly about imaginative writing, includes fascinating explorations of the many different facets of writing extended texts for others to read. If you are interested in this dimension of the research process, you will almost certainly identify with at least some parts of this book.

REFERENCES

The details of sources cited within quoted extracts are not included in this list of references.

Adolphs, S. (2009) Using a corpus to study spoken language, in S. Hunston and D. Oakey (eds) *Introducing Applied Linguistics: concepts and skills*, London: Routledge.

Al-Ali, M. N. (2006) Genre-pragmatic strategies in English letter-of-application writing of Jordanian Arabic–English bilinguals, *International Journal of Bilingual Education and Bilingualism* 9 (1), 119–39.

Alford, R. A. and Struther, J. B. (1990) Attitudes of native and non-native speakers toward selected regional accents of US English, *TESOL Quarterly* 24 (3), 479–95.

Allan, R. (2001) *A Wider Perspective and More Options: investigating the longer term employability of humanities graduates*, Southampton: Subject Centre for Languages, Linguistics and Area Studies, University of Southampton.

Alvermann, D. E., O'Brien, D. G. and Dillon, D. R. (1996) Conversations: on writing qualitative research, *Reading Research Quarterly* 31 (1), 114–20.

American Psychological Association (2009) *Learning APA Style*. Online. Available: www.apastyle.org/learn/faqs/effective-verb-use.aspx (accessed 4 August 2009).

Asprey, E. (2007) Black Country English and Black Country identity, unpublished PhD thesis, University of Leeds.

Baker, P. (2006) *Using Corpora in Discourse Analysis*, London: Continuum.

Baker, P., Gabrielatos, C., Khosravinik, M., Krzyzanowski, M., McEnery, T. and Wodak, R. (2008) A useful methodological synergy? Combining critical discourse analysis and corpus linguistics to examine discourses of refugees and asylum seekers in the UK press, *Discourse and Society* 19 (3), 273–306.

Bakhtin, M. M. (1981) *The Dialogic Imagination: four essays by M. M. Bakhtin*. Trans. C. Emerson and M. Holquist, Austin: Texas University Press.

Barton, D. and Hamilton, M. (1998) *Local Literacies: reading and writing in one community*, London: Routledge.

Battison, R. M. (2000) American Sign Language linguistics 1970–1980: memoir of a renaissance, in K. Emmorey and H. Lane (eds) *The Signs of Language Revisited: an anthology to honor Ursula Bellugi and Edward Klima*, Mahwah, New Jersey: Lawrence Erlbaum Associates.

Becker, H. S. (1986) *Writing for Social Scientists: how to start and finish your thesis, book, or article*, Chicago: University of Chicago Press.

Beebe, L. M. and Cummings, M. C. (1995) Natural speech act data versus written questionnaire data: how data collection method affects speech act performance, in S. M. Gass and J. Neu (eds) *Speech Acts across Cultures: challenges to communication in a second language*, Berlin: Mouton de Gruyter.

Bell, A. (1991) *The Language of News Media*, Oxford: Blackwell.

Biber, D. and Finegan, E. (1991) On the exploitation of computerized corpora in variation studies, in K. Aijmer and B. Altenberg (eds) *English Corpus Linguistics*, Harlow: Longman.

Billmyer, K. and Varghese, M. (2000) Investigating instrument-based pragmatic variability: effects of enhancing discourse completion tests, *Applied Linguistics* 21 (4), 517–52.

Birkbeck, University of London (2009) *Applied Linguistics MA*. Online. Available: www.bbk.ac.uk/study/pg/linguistics/TMALIAPP.html (accessed 12 October 2009).

Blaikie, N. (2000) *Designing Social Research*, Cambridge: Polity Press.

Blaxter, L., Hughes, C. and Tight, M. (2001) *How to Research*, Milton Keynes: Open University Press.

Block, D. (1996) Not so fast: some thoughts on theory culling, relativism, accepted findings and the heart and soul of SLA, *Applied Linguistics* 17 (1), 63–83.

Bloomer, A. (2009) Designing a questionnaire, in S. Hunston and D. Oakey (eds) *Introducing Applied Linguistics: concepts and skills*, London: Routledge.

Briggs, C. L. (1986) *Learning How to Ask: a sociolinguistic appraisal of the role of the interview in social science research*, Cambridge: Cambridge University Press.

Brumfit, C. (2001) *Individual Freedom in Language Teaching: helping learners to develop a dialect of their own*, Oxford: Oxford University Press.

Bucholtz, M. (2007) Variation in transcription, *Discourse Studies* 9, 784–808.

Burton, D. (ed.) (2000) *Research Training for Social Scientists: a handbook for postgraduate researchers*, London: Sage.

Cambridge University Press (2008) *Journal of Child Language: Instructions for Contributors*. Online. Available: http://assets.cambridge.org/JCL/JCL_ifc.pdf (accessed 14 October 2008).

Cameron, D. (1995) *Verbal Hygiene*, London: Routledge.

Cameron, D. (2001) *Working with Spoken Discourse*, London: Sage.

Cameron, D., Frazer, E., Harvey, P., Rampton, B. and Richardson, K. (1992) *Researching Language: issues of power and method*, London: Routledge.

Canagarajah, A. S. (1993) Critical ethnography of a Sri Lankan classroom: ambiguities in student opposition to reproduction through ESOL, *TESOL Quarterly* 27 (4), 601–26.

Carter, R. (2004) *Language and Creativity: the art of common talk*, London: Routledge.

Chiang, S.-Y. and Mi, H.-F. (2008) Reformulation as a strategy for managing 'understanding uncertainty' in office hour interactions between international teaching assistants and American college students, *Intercultural Education* 19 (3), 269–81.

Clark, M. J. and Hillenbrand, J. M. (2003) Quality of American English front vowels before /r/, *Journal of the International Phonetic Association* 33 (1), 1–16.

Clark, R. and Ivanič, R. (1997) *The Politics of Writing*, London: Routledge.

Coates, J. (1996) *Women Talk*, Oxford: Blackwell.

Coates, J. and Thornborrow, J. (1999) Myths, lies and audiotapes: some thoughts on data transcripts, *Discourse and Society* 10 (4), 594–97.

Cook, G. (1990) Transcribing infinity: problems of context presentation, *Journal of Pragmatics* 14 (1), 1–24.

Cook, G. (2003) *Applied Linguistics*, Oxford: Oxford University Press.

Cook, G., Pieri, E. and Robbins, P. T. (2004) 'The scientists think and the public feels': expert perceptions of the discourse of GM food, *Discourse and Society* 15 (4), 433–49.

Cook, V. (1986) The basis for an experimental approach to second language learning, in V. Cook (ed.) *Experimental Approaches to Second Language Learning*, Oxford: Pergamon Press.

Cumming, A. (1994) Alternatives in TESOL research: descriptive, interpretive, and ideological orientations, *TESOL Quarterly* 28 (4), 673–5.

Curzan, A. and Queen, R. (2006) In the profession: academic publication, *Journal of English Linguistics* 34, 367–72.

Dailey-O'Cain, J. (2000) The sociolinguistic distribution of and attitudes toward focuser *like* and quotative *like*, *Journal of Sociolinguistics* 4 (1), 60–80.

Deuchar, M. (2006) Welsh-English code-switching and the Matrix Language Frame model, *Lingua, Celtic Linguistics* 116 (11), 1986–2011.

Dörnyei, Z. (2007) *Research Methods in Applied Linguistics*, Oxford: Oxford University Press.

Duff, P. (2007) *Case Study Research in Applied Linguistics*, Boca Raton, FL: CRC Press.

EFA [Education for All] Global Monitoring Report Team (2008) *Overcoming Inequality: why governance matters*, Paris: United Nations Educational, Scientific and Cultural Organization (UNESCO).

English Subject Centre (2004) *Student Employability Profiles: English*, London: The Higher Education Academy English Subject Centre.

Fairclough, N. (2001) Critical discourse analysis as a method in social scientific research, in R. Wodak and M. Meyer (eds) *Methods of Critical Discourse Analysis*, London: Sage.

Fairclough, N. (2003) *Analysing Discourse: textual analysis for social research*, London: Routledge.

Fairclough, N. (2004) Critical Discourse Analysis in researching language in the new capitalism: overdetermination, transdisciplinarity and textual analysis, in L. Young and C. Harrison (eds) *Systemic Functional Linguistics and Critical Discourse Analysis: studies in social change*, London: Continuum.

Fairclough, N. (2009) Language, reality and power, in J. Culpeper, F. Katamba, P. Kerswill, R. Wodak and T. McEnery (eds) *English Language: description, variation and context*, Basingstoke: Palgrave Macmillan.

Feist, M. I. and Gentner, D. (2007) Spatial language influences memory for spatial scenes, *Memory and Cognition* 35 (2), 283–96.

Fink, A. (2005) *Conducting Research Literature Reviews: from the internet to paper*, Thousand Oaks, CA: Sage.

Fischer, S. D. (2000) More than just handwaving: the mutual contributions of sign language and linguistics, in K. Emmorey and H. Lane (eds) *The Signs of Language Revisited: an anthology to honor Ursula Bellugi and Edward Klima*, Mahwah, New Jersey: Lawrence Erlbaum Associates.

Fisher, A. (1988) *The Logic of Real Arguments*, Cambridge: Cambridge University Press.

Foddy, W. (1994) *Constructing Questions for Interviews and Questionnaires: theory and practice in social research*, Cambridge: Cambridge University Press.

Forsyth, R., Clarke, D. and Lamb, P. (2008) Timelines, talk and transcription, *International Journal of Corpus Linguistics* 13 (2), 225–50.

Foulkes, P. and Barron, A. (2000) Telephone speaker recognition amongst members of a close social network, *Forensic Linguistics* 7 (2), 180–98.

Gabrielatos, C. (2007) Selecting query terms to build a specialised corpus from a restricted-access database, *ICAME Journal* 31, 5–43.

Gabrielatos, C. and Baker, P. (2008) Fleeing, sneaking, flooding: a corpus analysis of discursive constructions of refugees and asylum seekers in the UK press, 1996–2005, *Journal of English Linguistics* 36 (5), 5–38.

Garrett, P., Coupland, N. and Williams, A. (2003) *Investigating Language Attitudes: social meanings of dialect, ethnicity and performance*, Cardiff: University of Wales Press.

Gee, J. P. (1996) *Social Linguistics and Literacies: ideology in discourses*, London: Taylor & Francis.

Gee, J. P. (1999) *An Introduction to Discourse Analysis: theory and method*, London: Routledge.

Gildersleeve-Neumann, C. E., Kester, E. S., Davis, B. L. and Peña, E. D. (2008) English speech sound development in preschool-aged children from bilingual English–Spanish environments, *Language, Speech, and Hearing Services in Schools* 39, 314–28.

Giles, H. and Powesland, P. F. (1975) *Speech Style and Social Evaluation*, Oxford: Academic Press.

Halliday, M. A. K. (1996) Literacy and linguistics: a functional perspective, in G. Williams and R. Hasan (eds) *Literacy in Society*, Harlow: Addison Wesley Longman.

Harley, D. and Fitzpatrick, G. (2009) Creating a conversational context through video blogging: a case study of Geriatric 1927, *Computers in Human Behavior.* Including the special issue: *Enabling Elderly Users to Create and Share Self-authored Multimedia Content* 25 (3), 679–89.

Harnsberger, J. D., Wright, R. and Pisoni, D. B. (2008) A new method for eliciting three speaking styles in the laboratory, *Speech Communication* 50 (4), 323–36.

Hart, C. (1998) *Doing a Literature Review: releasing the social science research imagination*, London: Sage.

Harwood, N. (2005) 'We do not seem to have a theory . . . the theory I present here attempts to fill this gap': inclusive and exclusive pronouns in academic writing, *Applied Linguistics* 26 (3), 343–75.

Hasan, R. (1996) Literacy, everyday talk and society, in R. Hasan and G. Williams (eds) *Literacy in Society*, London: Addison Wesley Longman.

Hatch, E. and Lazaraton, A. (1991) *The Research Manual: design and statistics for applied linguistics*, Boston, MA: Heinle & Heinle.

Hayes, J. and Flower, L. (1980) Identifying the organization of writing processes: an interdisciplinary approach, in L. Gregg and E. Steinberg (eds) *Cognitive Processes in Writing.* Hillsdale, NJ: Lawrence Erlbaum.

Hayes, J. and Flower, L. (1983) Uncovering cognitive processes in writing: an introduction to protocol analysis, in P. Mosenthal, L. Tamor and S. Walmsley (eds) *Research on Writing: principles and methods.* New York: Longman.

Hirst, E., Henderson, R., Allan, M., Bode, J. and Kocatepe, M. (2004) Repositioning academic literacy: charting the emergence of a community of practice, *Australian Journal of Language and Literacy* 27 (1), 66–80.

Hubbard, C. P. and Prins, D. (1994) Word familiarity, syllabic stress pattern, and stuttering, *Journal of Speech, Language and Hearing Research* 37 (3), 564–71.

Hudson, R. (2004) *Basic Statistical Treatments of Sociolinguistic Data*. Online. Available: www.phon.ucl.ac.uk/home/dick/stats.htm (accessed 17 July 2009).

Hulstijn, J. H. (1997) Second language acquisition research in the laboratory: possibilities and limitations, *Studies in Second Language Acquisition – SSLA* 19 (2), 131–43.

Irwin, A. (2006) London adolescents (re)producing power/knowledge: *you know* and *I know, Language in Society* 35, 499–528.

Johnstone, B. (2000) *Qualitative Methods in Sociolinguistics*, New York and Oxford: Oxford University Press.

Kachru, B. B. (1985) Institutionalized second-language varieties, in S. Greenbaum (ed.) *The English Language Today*, Oxford: Pergamon.

Kachru, B. B. (ed.) (1992a) *The Other Tongue: English across cultures*, Urbana, IL: University of Illinois Press.

Kachru, B. B. (1992b) World Englishes: approaches, issues and resources, *Language Teaching* 25, 1–14.

Karmiloff, K. and Karmiloff-Smith, A. (2001) *Pathways to Language: from fetus to adolescent*, Cambridge, MA: Harvard University Press.

Kennedy, G. (1998) *An Introduction to Corpus Linguistics*, Harlow: Longman

Kilgarriff, A. (2005) Language is never, ever, ever, random, *Corpus Linguistics and Linguistic Theory* 1 (2), 263–75.

Kuiper, K. and Flindall, M. (2000) Social rituals, formulaic speech and small talk at the supermarket checkout, in J. Coupland (ed.) *Small Talk*, Harlow: Longman/Pearson.

Kurimoto, Y. (2009) Mothers' regulation speech toward their children: a comparison between mothers in England and Japan, unpublished PhD thesis, University of Reading.

Kvale, S. (1996) *InterViews: an introduction to qualitative research interviewing*, Thousand Oaks, CA: Sage.

Labov, W. (1972) *Sociolinguistic Patterns*, Philadelphia: University of Philadelphia.

Labov, W. (2004) Ordinary events, in C. Fought (ed.) *Sociolinguistic Variation: critical reflections*, Oxford: Oxford University Press.

Larsen-Freeman, D. and Cameron, L. (2008) *Complex Systems and Applied Linguistics*, Oxford: Oxford University Press.

Lawson, S. and Sachdev, I. (2004) Identity, language use, and attitudes: some Sylheti–Bangladeshi data from London, UK, *Journal of Language and Social Psychology* 23, 49–69.

Lea, M. R. and Street, B. V. (1998) Student writing in higher education: an academic literacies approach, *Studies in Higher Education* 23 (2), 157–72.

Lillis, T. M. (2001) *Student Writing: access, regulation, desire*, London: Routledge.

Lindquist, H. (2007) Viewpoint-wise: the spread and development of a new type of adverb in American and British English, *Journal of English Linguistics* 35 (2), 132–56.

Ling, R. and Baron, N. S. (2007) Text messaging and IM: linguistic comparison of American college data, *Journal of Language and Social Psychology* 26 (3), 291–98.

Long, M. H. (1993) Assessment strategies for second language acquisition theories, *Applied Linguistics* 14 (3), 225–49.

Lorés, R. (2004) On RA abstracts: from rhetorical structure to thematic organisation, *English for Specific Purposes* 23, 280–302.

Low, G. (1999) What respondents do with questionnaires: accounting for incongruity and fluidity, *Applied Linguistics* 20 (4), 503–33.

Macken-Horarik, M. (2003) APPRAISAL and the special instructiveness of narrative, *Text* 23 (2), 285–312.

Macksoud, R. (2009) Using interview data in case studies, in S. Hunston and D. Oakey (eds) *Introducing Applied Linguistics: key concepts and skills*, London: Routledge.

Marshall, J. and Goldbart, J. (2007) Communication is everything I think: parenting a child who needs Augmentative and Alternative Communication (AAC), *International Journal of Language and Communication Disorders* 43 (1), 77–98.

Matoesian, G. M. (2008) You might win the battle but lose the war: multimodal, interactive, and extralinguistic aspects of witness resistance, *Journal of English Linguistics* 36 (3), 195–219.

Maybin, J. (2005) *Children's Voices: talk, knowledge and identity*, London: Palgrave Macmillan.

McDonald, C. (1992) *English Language Project Work*, London: Macmillan.

McDonough, J. and McDonough, S. (1997) *Research Methods for English Language Teachers*, London: Arnold.

McEnery, T. (2005) *Swearing in English: bad language, purity and power from 1586 to the present*, London: Routledge.

McEnery, T., Xiao, R. and Tono, Y. (2006) *Corpus-based Language Studies: an advanced resource book*, London: Routledge.

Meyer, C. F. (2002) *English Corpus Linguistics: an introduction*, Cambridge: Cambridge University Press.

Milroy, L. and Gordon, M. J. (2003) *Sociolinguistics: method and interpretation*, Oxford: Blackwell.

Myers, G. (1998) Displaying opinions: topics and disagreement in focus groups, *Language in Society* 27, 85–111.

Norrick, N. R. (2005) Interactional remembering in conversational narrative, *Journal of Pragmatics* 37, 1819–44.

Oakey, D. (2009a) Skills of expression, in S. Hunston and D. Oakey (eds) *Introducing Applied Linguistics: concepts and skills*, London: Routledge.

Oakey, D. (2009b) Editing skills, in S. Hunston and D. Oakey (eds) *Introducing Applied Linguistics: concepts and skills*, London: Routledge.

Olsen, W. and Morgan, J. (2005) A critical epistemology of analytical statistics: addressing the sceptical realist, *Journal for the Theory of Social Behaviour* 35 (3), 255–84.

Pancsofar, N. and Vernon-Feagans, L. (2006) Mother and father language input to young children: contributions to later language development, *Journal of Applied Developmental Psychology* 27, 571–87.

Papaioannou, V., Santos, N. B. and Howard, A. (2008) Data collection: real stories from the field, in B. Beaven (ed.) *IATEFL 2007: Aberdeen Conference Selections*, Canterbury: IATEFL.

Parker, M. D. and Brorson, K. (2005) A comparative study between mean length of utterance in morphemes (MLUm) and mean length of utterance in words (MLUw), *First Language* 25 (3), 365–76.

Pavlenko, A. (2007) Autobiographic narratives as data in applied linguistics, *Applied Linguistics* 28 (2), 163–88.

Peck, J. and Coyle, M. (2005) *The Student's Guide to Writing: grammar, punctuation and spelling*, Basingstoke: Palgrave Macmillan.

Petrić, B. and Czárl, B. (2003) Validating a writing strategy questionnaire, *System* 31, 187–215.

Phillips, N. and Hardy, C. (2002) *Discourse Analysis: investigating processes of social construction*, Thousand Oaks, CA: Sage.

Pinker, S. (1994) *The Language Instinct*, London: Penguin.

Piquemal, N. and Kouritzin, S. (2006) When 'history' happens to research: a tale of one project, two researchers, and three countries in a time of global crisis, *Canadian Journal of Education* 29 (4), 1271–94.

Polio, C. G. (1997) Measures of linguistic accuracy in second language writing research, *Language Learning* 47 (1), 101–43.

Popper, K. R. (1994) *Knowledge and the Body–Mind Problem: in defence of interaction*, London: Routledge.

Potter, J. (1996) *Representing Reality: discourse, rhetoric and social construction*, London: Sage.

Potter, J. and Hepburn, A. (2007) Life is out there: a comment on Griffin, *Discourse Studies* 9 (2), 276–82.

Poulson, L. and Wallace, M. (eds) (2004) *Learning to Read Critically in Teaching and Learning*, London: Sage.

Prabhu, N. S. (1992) The dynamics of the language lesson, *TESOL Quarterly* 26 (2), 225–41.

Pullman, P. (1995, 1997, 2000) *His Dark Materials* (*Northern Lights, The Subtle Knife, The Amber Spyglass*), Scholastic/David Fickling Books.

QAA (2007a) *Subject Benchmark Statements English*, Mansfield: Quality Assurance Agency for Higher Education.

QAA (2007b) *Subject Benchmark Statements Linguistics*, Mansfield: Quality Assurance Agency for Higher Education.

Rampton, B. (2007) Neo-Hymesian linguistic ethnography in the United Kingdom, *Journal of Sociolinguistics* 11 (5), 584–607.

Rasinger, S. M. (2008) *Quantitative Research in Linguistics*, London: Continuum.

Rayson, P. (2008) Wmatrix: a web-based corpus processing environment, Computing department, Lancaster University (http://ucrel.lancs.ac.uk/wmatrix/).

Reyes, I. (2004) Functions of code switching in schoolchildren's conversations, *Bilingual Research Journal* 28 (1), 77–98.

Richter, T. and Zwaan, R. A. (2009) Processing of color words activates color representations, *Cognition* 111 (3), 383–9.

Rubin, H. J. and Rubin, I. S. (2005) (2nd edition) *Qualitative Interviewing: the art of hearing data*, Thousand Oaks, CA: Sage.

Sampson, G. (1997) *Educating Eve: the 'language instinct' debate*, London: Cassell.

Schauer, G. A. and Adolphs, S. (2006) Expressions of gratitude in corpus and DCT data: vocabulary, formulaic sequences, and pedagogy, *System* 34, 119–34.

Schegloff, E. A., Koshik, I., Jacoby, S. and Olsher, D. (2002) Conversation analysis and applied linguistics, *Annual Review of Applied Linguistics* 22, 3–31.

Schiffrin, D. (1994) *Approaches to Discourse*, Oxford: Blackwell.

Schiffrin, D., Tannen, D. and Hamilton, H. E. (eds) (2003) *The Handbook of Discourse Analysis*, Oxford: Blackwell.

Scholfield, P. (1994) *Quantifying Language: a researcher's and teacher's guide to gathering language data and reducing it to figures*, Clevedon: Multilingual Matters.

Sealey, A. (1990) Magic words: helping young children to develop their knowledge about language, in R. Carter (ed.) *Knowledge about Language and the Curriculum: the LINC reader*, London: Hodder and Stoughton.

Sealey, A. (2000) *Childly Language: children, language and the social world*, Harlow: Longman/Pearson Education.

Sealey, A. and Carter, B. (2004) *Applied Linguistics as Social Science*, London: Continuum.

Sebba, M. (2000) *Focussing on Language: a student guide to research planning, data collection, analysis and writing up*, Lancaster: Definite Article Publications.

Semino, E. and Short, M. (2004) *Corpus Stylistics*, London: Routledge.

Semino, E., Heywood, J. and Short, M. (2004) Methodological problems in the analysis of metaphors in a corpus of conversations about cancer, *Journal of Pragmatics* 36 (7), 1271–94.

Sharples, M. (1999) *How We Write: writing as creative design*, London: Routledge.

Shriberg, L. D., Lewis, B. A., Tomblin, J. B., McSweeny, J. L., Karlsson, H. B. and Scheer, A. R. (2005) Toward diagnostic and phenotype markers for genetically transmitted speech delay, *Journal of Speech, Language and Hearing Research* 48 (4), 834–52.

Silverman, D. (2001) *Interpreting Qualitative Data: methods for analysing talk, text and interaction*, London: Sage.

Simpson, P. (2001) 'Reason' and 'tickle' as pragmatic constructs in the discourse of advertising, *Journal of Pragmatics* 33, 589–607.

Sinclair, J. McH. (2004) Corpus and text – basic principles, in M. Wynne (ed.) *Developing Linguistic Corpora: a guide to good practice*, Oxford: Oxbow Books. Online. Available: http://ahds.ac.uk/linguistic-corpora (accessed 3 June 2009).

Slobin, D. I. (1996) From 'thought and language' to 'thinking for speaking', in J. J. Gumperz and S. C. Levinson (eds) *Rethinking Linguistic Relativity*, Cambridge: Cambridge University Press.

Slobin, D. I. (2003) Language and thought online: cognitive consequences of linguistic relativity, in D. Gentner and S. Goldin-Meadow (eds) *Language in Mind: advances in the study of language and cognition*, Cambridge, MA: MIT Press.

Smagorinsky, P., Wright, L., Augustine, S. M., O'Donnell-Allen, C. and Konopak, B. (2007) Student engagement in the teaching and learning of grammar: a case study of an early-career secondary school English teacher, *Journal of Teacher Education* 58 (1), 76–90.

Smith, S. W., Noda, H. P., Andrews, S. and Jucker, A. H. (2005) Setting the stage:

How speakers prepare listeners for the introduction of referents in dialogues and monologues, *Journal of Pragmatics* 37, 1865–95.

Song, J. Y., Sundara, M. and Demuth, K. (2009) Phonological constraints on children's production of English third person singular –s, *Journal of Speech, Language, and Hearing Research* 52, 623–42.

Statistical Advisory Service, University of Reading (2007) Online. Available: www.reading.ac.uk/biologicalsciences/appstats/biosci-as_SAS_info.aspx (accessed 26 January 2009).

Stubbs, M. (1996) *Text and Corpus Analysis*, Oxford: Blackwell.

Stubbs, M. (1997) Whorf's children: critical comments on critical discourse analysis (CDA), in A. Ryan and A. Wray (eds) *Evolving Models of Language*, Clevedon: British Association of Applied Linguistics/Multilingual Matters.

Stubbs, M. (2001) *Words and Phrases: corpus studies of lexical semantics*, Oxford: Blackwell.

Taylor, J. R. and Pang, K.-Y. S. (2008) Seeing as though, *English Language and Linguistics* 12 (1), 103–39.

Teubert, W. (2005) My version of corpus linguistics, *International Journal of Corpus Linguistics* 10 (1), 1–13.

Thompson, P. and Sealey, A. (2007) Through children's eyes?: corpus evidence of the features of children's literature, *International Journal of Corpus Linguistics* 12 (1), 1–23.

Trudgill, P. (1972) Sex, covert prestige and linguistic change in the urban British English of Norwich, *Language in Society* 1 (2), 175–95.

Trudgill, P. (1983) *Sociolinguistics: an introduction to language and society*, London: Penguin.

Vold, E. T. (2006) Epistemic modality markers in research articles: a cross-linguistic and cross-disciplinary study, *International Journal of Applied Linguistics* 16 (1), 61–87.

Wallace, C. (2005) *Critical Reading in Language Education*, Basingstoke: Palgrave Macmillan.

Wallace, M. and Poulson, L. (2004) Critical reading for self-critical writing, in L. Poulson and M. Wallace (eds) *Learning to Read Critically in Teaching and Learning*, London: Sage.

Wallace, M. and Wray, A. (2006) *Critical Reading and Writing for Postgraduates*, London: Sage.

Wetherell, M., Taylor, S. and Yates, S. J. (eds) (2001) *Discourse as Data: a guide for analysis*, London and Milton Keynes: Open University and Sage.

White, P. R. R. (2005) *The Appraisal Website*. Online. Available: www.grammatics.com/Appraisal (accessed 10 July 2009).

Widdowson, H. (1990) *Aspects of Language Teaching*, Oxford: Oxford University Press.

Wikipedia (2008) *Wikipedia: about*. Online. Available: http://en.wikipedia.org/wiki/Wikipedia:About (accessed 16 October 2008)

Wiley-Blackwell (2009) *Journal of Sociolinguistics: author guidelines*. Online. Available: www.blackwellpublishing.com/submit.asp?ref=1360-6441&site=1 (accessed 14 October 2008).

Wodak, R. and Krzyzanowski, M. (eds) (2008) *Qualitative Discourse Analysis in the Social Sciences*, Basingstoke: Palgrave Macmillan.

Wolcott, H. F. (2001) *Writing Up Qualitative Research*, Thousand Oaks and London: Sage.

Wray, A. and Bloomer, A. (2006) *Projects in Linguistics: a practical guide to researching language*, London: Hodder Arnold.

Wynne, M. (ed.) (2004) *Developing Linguistic Corpora: a guide to good practice*, Oxford: Oxbow Books.

Yang, L. R. and Givón, T. (1997) Benefits and drawbacks of controlled laboratory studies of second language acquisition, *Studies in Second Language Acquisition – SSLA* 19 (2), 173–93.

Young, S. (2008) The broadcast political interview and strategies used by politicians: how the Australian prime minister promoted the Iraq War, *Media, Culture and Society* 30 (5), 623–40.

Ziegelbauer, K., Gantner, F., Lukacs, N. W., Berlin, A., Fuchikami, K., Niki, T., Sakai, K., Inbe, H., Takeshita, K., Ishimori, M., Komura, H., Murata, T., Lowinger, T. and Bacon, K. B. (2005) A selective novel low-molecular-weight inhibitor of IkappaB kinase-beta (IKK-beta) prevents pulmonary inflammation and shows broad anti-inflammatory activity, *British Journal of Pharmacology* 145, 178–92.

INDEX